RE-BISONING THE WEST

Restoring an American Icon to the Landscape

RE-BISONING THE WEST

Restoring an American Icon to the Landscape

Kurt Repanshek

TORREY HOUSE PRESS

SALT LAKE CITY • TORREY

First Torrey House Press Edition, September 2019

This book was published with support from
Furthermore: a program of the J. M. Kaplan Fund

Furthermore:
a program of the J. M. Kaplan Fund

Published by Torrey House Press
Salt Lake City, Utah
www.torreyhouse.org

International Standard Book Number: 978-1-937226-98-5
E-book ISBN: 978-1-948814-00-3
Library of Congress Control Number: 2018956436

Map used with permission from Wildlife Conservation Society
Cover design by Kathleen Metcalf
Interior design by Rachel Davis
Distributed to the trade by Consortium Book Sales and Distribution

MIX
Paper from
responsible sources
FSC® C011935

For my wife, Marcelle,
for her patience and ever-present encouragement,
and to the "red dawgs," that they'll find new room to roam

Acknowledgments

What is it about bison that so intrigues and entrances? Their innate power? Their place on the landscape? Their ancientness?

It's a question I hopefully answer in the following pages. And it's one no doubt that Theodore Roosevelt, William Hornaday, Charles "Buffalo" Jones, Michel Pablo, Charles Pablo, and others in the late nineteenth and early twentieth centuries answered for themselves and used to drive their efforts to keep the species from going extinct. Those individuals, and their peers, deserve our thanks for the groundbreaking work they did in maintaining bison on the landscape.

There are many individuals who helped me in detailing how bison avoided extinction and examining how their numbers can be increased on the Great Plains. Dr. James Derr at Texas A&M University patiently helped me understand, at least in passing, bison genetics and cattle introgression. Dr. Glenn Plumb, formerly the chief wildlife biologist for the National Park Service and now the Bison Specialist Group Chair for the International Union for Conservation of Nature, explained the work the Department of the Interior and National Park Service are doing to increase the federal government's conservation herds of bison, as did Greg Schroeder, the resource management chief at Wind Cave National Park.

I owe particular thanks to Philip Deloria, Harvard University's tenured professor of Native American studies; Robbie Magnan of the Assiniboine and Sioux tribes at the Fort Peck Reservation; and Jason Baldes of the Eastern Shoshone Nation on the Wind River Indian Reservation for help in understanding what bison mean to native cultures. Damien Austin, superintendent of the nonprofit American Prairie Reserve in Montana, allowed me to tag along on a hunt for two bison that needed new radio collars, and endured my questions as we slowly drove across the prairie.

Staff and officials at the Montana Department of Livestock and Department of Fish, Wildlife, and Parks lent their perspectives of the Yellowstone bison issue, and Bill Bates, formerly of the Utah Division of Wildlife Resources, and Bob Mountain of the US Forest Service, happily discussed bison on the landscape and where new herds might (or might not) be located. Longtime colleague Angus Thuermer, Jr., at WyoFile, who collaborated on the initial series of bison articles that appeared on NationalParksTraveler.org in September 2017 and inspired this book, provided great reporting and writing then that have been incorporated into *Re-Bisoning the West*.

Special thanks to Kirsten Johanna Allen at Torrey House Press for seeing value in this project, and associate editor Anne Terashima for her keen edits, suggestions, and patience in trying to get a writer who grew up, professionally, with *The Associated Press Stylebook*, to adopt *The Chicago Manual of Style*.

An immeasurable amount of thanks goes to my wife, Marcelle Shoop, for enduring her husband's writer's blocks, long road trips in search of bison and their history, and struggles with telling a story more than 200,000 years in the making.

A great many others responded with helpful information and answers to my questions. A topic such as restoring bison on the Great Plains cannot be completely covered in a single book or paper, as evidenced by the many that have been produced on bison. The next chapter, of course, will involve what success is met in both growing the herds in general and, more specifically, preserving the genetic blueprint that makes bison such incredible animals.

Kurt Repanshek
Park City, Utah
2019

Contents

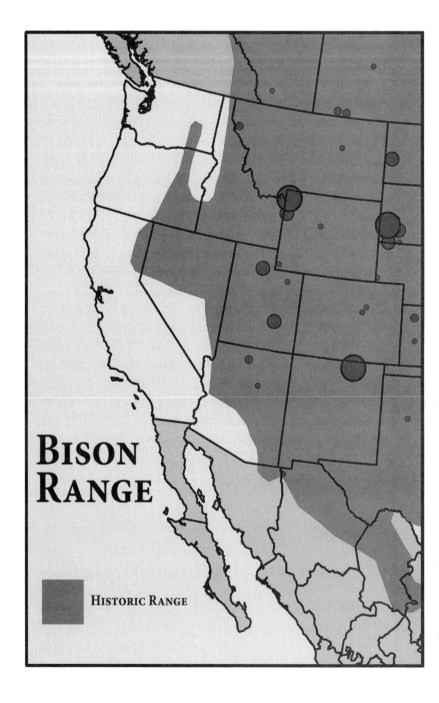

BISON
RANGE

HISTORIC RANGE

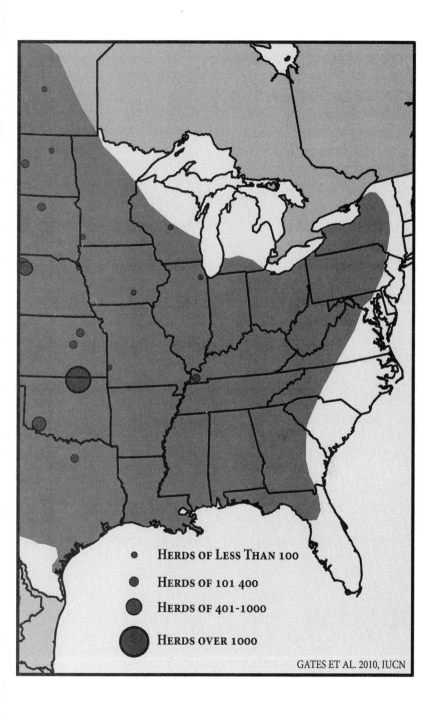

HERDS OF LESS THAN 100

HERDS OF 101 400

HERDS OF 401-1000

HERDS OVER 1000

GATES ET AL. 2010, IUCN

Prologue

A *vast, placid sea undulates slightly, as though to the rise and fall of the tide, staining the ground in all directions to the horizon. Though this sea contains no water, it moves in unison, rippling up and down, forging ever forward: herds of bison covering the landscape. Their dark brown shaggy humps rise not with a tide, but with the rolling hills. A dust cloud billows in their wake. Their baritone grunts, swelling and ebbing with the herd, carry across the Great Plains.*

Late September nights in the backcountry of Yellowstone don't hold warmth. They grow cold quickly. We had a reasonable pile of broken branches to feed the flames of our campfire until night called and we'd crawl into the down bags waiting inside our tent. Flickering shadows danced skyward against the lodgepole pine canopy, and an ebbing glow from the campfire leapt out across the forest floor. The snap and crackle of the fire was occasionally interrupted by nearby Lone Star Geyser as it fumed and sputtered and loosed a steaming *whoosh* of hot water, sending rivulets gurgling down to the Firehole River.

Though not our first backpacking trek through the park, we still had understandably nervous thoughts of grizzlies clacking teeth in the middle of the night, their low but unmistakable growl filling our ears. What we didn't count on was the bison. Here in the forest. As the animal ambled along the firelight's periphery, we couldn't tell in the fading twilight if it was a bull or a cow. But at a weight north of one thousand pounds, male or female, it didn't matter. It could inflict broken bones and trample our tent just by turning around. Nudging more wood into the flames, we watched the bison linger along the rim of firelight and then settle to the ground for the night.

Bison are deceptive. They are ponderous in their bulk, and their expressionless demeanor lends a certain stolidness. Matriarchal in herd structure, they are quick to defend their young, always conscious of nearby predators. They also are surprisingly nimble, capable of turning quickly and accelerating to forty mph. Bison are a mammalian relic from deep out of the past that are amazing to watch as they move in herds across the landscape or simply hunker down to bask in the sun while their calves frolic. They are powerful creatures, physically and iconically. Wander into an art gallery in the West and odds are good you'll find images of bison staring out from canvases. Potent images of stout, indomitable animals that are hard to turn your eyes from. They are portrayed as they stand on the landscape, and at times in surrealistic, neon hues as the artist strives to depict their spirituality.

Back in 2007, the folks in West Yellowstone, Montana, no doubt recognizing the representation of wildness and strength in bison, staged a "Where the Painted Buffalo Roam" fundraiser for their town. This campaign featured twenty-six three-quarter-sized fiberglass cow bison statues painted by select artists to reflect themes from Yellowstone and Native American people from the region. These bison stood in various public places around town for a period of months, and then were auctioned off. The paintings on the bison statues were wide-ranging. One depicted the park's Upper Geyser Basin in full steam mode, another feral horses at full gallop, another, the artist noted, "an attempt to portray part of the North Plains Indian belief in the legend of the Sacred White Buffalo Calf Woman, who came down from the heavens long ago to show the people the way to the sacred path." The highest bid, of $17,000, went for a bison painted on one side to show turn-of-the-century tourists exploring Yellowstone by tally-ho coaches, and on the other a scene of yellow touring buses. The project raised $161,500. Cattle canvases would not have fared as well.

That night in the backcountry of Yellowstone, the animal that shared our campsite was an ancient animal, figuratively. The *Bison* genus stretches back some two million years to Asia. Somehow, through all the ice ages and despite all the long-toothed predators, it never went extinct. It probably should have, at least once or twice, as did the camels, mammoths, and ground sloths. Bison somewhat recently arrived in North America, about two hundred thousand years ago during glacial periods that dropped sea levels and allowed a land bridge to surface and connect Asia to the land we know today as Alaska. By crossing the thousand-mile-long strip known as Beringia, which now has been underwater for about twenty thousand years, the animals reached a new continent with near-endless possibilities for their kind.

The bison in Yellowstone's Hayden Valley really don't look much different from those who made the crossing. Oh, they are smaller, their horns closer to their skulls, their bodies more compact. We know this thanks to Walter and Ruth Roman. The couple literally scraped, or, more precisely, blasted, a living from the land with their Lucky Seven Mining Co. Summer into early fall 1979 found the Romans at their placer mine along Pearl Creek above the Chatanika River, sixteen miles northeast of Fairbanks, Alaska.[1] Their tool of choice was a pressurized hose that spit out a nearly six-inch-wide torrent of water that could cut through the permafrost and, hopefully, expose gold-bearing rubble. This particular form of mining, known as "hydraulicking," dates to the Roman Empire. Those Romans didn't know everything, though, and miners during the California Gold Rush of the 1850s greatly improved the technology by adding a nozzle to create a more forceful jet of water to tear into hillsides.

What the modern-day Romans found as they slowly eroded the hillside into muddy torrents was not gold, but not entirely invaluable, either.[2] Under their watchful eyes, the powerful sluice of water raked back and forth and back across the slope, thawing, chewing, gashing, slashing, and washing away a slurry of sediments, pulling away rocks and soil and debris from the past thirty-six thousand years. No gold fell away, but mired in the muck were the hindquarters of a prehistoric creature jutting out like some massive tree trunk. With a tail. Dubbed "Blue Babe," in part for the color of the long-buried carcass, this steppe bison (*Bison priscus*), as paleontologists would later conclude, must have been a magnificent animal when breath filled its lungs, blood flowed through its veins, and rippled muscles flexed its hide as it walked. Blue Babe stood almost seven feet tall at the shoulder, weighed a ton or so, and had crescent-shaped horns ranging more than three feet from tip to tip. Those horns weren't for show, not at all, but for defense, for survival. Driven forward by two thousand pounds of bone and brawn and fury, they could be particularly effective. The animal's size and strength enabled it to endure on the mammoth steppe during the Pleistocene. It was a cold, somewhat arid place, covered with grasslands that wandered across the landscape then as they do today across the Great Plains of the United States and southern Canada. Forbs—herbaceous flowering plants—grasses, and perhaps willow shrubs provided the forage the great beast consumed and, in turn, transformed into muscle.

Blue Babe grazed this landscape with other bison, of course, but also with woolly mammoths, musk oxen, and horses. As they all fell into the category of prey for the carnivores of the day, they needed to keep watch for packs of dire wolves, short-faced bears, and American lions. The lions were among the big apex predators on the Pleistocene landscape, much larger than their relatives of today, though lacking the manes of African lions. The males that preyed on the likes of Blue Babe weighed more than 900 pounds, and possibly as many as 1,100 pounds.[3] Females were smaller by a few hundred pounds, but, like wolves today, their tendency to hunt in small groups enabled them to overwhelm their prey from all sides and tilt the battle in their favor. They'd stalk, feint, and charge, take swipes and bites, always searching for a weakness, for an opening to launch a fatal attack. The steppe bison had no chance. Blue Babe's death was, in the end, inevitable.

In that battle thirty-six thousand years ago, the bull bison was attacked from behind, either caught by surprise or run down by a lion, or lions, in flight. Claws raked its flanks, teeth pierced the thick hide that bore scars from past battles survived. Though the bison outweighed the lion by at least half a ton and had those massive horns, it nevertheless was at a marked disadvantage. Stumbling to the ground was fatal, as the predator tore at the bison's girth, determined to rip through the leathery hide to reach the muscle and organs shielded by the rib cage. The battle attracted scavengers, who patiently waited their turn. But was that how it played out? Was it that cut and dried, a fierce attack accomplished in a matter of minutes? That was the mystery that landed at the muddy feet of R. Dale Guthrie. Born in 1936 in Nebo, Illinois, a village of fewer than five hundred then and less now, he was educated in paleontology at the University of Chicago and went on to teach zoology and Arctic biology at the University of Alaska from 1962–96. Though arguably best known for a book he wrote on Blue Babe, Guthrie traveled extensively in the Arctic and to Europe and Asia to study and decipher prehistoric sites. His avocation, second to paleobiologist, was art lover. He especially enjoyed studying Paleolithic art and searching for connections to, or representations of, Pleistocene natural history. With no time machine to transport himself back to that epoch, what better way to understand its wildlife than through the art the hunters left behind? Guthrie came away from a 1979 conference in Switzerland determined to try "to place Paleolithic art in a larger dimension of natural history and [link] artistic behavior to our evolutionary past."[4] Among the professional papers that flowed from Guthrie's travels was one in which he wondered why the artists were drawn to create images of animals we refer to today as *charismatic megafauna*, the great beasts of their day thousands of years ago. Did the pinstriped horses and polka-dotted reindeer these people painted actually trot across the landscape, or were they embellished creatures the artists held in esteem? Why did so many scenes depict hunting?

In July 1979, when the Romans called Guthrie, the pale-ontological puzzle confronting him, quite ignominiously, was protruding butt-first from the hillside. Guthrie, assisted by his wife, Mary Lee, and son, Owen, walked up to the muddy, well-preserved but slightly frozen bison rump and was immediately struck by the smell, "a rich, pungent rottenness, like nothing else I have smelled."

"It was a rottenness aged for millennia in the frost—not a stench, but a sweet, intense tang," he recalled.

The source of that stench was thawing quickly, too quickly to study from its awkward resting place. When the rear half of the bison began to tear away from the front end that was still securely frozen in place, Guthrie arranged to have it carted off to the University of Alaska and the Institute of Arctic Biology. Once there, it was put in cold storage in a walk-in freezer. When the animal's head and shoulders melted free, they too went into deep freeze there. During an ensuing necropsy, the equivalent of a human autopsy, on the stunningly complete remains, Guthrie pieced together a theory for how Blue Babe died. And it wasn't what most of us would think. His conclusion did not support a quick death by a pride of lions that had little trouble tearing into the animal. This bull had dense neck muscles covered by thick, sheet-like layers of skin. They formed a tough physiological lam-inate that a lion couldn't easily clamp its jaws around. As a result, the cats would resort to smothering their prey. And that's what Guthrie figured had happened.

"Using claws for a secure hold, a lion will throw a buffalo down and clamp the buffalo's entire nose and mouth in a firm bite or clamp the trachea closed,"[5] he explained. With Blue Babe, the paleobiologist based his theory on puncture wounds coupled with stains left by blood clots that had formed around the bull's snout. But there was a twist in this case, which was unusual from the start. Why wasn't the carcass devoured? Guthrie theorized that fewer than three lions were involved in attacking the bison, and that the carcass froze solid before they could consume much of it. Lending credence to that theory was that a tooth fragment from one of the predators, possibly broken off as the lion tried to tear through the frozen hide, was later found in Babe's neck by a taxidermist.[6]

Because so much of the carcass was intact for the Romans to jet wash out of the hillside, Guthrie surmised that Blue Babe died early in winter. Bitterly cold temperatures turned the bison's skin into a sheet-metal-like barrier that no predator could penetrate.[7] Then, before spring thaw could arrive with warming temperatures that would soften the skin, bloat the carcass, and spew the odors that would bring the predators and scavengers back, Blue Babe was buried by sediments. Perhaps they came in one large swoosh of a muddy torrent unleashed by snowmelt. Or perhaps there was an avalanche that sent snow and soil down atop the carcass. And then some more layers were added for good measure, and they, in turn, froze. This process, repeated again and again, cemented the bison's remains in permafrost, out of reach of predators and scavengers and out of sight for tens of thousands of years until the Romans came along with their powerful hose in search of gold.

The preservation of the find, the seeming freshness of it, Guthrie later told a gathering at the thirty-second Alaska Science Conference in 1981, was simply amazing. And, no doubt surprisingly to most of us, appealing in a gastronomical context.

"Red meat in the mud. It is really a dramatic thing to all of a sudden fall into your lap, to see this coming out—an animal that no longer exists, with black hair, wool, and fat,"[8] he told his spellbound audience. While the remaining flesh might not have looked butcher-shop fresh, even after thirty-six thousand or more years it didn't look too far gone to sample. So one evening in 1984 Guthrie invited the taxidermist who was able to show-case Blue Babe in repose for the university's museum and some friends for bowls of Blue Babe stew. "The meat was well aged but still a little tough, and it gave the stew a strong Pleistocene aroma, but nobody there would have dared to miss it," said the paleontologist.

The bison's nickname, "Blue Babe," was derived from both the mythical, oversized ox that accompanied the legendary lum-berjack Paul Bunyan of American folklore[9] and from the bluish hue left on the bison's skin due to a chemical reaction between minerals in the surrounding soil, phosphorous from the skin, and the air. Babe was just one of the ancestors of today's *Bison bison.* Coexisting with the bull for a time, but eventually succeed-ing it, was the Ice Age *Bison latifrons,* or long-horned bison, a massive beast at more than eight feet tall and more than two tons on the hoof. It shared the landscape for about one hundred thou-sand years with *Bison antiquus.* Then arrived *Bison occidentalis* for a somewhat short period and, finally, today's *Bison bison.*[10]

Collectively, the various subspecies demonstrate how, down through the millennia, the populations of these now iconic ani-mals rose and fell and evolved, facing climate change and endur-ing predation by four-, and later two-, legged carnivores. Their numbers and physiques altered to suit the times, standing large and massive when the climate produced mild seasons of plen-tiful vegetation, and shrinking smaller and less hulking during glacial periods when forage was comparatively scarce and a smaller body size better maintained core temperature. No other land-based megafauna have endured through the ages as have bison. They are hard not to admire, not just for their appearance but also their perseverance and uncanny adaptability.

Early man venerated bison much as we do today, probably to a greater degree, because the animals provided food, shelter, and warmth. When Blue Babe was being attacked by that lion, or lions, on the other side of the world in Europe humans were accustomed to blocking the cold of winter with the heavy robes of bison and other furry ungulates and nourishing themselves with the equivalent of bison ribeyes.[11] Paintings adorning the walls of caves at Altamira, Spain, portray bold, handsome bison. Many of those sprawling images, some of which are life-size, were crafted in life-mimicking pigments.[12] These were not mere stick figures, not doodles to pass the time until the rain stopped. These were meant to show respect, even awe. Ochre, hematite, and manganese were used alone, or diluted or mixed with other substances, to produce varying shades of skin tones. These Stone Age artists put much thought into the images they wanted to create with the color palette and canvas at their disposal. If the image alone didn't reflect enough respect for the animals, it was further enhanced and given lifelike qualities by the artist's use of rippling rock wall contours to add heft, some muscular definition, to the paintings.

That idolization of, and reliance upon, bison came to North America with those humans who walked from Asia east to the continent. As in the old world, in the new one the beasts were hunted for food and shelter, clothing and fuel, even ornamentation. Evolving societies of native cultures were nothing if not inventive and practiced at finding what they needed. Bison hides were scraped clean of fat and muscle to become tepees and robes. They were stretched over curved tree limbs to form bull boats that could be paddled across a river. Bison ribs became runners for winter sleds, while sinews launched arrows from bows or served as thread. And, of course, the meat was about the richest protein around.

But bison were more than sustenance and shelter. Great Plains people viewed them almost as deities, and perhaps rightfully so, considering not only their sheer bulk and demeanor but also the reliance on them and their cultural significance. Bison were mythical, practical, spiritual, and transformative animals. Black Elk held bison in particular regard. Born shortly before the end of the Civil War, this Oglala Sioux holy man fell sick when he was nine years old and lingered for several days in a semiconscious state. During that period, he had a vision in which he was taken to the center of the Lakota world and instructed on the keys of earthly unity. "I was seeing in a sacred manner the shapes of all things in the spirit, and the shape of all shapes as they must live together like one being," he recalled.[13]

As a young man, Black Elk traveled for a while as part of Buffalo Bill's Wild West show, though he would later return to the Black Hills of South Dakota and Wyoming to describe for whites the traditions of the Lakota. In 1932, with his son acting as translator, Black Elk related his life story to a biographer. During hours of interviews, Black Elk explained the Lakota's reverence for bison. "The buffalo represents the people and the universe and should always be treated with respect, for was he not here before the two-legged peoples, and is he not generous in that he gives us our home and our food?" he asked rhetorically. "The buffalo is wise in many things, and, thus, we should learn from him and should always be as a relative with him."[14]

But human predators, primarily those with white skin, didn't always share that respect. Hunters hired by the railroads to provide meat for the gritty crews building the Transcontinental Railroad, military personnel working to deprive the native peoples of their foremost sustenance, and buffalo hunters making a living by selling bison robes and hides decimated the species in the nineteenth century, pushing it toward extinction. So great and widespread were the killing fields that a Paiute medicine man, Wovoka, near the end of the century instructed his people to perform a once-forgotten dance that he maintained would drive the whites from the landscape.

Wovoka had been born in Nevada, about seven years before Black Elk. Though his teenage years were spent living with a white family, a time during which he learned about Christianity, when he was about thirty years old he refocused on Paiute traditions and beliefs. A powerful vision he experienced during the total solar eclipse of January 1, 1889, spurred Wovoka to revive the Ghost Dance—which an earlier Paiute medicine man, or healer, had started in 1869. That man, Hawthorne Wodziwob, encouraged his followers to perform a circle dance. A series of visions convinced him that doing so would wipe the white people from the earth while native cultures would be left to prosper. Wovoka built on this message through his own vision, and promoted it as a way to cleanse the world of whites and renew the landscape and its wildlife, including bison. "All Indians must dance, everywhere, keep on dancing," urged Wovoka. "Pretty soon in next spring Great Spirit come. He bring back all game of every kind. The game be thick everywhere. All dead Indians come back and live again. They all be strong just like young men, be young again."[15]

But the return of bison was not spawned by these visions or Ghost Dance rituals. Late nineteenth-century technological advances gave buffalo hunters even more reason to kill bison. These advances seemed ready to doom both the species and the native peoples who relied upon it. As more and more bison were killed, the people who once followed the great herds through the seasons continued to lose hold of the Great Plains as their homeland and were being pushed into reservation life. The downfall of bison herds was dynamic, though not accomplished solely by two-legged white predators. Other factors included the hunting by native cultures and even predation by wolves and grizzlies. Some think disease may also have played a role. Myriad factors contributed to the Great Slaughter.

Bison miraculously did come back, but not due to a prophecy. Their future was ensured by a handful of players, of white and native cultures, who sensed the demise of the great animals and worked to prevent it. There were men whose names stand out in American history, as well as some who have been over-looked. Among those often relegated to the back of the story are several men with Native American blood, including two who built a turn-of-the-century herd of several hundred bison that today is key to the return of purebred bison to the Rocky Mountain Front that sidles up to Glacier National Park. Still, it was a modest number of players, a small, far-flung group in a sparsely populated, far-stretching nation at the turn of the twentieth century, that crossed paths and collaborated as they worked to preserve bison. Today we see their success in small but strikingly rich, diverse pools of bison genes nurtured from Canada to Mexico, from Iowa to California. These men had no template to work from, no previous conservation mission or map that they were trying to emulate. There were no instructions, no how-to manuals. They were acting upon their own instincts, developing their own theories, arguing when necessary to gain some forward momentum in securing a place in the country where bison could survive.

Their timing coincided with a national consciousness welling up around the conservation of wildlife and natural spaces. John Muir had been praising the values of nature in promoting the High Sierra and what would become Yosemite National Park. His efforts corresponded with the rise in the 1870s of magazines such as *American Sportsman*, *Forest and Stream*, and *American Angler* that cultivated national audiences concerned about wildlife. Emerging at the same time were various organizations dedicated to wildlife and conservation, groups such as the League of American Sportsmen, the Camp Fire Club, and the Audubon Society.[16]

Four of the actors who had key roles in engineering the recovery of bison had big, oversized personalities; they were proud of their accomplishments, and not shy about announcing them. Each had hunted bison. Yet each came to recognize the dark fate bison faced, and was determined to see the animals avoid it. To a large degree they succeeded, as bison numbers rebounded from dozens to hundreds to thousands and then tens and even hundreds of thousands. Not to the millions that once roamed the West, but to herds that today ostensibly will prevent the species from vanishing.

But while the numbers are impressive, the touted recovery of bison as a unique, genetically pure species is not that simple and not so certain. Arguments have been made over whether the species is indeed recovered, saved from extinction, and some courts have entertained those arguments. At the moment, there doesn't seem to be any great urgency to resolving them, thanks to an estimated half-million bison in North America. Those animals are divided into two groups: commercial herds, raised for meat, their decorative hides, and even their heads as Western chic mounts on display in homes, hotels, and lodges; and conservation herds, which are viewed as inviolate reservoirs of pure bison genes intended to preserve the species. Media mogul and philanthropist Ted Turner owns the largest commercial bison herd, some fifty-one thousand head,[17] while conservation herds are scattered across the West and the Great Plains states, most often in units of the National Park System but also in preserves such as those managed by the Nature Conservancy and on Native American reservations.

Conservation herds stretch from Canada's Wood Buffalo National Park in the Northwest Territories south to Yellowstone, and from California to Iowa. State parks from Florida to Utah and even "landscape zoos"—with enclosures of tens of acres—in California feature bison. The National Bison Association, a non-profit organization that promotes commercial bison operations, has a goal of seeing bison numbers reach one million, possibly as soon as 2025. And yet, the International Union for Conservation of Nature and Natural Resources lists bison as near threatened.

Many scientists accept that the plains bison is an ecological relic, one effectively extinct within its historic range.[18] There are scant few bison roaming wild as they did 150 years ago, and the bulk of bison in North America are in commercial herds often managed to a degree as if they were cattle. Some of these captive bison face selective breeding, are moved through rotational pastures depending on the season, and are provided veterinary care on occasion. Altogether, that approach to managing bison threatens to move them away from their *Bison bison* ancestors both physiologically and behaviorally. At the same time, suitable land for bison is disappearing quickly. Two-and-a-half-million acres of shortgrass prairie were lost to agriculture between 2015 and 2016.[19] Another 1.7 million acres were transformed in 2017.

The species' future depends on our best animal husbandry, for both commercial and conservation herds. Without dinner-table appeal for bison ribeye steaks, tenderloins, and tri-tips and the desire to mount their heads over fireplaces in trophy homes, there would be little incentive to ranch bison. Were it not for the Interior Department's determination to preserve bison as genetically pure, or as pure as possible, and the resolve by native peoples to connect with their spiritual past, the number of conservation herds very possibly would struggle to grow in number with healthy genetic diversity.

Compounding the threat of genetic pollution and pocket conservation herds is the reality that bison have been removed from all but a sliver of the Great Plains. Bison in large numbers don't seem to mesh with our societal explosion of cities and towns, industrial zones, agricultural conglomerates, and even ranchettes. Without room to roam, conservation herds are limited in number of both herds and individuals. The removal of bison from the landscape also has affected the region's ecosystems by disrupting natural processes that other native species thrive in and rely upon. The cascading ecological impacts are clearly visible, both in terms of fauna and flora. As bison go, so, too, go a number of other species that evolved alongside these cloven-hoofed creatures and which also have been slowly squeezed by development that turned the Plains into suburbia and conglomerate agricultural tracts. Swift fox, black-footed ferrets, and greater sage-grouse all face precarious futures without society's intervention.

There are reasons for optimism. After all, bison have great public appeal. *Tatanka*, the Lakota word for buffalo, entered into popular lexicon in 1990 via the Oscar-winning movie *Dances with Wolves*. The designation of bison as the national mammal in 2016, along with the arrival of ground bison and bison steaks in groceries, raised the visibility of an animal that once was more numerous than any other ungulate on the North American landscape. The federal government's efforts to see bison as a pure species remain on the landscape is a huge plus in their favor. But now, little more than a century after efforts to preserve bison began, the species faces a puzzling legal and biological predicament. Though sheer population numbers early in the twenty-first century placed an estimated five hundred thousand plains bison in North America, 96 percent of those animals are in commercial herds and lack genetic purity due to century-ago experiments to blend bison and cattle into some sort of super-livestock. Those experiments were conducted, ironically, by some of those who also worked so very hard to preserve the pureblood species. Today some conservationists argue the species, in a genetically sound form, needs the protection of the Endangered Species Act to survive. Some scientists view that as hubris, a grand measure of hyperbole. If a bison is 99 percent pure, containing just 1 percent cattle genes, does that weaken the species? That debate can, and will, continue without immediately dooming bison. But society must be willing to allow bison to recoup some of the landscapes they've been removed from if we want the species to succeed. There is a large amount of shortgrass and tallgrass prairie lands outside the National Park System that, in theory at least, could be opened to bison. Native peoples have nearly one hundred million additional acres on their reservations that could help support the animals. More acreage could be found on public lands held by states and the federal government. The era of large-scale conservation does not have to be a vestige of history or victim of development. We just need to be more creative and willing to forge alliances that would benefit from wild bison. In turn, bison would benefit the landscape, as it has been demonstrated that they are ecologically better than cattle or sheep. Bison are icons not just of the West but of the entire country. They are cultural centerpieces and are seen as key to lifting up native peoples spiritually, economically, and in terms of longevity. They should be given the opportunity to thrive not as open-air zoo specimens but as ecologically functioning biological engineers on the land.

Those sentiments are shared half a world away. In Romania, in the Southern Carpathian Mountains, European bison, or wisent, vanished from the landscape two centuries ago. But work is underway to release at least one hundred of the species by the end of 2020. Those pushing the initiative point to many of the same reasons for their recovery operation: European bison create a mosaic landscape with their grazing, which in turn benefits biodiversity. Part of the region targeted for wisent encompasses the Țarcu Mountains, which are a component of one of Europe's last significant wilderness areas. Successful recovery of the species would not only be an environmental victory, but is seen as a way to benefit the region economically, as well.[20]

The Landscape

The region, once labeled "the Great American Desert," is now more often called the "heartland," or, sometimes, "the bread-basket of the world." Its immense distances, flowing grasslands, sparse population, enveloping horizons, and dominating sky convey a sense of expansiveness, even emptiness or loneliness, a reaction to too much space and one's own meager presence in it.

—Encyclopedia of the Great Plains

The Great Plains is a topographical tabletop, one about five hundred miles east to west and two thousand miles north to south. Though not as flat as a table, the region nevertheless lacks a substantial range of mountains like the Appalachians, the Rockies, or the Sierra. It quite understandably could have developed an inferiority complex, for the East and West coasts urbanized much more quickly than this heartland, and across a much greater area. It took the 1862 Homestead Act, a legislative tool for encouraging the nation's westward expansion, to see what was possible out on the Plains. But for more than a few, taming this landscape proved impossible. Even today, more than 150 years after the Homestead Act ignited a land rush where settlers who could tame 160 acres of land for five years received it free and clear, the Plains are a tough place to live.

This is a breathtakingly wide expanse of land, as I discovered after graduating from college. Determined to see, and more specifically ski, the Rockies, I stuffed my few belongings into the back of my boxy 1978 Subaru wagon and headed west from New Jersey, only to run into the Plains on the other side of Missouri. I didn't find many trees to slow the wind or soften the sun's glare. Park your car along I-70 after leaving Topeka, Kansas, and stand on the highway's shoulder and you'll be awestruck by a setting that runs to, and then bends off, the horizon in all directions. Touching all, or parts, of a dozen US states, the roughly five hundred thousand square miles within the Great Plains province wash ashore at the foothills of the Rockies on its western edge and dip into the Missouri River on its eastern boundary. But it is bigger still, two thousand miles north and south, extending from the prairies of Canada's Alberta, Manitoba, and Saskatchewan provinces, all the way south to the banks of the muddy Rio Grande River.

Stand on the Wyoming prairie, or on that in Kansas, the Dakotas, Nebraska, or Oklahoma, and the open country flees from you in all directions. The plains cower from the Rocky Mountain Front in Colorado and Montana, but only in physical relief. There are no majestic peaks here, and yet, the Great Plains, with sun beating down, scant water, and seemingly perpetual wind, is as demanding a place as one of Colorado's fourteeners for those unprepared.

When I first ventured into the Great Plains, a young man making his first encounter with what lay west beyond West Virginia where I spent my college days, the contrast in landscapes was startling. Behind me were heavily treed mountains with leaping streams. Spread out before me were endless, mountainless plains rolling in all directions. A sea floor without the sea. Cattle, not bison, dotted the prairie on either side of I-70 for much of the 603 miles from Kansas City all the way to Denver.

To begin to appreciate this landscape, you must understand how it came to be. The Rocky Mountains, and even the Appalachians, are easier to admire and grasp than the Great Plains because of the sheer bulk that they send up and the geology that they expose. The Great Plains is a subtler region, or *physiographic division*, as topographers would tell you, one in need of both a geologic and geographic primer. North America's geologic contortions imbued the Plains with rich soils. During the Cretaceous Period more than sixty-five million years ago, an immense inland sea, the Western Interior Seaway, sloshed across the region. Into its warm waters sank the organic detritus of fish, amphibians, reptiles, seaweeds, and any land-rooted vegetation that was washed into the sea. Then came the slow ratcheting up of the Rocky Mountains. Geologists continue to puzzle over the exact mechanism that served as the jack, but some speculate that as the oceanic tectonic plate was forced to the east it didn't sink deep below the North American plate, but took a shallower pitch. As it did, it pushed up the mountains, much as a throw rug scooches up when your foot catches the edge. These riveting mountains, with their steep, canyon-incised flanks, drained rains and snowmelt through the foothills, carrying soils and other vegetative flotsam into rivers that then deposited them on the Plains. As the Cretaceous faded after its seventy-nine-million-year run and transitioned into the Paleogene, and it into the Neogene, the evolution brought glacial episodes with towering rivers of ice bulldozing additional soils and silts into the region. They even remodeled the landscape in places. Streams were pushed into different directions; the mighty Missouri River was shunted roughly 180 degrees, shoved away from its northward flow and sent off to the south.[21] All the while, more sediments were carried to the region on the breezes. Mineral-rich grains blasted into the sky by volcanic eruptions rode the winds to the Great Plains from the Great Basin far to the west.

Prehistoric life became imprisoned in this geology. Microscopic plankton, both from flora and fauna, that were buried deep by other layers of sediments and eventually placed under great pressure and heat, turned into oil and natural gas. Dinosaurs turned into fossilized remains. The fossils in the Plains led to the great bone wars of the nineteenth century in places such as southern Wyoming, Colorado, and Nebraska, while the oil and gas continue today to be pulled from below the Plains states for energy. All these geologic perturbations over tens of millions of years produced an incredibly diverse topography. Along with the Missouri, the Milk, Yellowstone, Powder, Cheyenne, Platte, and Dakota rivers carve through the country. So, too, do the Medicine Bow, the Tongue, Arkansas, and Niobrara rivers. Mountains are not a hallmark of the Plains, but a few provide geographic relief, poking up as inland islands above the prairie sea. Along with the Black Hills in today's South Dakota and Wyoming, there are the Snowy (Big and Little) and Judith Mountains in Montana, as well as the Little Rocky Mountains. But that's about it.

This is a very big place with a very complex personality. Despite its identifying name, the Great Plains is not self-defining, is not solely a flat, mid-continental placeholder. It climbs in elevation from a reasonable two thousand feet above sea level to a lung-testing—for true flatlanders—seven thousand feet. It embraces the rolling hill country of the Black Hills, the flat prairies with "amber waves of grain" that stir in the breezes that sweep Kansas and the Dakotas, and even the volcanically puckered landscape of eastern New Mexico. Steady erosion for the past five hundred thousand years sculpted the intricate formations found in Badlands and Theodore Roosevelt national parks.

Patches of ponderosa pine forests, buffalo grass and wheatgrass prairie, a mix of bluestem and sandsage prairie, and even oak-hickory forest appear along the eastern edge of the

Great Plains. There are expanses of fescue prairie, sections of mesquite and aspen, and some juniper-oak savanna.[22] There are draws, washes, gullies, ravines, coulees, arroyos, and canyons. Topographical quirks—cliffs and sinks—were used by Native Americans when it came to hunting bison. Bison herds would be chased by the hunters up to, and then over, these geologic "jumps" to their death. These death traps still stand out today near Chugwater, Wyoming, and on the Sanson Buffalo Jump within Wind Cave National Park in South Dakota. Some outcrops run a mile in length and stand fifty feet tall, and many are still littered with bones.

But the "plains," the mostly flat sections, are what come to mind when you hear the term uttered. At first glance, this can appear to be a desolate place, especially if it's winter and a thirty-mph wind blows snow in your face, or if it's summer and the cloudless sky offers no relief from the hundred-degree heat. Trees are few and far between in the heart of the Plains, too. Instead, you're greeted by a mix of shortgrass and tallgrass species that are the dominant vegetation. The eastern slash of the Great Plains province that greeted whites three centuries ago gained a bit of height and structure with switchgrass that reached ten feet into the sky, and big bluestem, another prairie grass that rose eight feet above the soil. During the growing season, asters and sunflowers brought more color and some height. Perennial bunchgrasses still today are found in most, if not all, states east of the Rockies. Along with providing forage for bison, pronghorn, and deer on the Plains, the grasses offer cover and nesting habitat for a variety of bird species. Ample rainfall drives the vegetation's growth. These plant species anchor deep root networks, locking the soil in place while also adding organic matter that encourages farming. On the more arid western half of the Plains grows sagebrush and grama-buffalo grass, the latter a runt compared to switchgrass and big bluestem. While it can struggle to reach ten inches in height, the buffalo grass carpets the prairie with a rich mix of other grasses: western wheatgrass, needlegrass, bunchgrass, and fescues.

Walk the prairie and, if you come after a soft, pattering rain, with the clouds clearing and the sun streaming through, the essence of the landscape rises up. Breathe deeply and fill your lungs with it. The moist air wicks up the pungent scent of sagebrush. As you stride through acres of this woody shrub, your legs brush the branches and their aromatic leaves release an indelible piquant fragrance. If you're on the far western edge of the Plains, or perhaps in the Black Hills, you also might inhale a sweet, piney bouquet courtesy of ponderosa pines. Along the Plains' eastern half, there might be a buttery scent, from prairie dropseed. All this vegetation, as it always has, provides food and habitat for pocket gophers, prairie dogs, and prairie chickens. They, in turn, are prey for black-footed ferrets, swift foxes, coyotes, bobcats, ferruginous hawks, golden eagles, and other raptors. Pronghorn antelope—North America's fastest creature, able to accelerate to fifty-five mph in prairie sprints—and white-tailed deer rove the Plains as well. A mysterious herd of elk drifts through the Red Desert dune fields of southwestern Wyoming.

A well-aged, faded map hanging on a wall in my home locates the many native cultures that historically called the Plains home. People now known as Kickapoo Shawnee, Omaha, and Winnebago lived on the eastern edge where the states of Minnesota, Iowa, and Missouri have been carved out of the country. The Mandan, Brule, Ponka, Yankton, and other Sioux communities made the middle of the Plains home, while the Crow, Gros Ventre, Blackfoot, Shoshone, and Assiniboin peoples claimed the western side. Cheyenne and Arapahoe people also lived on part of this landscape, as did the Minnetarees.

For tens of thousands of years, and still today, the largest animal on this landscape has been the plains bison, known to most people as buffalo. Biologists classify the species as *Bison bison*, or even *Bison bison bison*. But the animals were tagged as "buffalo" by the *coureurs de bois*, the French-Canadian trappers of the seventeenth and early eighteenth centuries. The name stuck with the *voyageurs*, fur traders who worked for the Hudson Bay Co. and the North West Co. and who called beef *boeuf*. Whichever name you choose, these animals are impressive to behold. Spend enough time in the Plains states and exploring their landscapes and you're bound to encounter bison. Growing up in New Jersey, the only bison I encountered were pictured in magazines and sequestered in zoos. Not until my first visit to Yellowstone, in the mid-1980s, did I see bison in the wild. Driving through the park's Hayden Valley for the first time is an experience you don't forget, both because of the hundreds of bison and the traffic jams. Why some people think the hulking animals are tame is impossible to answer. Even after stopping at one of the park's entrance stations and being handed a flyer warning them of the unpredictable nature of bison and how they like their space—move closer than twenty-five yards to these animals and you could be ticketed by a ranger—visitors pull over and park on the road's shoulder, get out with their cameras and, with each successive shutter click, take a step or two closer to the bison that seems so small in the viewfinder. Or they'll remain in their vehicles, slowly inching forward in the "bison jam," and roll down their windows to snap a close-up of the bison alongside their rig. Rangers try to stop these behaviors, knowing full well how unpredictable, cantankerous, and dangerous bison can be.

There are times when the bison come to you, as was the case with my experience camping near Lone Star Geyser. I've also shared a campground with them in Theodore Roosevelt National Park in North Dakota. Crawling out of my tent one morning, I found about a half-dozen bison milling about the Cottonwood Campground. Some were munching the green grass for breakfast, while a big bull was using a tree as a backscratcher. Later in the day, while hiking toward Wind Canyon, I watched as a herd spilled through a mountain pass and rumbled down into the canyon. Standing on the trail, I knew that this scene had been repeated across the Plains for thousands of years. Bison close-ups also abound in Wind Cave National Park, and there's little that compares with watching small bands moving freely across the prairie, or grazing the flats above the Snake River in Wyoming as the morning sun's rays paint the Tetons.

You don't easily confuse bison with cattle. Bison are taller at the shoulder and greater in girth, woollier, and not often swayed or intimidated by human onlookers. In Yellowstone's expansive Hayden Valley, herds of bison loll about at midday, chewing their cud, swatting flies with their tails, gazing about. And of a sudden, they'll take up en masse and move in late afternoon, browsing slowly as they go. As the tourist traffic slows on the Grand Loop Road and then stops, often in the middle of the road, cameras snapping and rolling, bison keep moving. Driving by these shaggy animals, they do look tame, and even willing to let you reach out your vehicle's windows to scratch behind their ears. It can take a concerted effort to spook the big bulls and cows, who seem to consider us with disdain, an inferior species. An Oregon man discovered this in August 2018 when, emboldened very possibly by a fermented beverage or three, he got out of his vehicle and pranced and preened and hooped and hollered, taunting a bison that was slowly moving across the park road. When the bison finally half-heartedly charged him, the man somehow managed to avoid the animal. He was not lucky enough, however, to evade law enforcement rangers, who arrested him two days later at the Many Glacier Hotel in Glacier National Park where, rangers said, he again was taunting, but this time with other human visitors. A few weeks later Raymond Reinke, fifty-five, of Pendleton, pleaded guilty to four charges, including one for having an open container of an alcoholic beverage in his vehicle and another for disturbing wildlife. He was handed a 130-day jail sentence, a bargain compared to what he might have encountered on the end of the bison's horns.

Most people who view bison do it sensibly, from a distance. It's usually a subconscious, or even conscious, matter of self-preservation. Even though the modern-day bison are smaller than their Pleistocene ancestors, they still are imposing at more than six feet tall at the shoulder, ten or more feet long from nose to rump, and weighing as much as two thousand pounds as adult bulls. Females are roughly half as large, which is still too large for you to mock within striking range.

Why add more bison to the landscape? Because they belong there. They once were an integral part of the landscape. They evolved with it, tilled it, manipulated it, engineered it. They were then, and remain today, ecological engineers. They mow the land differently than domestic livestock, often in a healthier fashion if they are left alone. Bison don't graze as hard as cattle; instead, appearing finicky, they browse and move frequently. The grass always is greener over there. Grazers such as cattle and sheep nip the vegetation off at or near ground level, while browsers like bison eat green stems and leaves. As a result, they leave behind grasses of varying heights, while the grazers often settle in for their meals and leave stubble in their wake. Bison also tend to pass over forbs, a choosiness that increases plant diversity. They spend less time than cattle around water sources, and so don't trample riparian areas or graze the surrounding vegetation down to the ground. All things being equal, cattle will spend hours around water; bison take a drink and move on.

These big animals don't require dietary supplements to remain healthy or to pack on weight for market.[23] They'll move with the seasons across their habitat. Some herds historically moved as much as two hundred miles to retreat to lower elevation winter habitat with lower snowfall, and so less work for a meal. That big hump on their backs? It is a mass of muscle that evolved as bison plowed their heads through the snows of winter to reach summer's leftover meals. When driven by hunger, these animals can shovel through eighteen inches of snow with their heads.[24] Hunger can be a powerful motivator, as bison generally require a daily diet of thirty pounds or so of grasses, sedges, willow, and even the occasional wildflower, such as a bouquet of scarlet globemallow. [25]

Their size, and tendency to group together against threats, makes it hard for wolves to take healthy bison down. Elk and deer are much easier prey. Still, some wolves in Yellowstone's interior have figured out how to survive on bison. The Mollies pack, whose territory is deep in the park's Pelican Valley, is the only pack that regularly preys on bison. That choice was in part due to the fact that while elk leave the park's interior for lower-elevation wintering grounds, these wolves stay behind to endure the winter along with the bison that stay put. The wolves have figured out how to take down bison, usually without getting injured or killed in the process. But it's still not easy. While the predators can kill an elk in roughly four minutes, it can take fourteen hours for fifteen wolves to kill a bison.[26] Elk run, hoping to outdistance wolves. That leaves them defenseless to predators looking to hamstring their prey. Bison, however, stand their ground and rely on their horns and hooves for defense. The resulting need for more muscles, and the protein-rich diet of bison, has produced wolves in the Mollies pack that are 5 to 10 percent larger than wolves that concentrate on elk down along the Lamar River. One male measured by researchers weighed nearly 150 pounds.

Wolves might be the consummate killing machines in the wild kingdom, but bison are the apex creatures. Everything about them affects all other life-forms on the Plains. Their habit of rolling on the ground to shed fur, crush biting flies, and, for males, embed their scent in the dirt, creates "wallows," small craters in the earth. These wallows are no small depressions, and at times bison might seem fastidious in creating them. Some bulls will seek ground softened, perhaps thanks to a seep or rain puddle, and then thrust a horn into the dirt like a pick. With growing vigor the animal then drops to the ground and uses both horns as well as the hump on his back to grind his desired indentation into the earth.[27] Repeated use by any number of bison can grow some wallows to about nine hundred square feet—roughly the size of half a volleyball court.[28] And because wallows are returned to again and again by bison that squirm about on their backs, grating their spines, humps, and flanks into the ground, the dirt is compacted. The result, when rains come, is that these depressions can turn into ephemeral water holes. These oversized puddles are used by the Plains spadefoot toads as nurseries, they nourish wetland plants, and they can even influence runoff. Botanists for the National Park Service have found that wallows can aid prairie plants that grow in moist settings and that, overall, they contribute to prairie biological diversity since their size, shape, and water-retention capabilities attract different grasses and forbs. Miniature wetland gardens, if you will. National Park Service researchers calculated that at the pinnacle of the bison population there might have been more than 1.5 billion wallows. Some of these relic depressions can be seen from the air today.[29] In some areas, once you know what to look for, you can find yourself surrounded by them. You won't find them in cattle pastures. Cows don't wallow.

Bison are not averse to showing wolves a thing or two about dominance. In 2002, researchers in Yellowstone watched bison drive wolves away from recent kills the wolves had made, and saw a herd of nearly forty bison chase off eleven members of the Druid Peak pack that had pulled down a cow elk. The bison then surrounded her to keep off the wolves. Another time, onlookers watched as a half-dozen bison repeatedly scattered eight napping wolves.[30] Videographers in the park even captured a week-old calf hold off an attacking wolf long enough for mom to arrive.[31] And, at a state park in Florida, a bison was photographed running off an alligator. Some Yellowstone visitors have experienced the temper of bison firsthand, having been gored and even flipped into the air by those that they approached for photos too closely.

Bison are community builders, too. The grazing of their herds assists prairie dogs in building their colonies, and provides nesting habitat for the melodious western meadowlark, chestnut-collared longspur, and other songbirds. Explore prairie grasslands and you'll find the mountain plover, lark bunting, and ferruginous hawk. More than three dozen bird species are associated with grasslands once tended to by millions of bison.[32] Some birds have something of a symbiotic relationship with bison. Starlings and cowbirds will hop a ride on the back of bison, in part to be close by when the animals kick up insects out of the prairie grass, and also to pluck insects out of the fur they're clinging to. It's also thought that there is a collaborative relationship between bison and prairie dogs, as the dogs' constant nibbling on grasses in their sprawling colonies spurs fresh growth, even into the fall, that bison relish.

Through their grazing, bison also stimulate vegetative growth, and they inhibit the spread of woody vegetation by rubbing not just their horns on shrubs and trees but their entire bodies as they scratch a massive itch. If there are no trees around, a nice boulder will suffice. The grazing habits of bison created de facto firebreaks on the prairie, as flames would run up to the vegetative mosaics bison formed with their shifting meals and sometimes stall, diverting into areas with heavier vegetative fuels.[33] While bison cows can live to twenty years—with many of those years prime for producing offspring—males are into old age by their twelfth year. Hard winters with deep snow can quickly cut those limits.[34] But even in death bison give to the landscape, their bodies feeding wolves, bears, coyotes, and the various scavengers that trail those predators, and returning nutrients to the soil, nourishing fungi and microbes.

On North America, the descendants of Blue Babe eventually separated into two subspecies, the plains bison and the wood bison. The two are similar in appearance, though the plains bison are a bit smaller and stockier with thick "chaps" of hair down their forelegs. The taller, more angular wood bison carry a more square hump, have a darker pelage, and tend to have straighter, less frizzy hair on their heads. While Yellowstone is home to the largest wild herd of plains bison, Canada's Wood Buffalo National Park claims that distinction for wood bison. But outside of national parks and some state parks, the loss of grasslands to settlement and agriculture has affected many of these species. Bison, of course, have lost vast landscapes they once roamed at will. So, too, have black-footed ferrets, small, slinky, carnivorous cousins of weasels, that were thought extinct until 1981. That's when a ranch dog in Meeteetse, Wyoming, trotted home with one in its mouth, happy but ignorant of the significance of its catch. An ambitious captive breeding program has boosted their numbers. And yet, while recovering ferret colonies today can be found in Badlands and Wind Cave national parks in South Dakota, the Fort Belknap Indian Reservation and the UL Bend National Wildlife Refuge in Montana, and more than a dozen other locations in the Plains states, they remain endangered as a species.

The examples of negatively affected species go on. The US Fish and Wildlife Service considers swift fox populations to be ample, but their natural habitat on the Plains has been cut by about 60 percent due to growth of the human footprint.[35] Also struggling to survive against this loss of room is another Great Plains native, the mountain plover. The transformation of grasslands into industrial agricultural plots and asphalt rectangles surrounding big box stores has plovers heading toward threatened species status, something their East Coast and Great Lakes relatives already have. These diminutive birds are known to some as "prairie ghosts," as their dusky coloration helps them blend almost seamlessly into the landscape. The name could be prophetic if their habitat continues to shrink.

As land has gone into agricultural production, or been cleared for other development, non-native bird species in the

Plains have increased in number as the native vegetation that many species evolved with has been lost. Ring-necked pheasants, gray partridges, and house sparrows are among the invasive species competing with native species.[36] But if we could give bison a larger slice of the public landscape, some of these other species just might expand, as well. Because bison utilize the landscape differently than cattle—moving more often, not lingering around water sources, favoring a different vegetative menu—native vegetation would gain an ally against invasive species, riparian areas wouldn't be so trampled, and the prairie not so heavily grazed. Wildfires, more likely in a warmer, drier climate, might not be as destructive on the Plains thanks to the vegetative patchwork left by bison.

Though the Great Plains is defined by prairie and sometimes referred to as the Great American Desert, it is an arid but not a waterless region. The Missouri and Platte rivers and their tributaries funnel snowmelt through the Plains. For early nineteenth-century explorers, these rivers provided access to the unknown West as they traveled by canoe, keelboat, and pirogue. These waters also provided the explorers' larder, as lakes, oxbows, and kettle ponds lured deer, elk, and bison, as well as mallards, pintails, teal, and Canada geese, among other species. Beavers were the engineers of the water world of the Plains. Their dams affected water flows, created ponds that in turn became lush riparian areas, and even "managed" woodlands to a certain extent by chewing downing trees.

Considering their size, horns, demeanor, and long, indomitable presence on the continent, it's understandable that bison for so long have been held in esteem. We marvel at their long history, how their very being exudes the concept of wildness in today's over-populated and developed world, their encapsulation of raw power. They appeared on the back of the Indian Head nickel that was minted from 1913 to 1938, became a symbol of the Interior Department in 1917, and have been part of the

National Park Service arrowhead emblem since 1952 because of bison's reflection of conservation. They were designated the national mammal of the United States in May 2016. But admiration for bison goes much further back. They played a key role in nourishing civilizations, literally and figuratively. For more than ten thousand years they were a veritable cupboard for Paleo-Indians, Native Americans, and settlers, providing food, clothing, and shelter. At day's end, Native Americans would return to tepees made with bison hides, use bison robes as insulating carpets and as blankets, and cook meals in massive bison stomachs. They and mountain men alike would use bison sinews for thread; turn horns into goblets, powder horns, and ladles; and reduce hooves through boiling into glue for attaching arrow points to shafts. Bison fur—fine, insulating hairs close to the body covered by more coarse outer hairs that provided a layer of protection against rain and snow—filled pillows, was woven into ropes, and adorned headdresses. For some, it even found new life as human hairpieces.[37] The coarser outer hairs also were used to fashion horse halters. Not overlooked were bison tails, which became fly swatters.[38] Portions of hide served as saddle blankets, were fashioned into moccasins as well as drums, and used as palettes. Bison brains tanned these hides, while hearts became pouches. The animals' manure, plopped down as patties on the prairie, when dried became fuel for fires when wood was not available.

Meat was not just a given, it was survival and a daily meal for many native cultures.[39] That which wasn't to be eaten promptly had to be cured, and that meant hours carving thin strips from the carcasses to hang in the sun. This work was done by the women, who also spent hours fashioning tools and utensils from bison bones, and more time adding artistic flare to both clothing and tepees.[40] Sections of the hide were fashioned into "parfleches," early storage trunks. In North Dakota, I gazed at one of these handsomely decorated bags that was hanging from the roof of an earth lodge at Knife River Indian Villages National

Historic Site. Geometric designs painted in vivid reds, blues, oranges, and whites covered the hide. These nineteenth-century suitcases safely stored clothes, dried foods, and trade items. In an effort to keep the parfleches safe from rodents and any rain that might leak through the lodge ceiling, rawhide swatches were threaded onto the cord that suspended the bags.[41] Two centuries ago, George Catlin saw parfleches and more in person. Raised in the heart of New York State on the family farm, he set out in life to follow in the footsteps of his father, a successful attorney. But his passion to paint prompted Catlin to shelve his law books and take up brush and palette with a studio in Philadelphia. Though he initially concentrated on small portraits, one day he was awe-struck by a delegation of Native Americans that passed through Philadelphia on their way to Washington, DC.

He recalled this incident in *Letters and Notes on the North American Indians*:

> A delegation of some ten or fifteen noble and dignified-looking Indians, from the wilds of the 'Far West,' suddenly arrived in the city, arrayed in all their classic beauty—with shield and helmet—with tunic and manteau—tinted and tasseled off, exactly for the painter's palette. In silent and stoic dignity, these lords of the forest strutted about the city for a few days, wrapped in their pictorial robes, with their brows plumed with the quills of the war-eagle. . . . Man, in the simplicity and loftiness of his nature, unrestrained and unfettered by disguises of art, is surely the most beautiful model for the painter—and the country from which he hails is unquestionably the best study or school of the arts in the world . . . and the history and customs of such a people, pre-served by pictorial illustrations, are themes worthy the life-time of one man, and nothing short of the loss of my life shall prevent me from visiting their country, and becoming their historian.

Catlin let go of miniatures and instead worked on detailing the history of Native Americans by traveling the West.

From 1832 to '37 Catlin made forays into the West and Midwest, visiting dozens of tribes to record their lives on canvas. He spent time with the Blackfoot, Crow, Cree, Sioux, Mandan, Cherokee, Choctaw, Creek, Osage, Chippewa, Sauk, and Fox. The artist produced more than three hundred portraits during his journeys, as well as a couple hundred related paintings. He marveled at the native languages, noting at one point that the Crow and Blackfeet speak completely different languages, that the Dakotas have a different language than the Mandans. His portraits of two Mandan chiefs on the Upper Missouri so impressed the chiefs that they named Catlin *Teh-o-pe-nee Wash-ee*, or medicine white man. Catlin's words and paintings captured the Great Plains in its pre-development rawness and magnificence before settlers swept over it.

"In looking back from this bluff, towards the West, there is, to an almost boundless extent, one of the most beautiful scenes imaginable," he wrote in 1832 as he gazed out from the Lower Missouri River. "The surface of the country is gracefully and slightly undulating, like the swells of the retiring ocean after a heavy storm. And everywhere covered with a beautiful green turf, and with occasional patches and clusters of trees."

You can find such settings in some places today, but very few with bison on them.

Tatanka

Historically the buffalo had more influence on man than all other Plains animals combined. It was life, food, raiment, and shelter to the Indians. The buffalo and the Plains Indians lived together, and together passed away. The year 1876 marks practically the end of both.

—Walter Prescott Webb, *The Great Plains*

For many of us on our first, and perhaps only, visit to Wind Cave, Yellowstone, Badlands, Theodore Roosevelt, or other national parks or preserves with bison, that first glance of the animals in the wild can be startling and enamoring at the same time. It's a fleeting connection with something truly wild that lives on the landscape as it has for tens of thousands of years. We ooh and ahh, take some photographs, and head down the road. End of connection.

Native Americans and bison, however, are intertwined, and always have been. Bison are *iinii* to the Blackfeet Nation, *hotova'a* or *hotoaao'o* to the Cheyennes, depending on the sex of the animal, and *kúcu* to the Utes. The Cherokee people know bison as *ya-na-sa*, while in the Pawnee language they are *tarha*, and in Navajo *ayani*. But regardless of what they are called, bison were, and continue to be, celebrated by these cultures. They not only gave life through their meat but they represented a linkage, a fastening with the earth and freedom that native cultures seek. Stories told by elders through the generations tell of bison coming from the underworld, from caves, caverns, and grottos winding deep into mountainsides. In South Dakota, on the western edge of the state that features the undulating pine country known as the Black Hills, you can walk right up to the narrow, rocky hillside crevice where, a Lakota creation narrative tells us, bison streamed out into the sunlight: hundreds and thousands of animals stretching across the prairie in a dark brown rising tide. These *Pte-O-ya-te* were "relatives, who provided humans with food, clothing, shelter, tools, medicine, and many other necessities."[42] The connection was further enforced by the story of White Buffalo Calf Woman, who taught the Lakota to be honorable, respectful, and self-disciplined.[43] Not only did the Buffalo People stampede from that crevice which led to making Wind Cave a national park, but the Lakota view the air that rushes out of that small hole as "the breath of life."[44]

Similar creation narratives have been handed down by native peoples across the West, telling of bison spewing forth from a cave in Texas and in the Crazy Mountains of Montana.[45] The herd that spilled out of the Crazy Mountains "spread wide and blackened the plains," according to Crow chief Plenty Coups. "Everywhere I looked great herds of buffalo were going in every direction, and still others without number were pouring out of the hole in the ground to travel on the wide plains."[46] Pawnee narratives also tell of spirit animals that live in caves, waiting for the time when they will be granted access to the surface.[47]

The depletion of the great herds in the nineteenth century deprived native peoples of food and shelter, and was also a spiritual loss. Bison represented the universe and superseded the arrival of humans. Unlike many of the whites who came west, native peoples viewed bison with honor and dignity. Just as Lakota and other native cultures believed bison had come from the underworld, they also believed they returned to that protective dwelling place after the whites decimated the great herds. A Kiowa narrative tells of a woman who woke one morning shortly before sunrise and went to a spring to get some water. As the growing predawn light began to illuminate the wafting mists filling the valley, she saw an old bison cow walk out of the vapors. Trailing her were more bison, some old and weary, some wounded, some young calves.

"As she watched, the old buffalo cow led the last herd through the mist and toward the mountain," goes the traditional story. "Then the mountain opened up before them, and inside of the mountain the earth was fresh and young. The sun shone brightly and the water was clear. The earth was green and the sky blue. Into this beautiful land walked the last herd of buffalo, and the mountains closed.

"The buffalo were gone."[48]

Even before President Thomas Jefferson sent Meriwether Lewis and William Clark west in 1804 to find out exactly what he had purchased from the French via the Louisiana Purchase of 1803, bison figuratively have been going into the mountain, literally heading toward their demise. Once the horse reached the Plains with Spanish conquistadors, native peoples' ability to travel expanded. Before the horse, dogs had pulled the travois carrying family belongings. The arrival of the horse made it possible to carry more, carry it farther, and carry it more quickly. Horses enabled these peoples to become nomads, to follow the bison on their migrations and so always have food and shelter nearby. If winter's snows made it difficult for horses to carry warriors all the way to the bison, the hunters could dismount, don snowshoes, and drive bison into drift-clogged ravines. There the snowbound bison met their fate at the hands of hunters with their lances.[49]

As went the bison, so too did the Native Americans. The prediction by William Tecumseh Sherman, one of the Union Army's heralded Civil War generals, that the destruction of the great bison herds would directly impact Plains native peoples, proved true. It has been debated whether the US military formally set down a strategy to wipe out bison herds specifically to subjugate the Plains cultures, or whether it was a word-of-mouth strategy. Regardless, General Sherman was determined to reduce bison herds. "As long as Buffalo are up on the Republican [River], the Indians will go there," the general wrote to his friend, General Sheridan, in 1868 from Fort Laramie in the Wyoming Territory. "I think it would be wise to invite all the sportsmen of England and America there this fall for a Grand Buffalo hunt, and make one grand sweep of them all. Until the Buffalo and consequent(ly) Indians are out (from between) the Roads we will have collisions and trouble."[50] The army was so intent on gaining the assistance of buffalo hunters to kill bison that it gave them ammunition for free.

Sherman's proposal was not made jokingly, notes David D. Smits. A historian focused largely on the American frontier following the Civil War, Smits's research revealed that the upper echelon of the army "routinely sponsored and outfitted civilian hunting expeditions onto the plains." "Buffalo Bill" Cody's reputation and nickname was built on killing bison, and he often lived up to that repute. In the fall of 1871, he led a group of newspaper editors from New York and Chicago, businessmen, General Sheridan, and fellow soldiers into the prairie not far from present-day North Platte, Nebraska, for a hunt. They wound up slaughtering more than six hundred bison, taking only the tasty tongues and leaving the rest for scavengers.[51]

Robert Utley long served as chief historian for the National Park Service. One of his favorite topics, despite the many possibilities that the far-flung reach of the National Park System afforded him, was the American West, about which he wrote more than fifteen books. His examination of the frontier between 1846 and 1890 called the loss of bison a "cultural catastrophe."[52] It left Plains peoples with little option but to settle on reservations.

Their daily lifeblood had been wiped out, and other wild game was following that path, too, as whites moved west. The meager prospects of living off the land as they had for generations left those placed on reservations with little incentive to flee. The cultural dynamics of western life had swung; nomadic peoples were doomed, settlements were growing. It's been an ongoing story through history: the conquerors dictate to the conquered. As whites moved west, striving to tame the landscape, game was becoming harder to find and the nomadic life of many cultures was not just threatened but ended.[53] John Fire Lame Deer didn't know Utley, but shared his opinion. A Lakota Sioux born on the Rosebud Reservation in South Dakota in 1906, Lame Deer struggled with finding his identity, as many young men and women of any culture commonly do. He tried his hand on the rodeo circuit as both competitor and clown, and struggled with alcohol, gambling, and chasing women. Not unlike Wovoka and Black Elk before him, when Lame Deer reached his mid-fifties he found his calling as a Sioux holy man, one who embraced his Native American upbringing and background after an early-in-life introduction to the white culture. It was an encounter with "civilization" that soured Lame Deer on whites as a nearsighted culture that failed to appreciate the wonders and beauties the natural world offered.

Lame Deer's affinity with the natural world gave him empathy for bison. "If brother buffalo could talk," he said, "he would say, 'They put me on a reservation like the Indians.' In life and death we and the buffalo have always shared the same fate."[54]

That fate was destined, directly and indirectly, by the white settlers, traders, mercantilists, and opportunists looking to make a buck however possible. Those who sold liquor, brought disease, and were determined to claim lands for themselves effectively brought down the native cultures just as they contributed to the fall of bison. The disappearance of bison, it seemed to John Fire Lame Deer, would be coupled with the disappearance of tribal cultures. "The buffalo gave us everything we needed. Without it we were nothing. Our tepees were made of his skin. His hide was our bed, our blanket, our winter coat. It was our drum, throbbing through the night, alive, holy," he said.[55]

The sudden loss of bison—there are estimates that bison numbers dropped from millions to hundreds in just a decade late in the nineteenth century—was crippling economically as well as physically to native cultures. Three university economists, Donna Feir and Rob Gillezeau of the University of Victoria and Maggie E. C. Jones of Queens University, described those cultures that revolved around bison as "once the richest in North America, with living standards comparable to or better than their average European contemporaries."[56] Once the bison were gone, however, these cultures became some of the poorest. The economic blow continues even today, more than a century after the Great Slaughter. Communities that depended on bison for just about everything in life—food, housing, clothing, and some medicines—had per capita income levels in 2000 that were roughly 30 percent lower than those native peoples who were not so dependent on bison. Within a generation the average heights of members of "bison-dependent nations" dropped as many as two inches due to nutritional losses. "One way to understand the effects of the decline of the bison is as one of the most dramatic devaluations of human capital in North American history," the economists held.

At the turn of the twentieth century, the future of bison would have been assured if the great herds could have been replenished simply by driving them out of caves. It was thought that there were only about 1,110 pureblood bison in private, captive, ownership in the United States on January 1, 1908, and no more than twenty-five thought to ramble wild in Yellowstone's interior. There were another fifty-nine bison in the park at the time, but they lived essentially as domestic livestock in a fenced pasture in the Lamar Valley.[57]

There was a time when bison were apex creatures on the landscape. They can regain that role, though it won't come overnight, and it certainly won't be easy. Cattle long have owned the open range—during a six-year period, from 1874 to 1880, Wyoming's cattle census alone reportedly jumped from ninety thousand to more than five hundred thousand[58]—and while bison might offer a better economic return, turning a thousand-head cattle operation into a thousand-head bison operation comes with significant costs. But incremental steps are being taken to regain a prominent role for bison. Today, more than a century after the Great Slaughter, native peoples are working hard to reawaken and strengthen their cultural, spiritual, economic, and health connections with bison. Some tribal governments have exerted their rights to hunt bison that move out of Yellowstone; since 2006, a small handful of tribes have been given permits from the state of Montana to hunt bison outside Yellowstone borders. In 2014, the Cherokee Nation in Oklahoma brought an end to a four-decade absence of bison on its reservation by accepting animals from Badlands and Theodore Roosevelt national parks.[59] Three years later, the Kalispel Tribe of Washington State received three bison from Wind Cave.[60] The Blackfoot Nation in Montana has grown its own herds with bison from Canada.

Helping orchestrate some of these bison transfers is the InterTribal Buffalo Council, a collective organization of more than sixty tribes whose mission is to put bison back on reservations to foster their cultural, traditional, and spiritual relationships with the animals.[61] But there's a larger effort underway: to see one million bison roaming North America in the coming decades. As with other efforts through the past century, it's an ambitious goal, driven by the InterTribal Buffalo Council, the National Bison Association, the Canadian Bison Association, and the Wildlife Conservation Society. While achieving such a goal—roughly doubling the current number of bison on the continent—could bring recognizable economic rewards to commercial operations, tribes also see the cultural benefits they would receive from having bison to use in ceremonies and pow-wows, and to improve the diets of their members.[62]

Each year the Council works to obtain surplus bison from parks and other conservation herds for its member tribes. It has landed federal grants to underwrite a program that supplied bison to school lunch programs on reservations in South Dakota.[63] But bringing bison to the table is just one element of reawakening Native American culture among tribal youth. In 2017, 2,300 acres of federal lands were set aside in the Black Hills for the Sioux to both preserve the past and look to the future. Without a connection to their cultural past, younger generations of Sioux could struggle to define what they want in their future. Land tied to their cultural history is, of course, a solid connection. As is regaining the Sioux language. And, understandably, so are the bison that once again roam this corner of the Black Hills, the Pe' Sla grasslands.[64] But obtaining bison and renewing traditions are not always easily done, even now in the twenty-first century. Sometimes there is a will, but not a way to success. Sometimes the way that seems obvious is blocked.

The Fort Peck Indian Reservation in northeastern Montana is home to the Assiniboine and Sioux peoples. Its rolling prairie straddles parts of four counties, and with more than two million acres, it is the ninth-largest reservation in the country. The Missouri River traces the southern boundary of the reservation before drifting off into North Dakota. Looking at a geographic map of the reservation, it's not hard to see the outline of a bison created by drainages that feed into the Missouri. Though located nearly 425 miles from Yellowstone, the reservation stands ready as an incubator of sorts for bison that many groups are seeking. But, unfortunately, a series of hoops must be jumped through to obtain park bison. First, the park service needs to quarantine surplus Yellowstone bison for up to five years, on average, and test them regularly for brucellosis. If the animals are still disease free after that period, they can, in theory, be shipped to Fort Peck, where the reservation has a five-hundred-thousand-dollar quarantine facility of its own. Once bison arrive there, they must be held for another year in quarantine. The long quarantine periods are necessary because the disease can lie latent. Bison that pass through those hoops can be released onto the reservation's bison pastures or, in theory, shipped to other destinations. That protocol works. It's been tested. More than sixty Yellowstone bison initially were sent through the quarantine process that started in 2012. All came through without testing positive for brucellosis. And yet, Montana officials have been hesitant to approve an ongoing bison transfer program. Reservation staff are ready. They've developed a memorandum of understanding with Montana and federal officials to routinely test any bison they would get from Yellowstone for brucellosis. They've written the procedures for capturing any park bison that escape from the roughly fifty thousand acres the Assiniboine and Sioux have set aside for bison.

Montana's political and legislative roadblocks frustrate Robbie Magnan, a barrel-chested army veteran who has grown the reservation's bison herds to some seven hundred animals since 2000. He is not one to mince his words.

"Everyone else we talked to is on the same page, with the exception of Montana," he replies when asked if he was optimistic the quarantine protocol would be approved. "We jumped through every hoop they wanted us to go through, and yet they create more and more."

Federal officials seemed to add another hoop late in 2018 when they offered to send five Yellowstone bison to the reservation. The catch? They wanted reservation officials to sign off on a memorandum of understanding that they would put the animals through only the last of three steps of quarantine monitoring. Lawyers for the reservation feared that the MOU forever would be an impediment to having the quarantine facility approved to handle all phases of quarantine. The impasse might be viewed as a twenty-first-century white man's slight of native peoples if the National Park Service at Yellowstone wasn't so willing and even anxious to see the program succeed. Montana's position seems illogical, even blockheaded. Why oppose a program that would send brucellosis-free bison from Yellowstone, via truck, padlocked if need be, to Fort Peck, where they would go through another five-year confinement period to double-down on their brucellosis-free status? The program would help reduce Yellowstone's bison population to a number more in line with what Montana officials prefer, and provide an economic, cultural, and dietary boost to the Assiniboine and Sioux.

Just as John Fire Lame Deer feared many years ago, that Native Americans and bison shared the same fate at the hands of whites, today's tribes see a lack of justice in how Yellowstone bison are being treated. Park-service staff attest to that. P. J. White, Rick L. Wallen, and David E. Hallac, park-service wildlife biologists, presented that concern in their 2015 book, *Yellowstone Bison: Conserving an American Icon in Modern Society*. They wrote that some Native Americans believe the stigma brucellosis has attached to Yellowstone bison is in some ways equal to the disparaging attitudes white settlers had toward native peoples. It's a view long held by the Lakota, who see their culture and trajectory intertwined with that of bison. That belief was voiced by Oglala Sioux leader Red Cloud in 1903 when he told his followers of meeting with representatives of President Theodore Roosevelt. "We told them that the supernatural powers, Taku Wakan, had given to the Lakota the buffalo for food and clothing. We told them that where the buffalo ranged, that was our country," he said. "We told them that the country of the buffalo was the country of the Lakota. We told them that the buffalo must have their country and the Lakota must have the buffalo."[65]

Ninety-six years later, on a dry, unseasonably mild February 7 when the temperature climbed to sixty degrees in Rapid

City, South Dakota, representatives from a handful of Native American tribes set out to walk and ride (in vehicles as well as atop horses) nearly five hundred miles to Gardiner, Montana, and Yellowstone's north entrance. The Buffalo Walk, as their mission was called, was seen as a way to show solidarity with park bison that were being gunned down as they migrated out of Yellowstone.

"Now our Buffalo brothers are being mercilessly slaughtered close to extinction and need our help," said Everett Poor Thunder in rallying for the cause. "To give our help we must walk, and through this walk of unity and solidarity will come a healing blessing for those involved."[66] It was an arduous pilgrimage, at times into the brunt of blizzard-like conditions, that united fifteen Native American tribes together in protest over the bison's plight.

The journey culminated with a ceremonial dance out of the long-ago past to venerate both warriors and bison. The Sun Dance has been called the preeminent religious ceremony of Plains tribes. Historically, it tested the stamina of warriors as they made a personal sacrifice through self-mutilation, marked the summer solstice, a time of renewal, and reconnected the people to the earth. The Lakota people revered the ritual as a physical sacrifice to summon population growth among their people and the bison.

The Buffalo Dance is a precursor to the main Sun Dance. Done as a lure for bison, warriors scrape at the ground with their feet, to imitate bison. Central to the Sun Dance is the piercing of a warrior's chest or back muscles for placement of bones or sticks. Cords would be attached to these items and then tied either to a Sun Dance pole or a bison skull.

On February 27, 1999, Gary Silk of the Standing Rock Sioux performed this key segment of the dance near the Roosevelt Arch at Yellowstone's north entrance. Slits were cut into his back, and then wooden sticks were threaded through them. To each stick, a cord that had been tied to a buffalo skull was attached. As painful as it was for Silk, it brought to life a vision he had had. "I kept having these dreams that this buffalo was laying there . . . I don't know if he was dying, or shot . . . but he was trying to get up. So in this dream I had, I hooked [myself] up to him and tried to pick him up."[67] Silk then circled those who had made the walk, dragging the skulls behind him, stopping briefly at each compass point to sing a prayer. After seven such circles, he stopped so his young daughter could sit on the two buffalo skulls. Silk took hold of the tail of a horse that was brought to him. A sharp slap on the horse's rump sent it, and Silk, bolting forward, the momentum pulling the sticks from his back.

During Yellowstone's fiery summer of 1988, I tagged along with a park archaeologist when she went out to mark the forest locations of ancient wickiups still standing, though in a state of collapse. These temporary shelters, constructed by leaning long saplings together in tepee fashion, were thought to have been used by Sheep Eater, or Tukudeka, communities. The Tukudeka people made Yellowstone more of a permanent home than the other native peoples that passed through hunting or to collect obsidian at Obsidian Cliff in the northwestern section of the park. If forest fires that summer consumed the wickiup remains, at least the park would be able to locate where they had stood by the metal stakes this woman drove into the soil.

Down through the centuries, more than two dozen native cultures have established some connection with the Yellowstone landscape, either as a place to hunt or gather obsidian, or as a landscape their trails passed through. Crow, Blackfeet, Shoshone, Flathead, Nez Perce, and other Plains tribes were given use of the lands by the 1851 Treaty of Fort Laramie. Seventeen years later, another treaty, also reached at Fort Laramie in southeastern Wyoming, revoked many of the provisions of the earlier treaty. The Bannock communities that resided west of the park routinely traveled through the area to reach hunting grounds to the north-east of Yellowstone. Most of these passages went without inci-dent. But in 1878, a band of Bannock warriors fled through the park, intent on reaching Canada where they would join up with Lakota leader Sitting Bull. During their passage they surprised a surveying team and absconded with some stock and supplies. In early September, a military party that was providing protection for visitors on vacation encountered the warriors to the east of the park and killed eleven. Another thirty-one were captured, along with about two hundred horses and mules. While some Bannock and Shoshone bands still hunted in the southern areas of the park in the mid-1890s, by 1895 the native peoples that had long utilized the landscape now embraced by the park for hunt-ing and gathering had been forced onto reservations.

A century later, many Native Americans are working to renew their connections to the park's landscape, its flora, and its fauna. They are focused particularly on bison because of the ani-mals' manifestation of power and strength as well as their spiri-tual connection to native peoples. That relationship was formally recognized by the InterTribal Bison Council in 2014 through a treaty "of cooperation, renewal and restoration" signed by eight tribes (others have signed on in the ensuing years). One section of the treaty reads:

> it is the collective intention of WE, the undersigned NATIONS, to welcome BUFFALO to once again live among us as CRE-ATOR intended by doing everything within our means so WE and BUFFALO will once again live together to nurture each other culturally and spiritually. It is our collective intention to recognize BUFFALO as a wild free-ranging animal and as an important part of the ecological system; to provide a safe space and environment across our historic homelands, on both sides of the United States and the Canadian border, so together WE can have our brother, the BUFFALO, lead us in nurturing

our land, plants and other animals to once again realize THE BUFFALO WAYS for our future generations.

The treaty is working in Wyoming, bringing bison back to a landscape that last saw them in 1885. That year marked the last time the Eastern Shoshone were allowed to hunt bison on their land, the Wind River Indian Reservation. Twenty-two years before, in 1863, the federal government had promised the Eastern Shoshone a landscape of 44.6 million acres that touched parts of Utah, Idaho, Montana, Wyoming, and Colorado for their homeland. In 1868, the government greatly reduced that to 2.7 million acres under the second treaty of Fort Bridger. Bison still were prolific on that landscape; in 1881, Shoshone hunters took thousands of bison. But in 1885, just ten were counted on the reservation.

Today, the bison population is going in the opposite direction. Jason Baldes has been working side by side with the Eastern Shoshone and Northern Arapaho peoples to place bison on the west-central Wyoming reservation. Growing up as a member of the Eastern Shoshone people, Baldes and his father, Dick, a biologist with the US Fish and Wildlife Service, spent countless days in the saddle exploring the Wind River Range that towers over the reservation's western border. After graduating high school, Jason navigated a series of community colleges and universities searching for the right fit for his Native American background. He finally found it at Montana State University, where he obtained both a bachelor's and master's degree in land resources and environmental sciences. Driving his interest in that field was a desire to see bison returned to the reservation. It was a thought that burrowed into his mind in 1997 when he and his father traveled to East Africa and witnessed a massive wildebeest migration. The idea wasn't simply to see bison as part of the reservation's landscape, but as a cultural, ecological, and nutritional fixture. What he calls "life's commissary."[68]

Baldes worked to develop the draft management plan for bringing bison back to the reservation with the goal of establishing a genetically pure, disease-free herd that would be managed as wildlife under the Shoshone and Arapahoe Tribal Game Code. Working with the National Wildlife Federation and the Eastern Shoshone's *Boy-Zhan Bi-Den* (Shoshone for "buffalo return") effort, Baldes saw the regeneration of a reservation herd in 2016 when ten bison from the Neal Smith National Wildlife Refuge in Iowa were freed. Another ten, from the National Bison Range in Montana, arrived in 2017. Both arrivals were momentous occasions, but the 2017 transplant was an afterthought in light of the birth early that year of the first bison calf on the reservation in 130 years. That calf's arrival was a significant event for the two tribes that have shared the reservation since 1878. Three more calves were born in 2018. The reservation herd is still small, fewer than two dozen animals early in 2019, but the hope is that eventually the Eastern Shoshone will once again be able to rely on bison for both cultural and dietary needs. Though other native cultures with bison also supplement revenues by selling bison meat and robes, Baldes views the animals more holistically, more reverently.

"If we have the cultural appreciation for this buffalo, why would we want to treat it as a monetary commodity?" he told me. "It's more important than that for me. Of course, economic development is a huge issue and tribes need access to capital, but for me, we have the opportunity to treat buffalo as wildlife with the greatest respect potentially available of any reservation. The cultural benefit for having buffalo and having access to them for sustenance, that's more important than the monetary gains of marketing the meat."

With 2.2 million acres on the reservation, acreage in the form of prairie as well as forest and mountains soaring to thirteen thousand feet, the plan is to grow the bison herd to one thousand or more and let it wander across four hundred thousand acres. Baldes would like to see reservation bison return to the nearby Wind River Mountains to the west and even the Owl Creek Mountains to the north. It's a vision of sustainability, both ecologically as well as for the health of Eastern Shoshone members. The average life expectancy of tribal members is just forty-nine, more than a quarter-century less than that of Wyoming's general population. Infant mortality, at nearly fifteen out of one thousand births, is more than double of that experienced by white Wyoming residents. As bison meat is higher in protein and lower in cholesterol than beef, making it a mealtime mainstay could help combat type 2 diabetes on the reservation. But there are other problems on the reservation that Baldes believes bison can help cure. High youth suicide rates, high school dropout rates, and unemployment rates.

"We have a lot of social problems that affect us. Buffalo is always seen as a way to help us heal from some of these atrocities of the past," he told me. "We're doing everything we can to create opportunities for our young people, who will become our leaders. And so whether it's language, whether it's substance abuse, health, we're doing everything we can socially to improve the lives of people on the reservation. Buffalo are integral to that, because it's not just an animal to us. It's kin. Every tribal member knows innately how important this animal was to our ancestors. We likely wouldn't be here if not for the buffalo, and so it's central to our ceremonies, the Sun Dance, the sweat ceremonies."

The same can be said at Fort Peck, where the integration of bison back into daily life involves programs for schoolchildren that connect them with the traditional, as well as modern-day, role of the animals. More than 1,500 children have participated. If state and federal authorities ever approve the quarantine protocol that Yellowstone officials developed and which in early 2018 gained the National Park Service's final go-ahead to put into operation, more tribes could see bison back on their lands. The Fort Peck quarantine facility, the first in North America operated by a tribal government, could once again be holding bison to complete the infection-monitoring period. Other sources of brucellosis-free bison include Elk Island National Park in Canada and, according to National Park Service officials, Wind Cave National Park. But the purity and historic content of genes from Yellowstone bison, their rich diversity that would benefit herds that lack those genes, make the park's bison highly sought. But Montana officials don't seem interested in seeing Yellowstone bison leave the park and cross their state to Fort Peck. They worry for the well-being of their livestock, even though there have been no documented cases of bison transmitting brucellosis to cattle. The problem, Robbie Magnan told me, is that Montana officials are "basically anti-buffalo." The cattle industry's grip on the state's livestock and wildlife interests is too strong. He's convinced that Montana officials "don't want to see buffalo on the landscape. And they use brucellosis as a scapegoat. They make it sound like it's so contagious it's almost like yellow fever."

A National Academies of Science report released early in 2017 supports Magnan's contention. A genetic mapping of brucellosis in northwestern Wyoming and into Montana traces the disease's spread to elk, not bison. The scientists found that while there has been no conclusive transmission of brucellosis from bison to cattle in the Greater Yellowstone Ecosystem since 1998, "direct contact of elk with cattle is more prevalent than contact of cattle with bison. As a result, the risk of transmission from elk to cattle may be increasing."[69]

"Montana makes me laugh because they make [bison brucellosis] sound so bad," Magnan told me. "If it was really that bad you would prohibit the movement of elk. But they don't. [Elk hunting] is such a big industry, they leave it alone."

The maligning of Yellowstone bison goes further when you consider that Montana does a poor job monitoring cattle in the greater Yellowstone area for brucellosis. Magnan cited an audit into how the state Livestock and Fish, Wildlife and Parks departments oversee the disease. Those studies documented that nearly 40 percent of the cattle shipped from ranches near Yellowstone was not tested for brucellosis. "The state really failed bad on it, but yet they can predict to us that it's not safe for us to bring buffalo up here," Magnan said with a sigh.

Perhaps in recognition of the National Academy of Sciences' report, Montana officials are quick to point out that a two-thousand-pound bison standing in the middle of a road in the middle of the night can be a pretty deadly object. Bison don't immediately flee from an approaching vehicle like elk or deer. A resulting collision can be deadly for both motorist and bison. Of course, a black Angus bull in the middle of the road can be just as deadly. Another issue is that bison usually go where they want to, and eat what they find. Defenders of Wildlife, a nonprofit wildlife conservation organization, along with some other conservation groups has created a compensation program for property owners who can prove bison damaged their property, whether it's a mailbox they pushed over or a field they wallowed in. If landscaping is damaged, gardens rototilled by hungry bison, or trees damaged by an animal looking for a scratching post, these conservation groups would step up with as much as one thousand dollars per landowner to compensate for the damage. It's one small way to buy some tolerance for free-range bison.

Further muddling the bison issue in Montana is that the animals are treated by state law as livestock, not as wildlife. As livestock, the animals technically need a clean bill of health from veterinarians. They also are classified as a "species in need of management" under the oversight of the Montana Fish, Wildlife and Parks Department, as well as the Montana Department of Livestock. While optimism was building in 2018 that this obstacle would be overcome, the year ended without resolution, and without the Fort Peck Reservation receiving more Yellowstone bison.

In late February of 2019, though, approval came for five Yellowstone bulls to be shipped to Fort Peck. Whether this marks the end of the intransigence remains to be seen. Cam Sholly, who arrived as Yellowstone's superintendent late in 2018, called the shipment "very important to the future success of the quarantine program." There were talks about sending another fifty-five park bison to Fort Peck near year's end, and Sholly was hopeful that more bison would be transferred in 2020. Still, "while this is a good start," he told me, "these numbers are largely symbolic. If this is going to succeed, more capacity and partner involvement will be necessary in the future." Yellowstone itself simply does not have the resources to process the numbers of bison through the initial stages of quarantine to meet the demands for park bison. But with the Blackfeet Nation working to increase the number of bison it runs on its reservation to the east of Glacier, and with the National Park Service eyeing that park as a candidate for another federally owned conservation bison herd, the pressure is increasing on Montana officials to compromise for the good of bison.

The Great Slaughter

There is no question that, so long as there are millions of buffaloes in the West, the Indians cannot be controlled, even by the strong arm of the government. I believe it would be a great step forward in the civilization of the Indians and the preservation of peace on the border if there was not a buffalo in existence.

—Democratic Congressman James Throckmorton,
of Texas, 1873

Stand on the plains of eastern Wyoming in the wind and look about. You might see no living thing but vegetation, some of it tumbling by. I have driven the southern stretch of the state on I-80 in all seasons of the year, and seen nothing but other motorists, vegetation, and ubiquitous ravens and magpies darting onto the highway to snag a piece of roadkill. To travel this same landscape in 1750 would have been like visiting a different world. You very likely would have been surrounded by bison. Tremendous herds roamed North America long before Columbus reached the New World, and they thrived until shortly after the Civil War. They came to the attention of Spanish explorers in the 1540s when Francisco Vázquez de Coronado led an expedition north from Mexico into the Southwest in search of the fabled Seven Cities of Gold. Coronado's mission to find and seize golden, bejeweled riches led him on a two-year odyssey all the way north into present-day Kansas with a military force of roughly 325 soldiers, several hundred Mexican-Indian allies, and perhaps 1,000 slaves and servants, along with roughly 1,500 stock animals. Though they roamed the Southwest for two years, they never did find the fabled cities. We know this thanks to Pedro de Castañeda de Nájera. Born in northern Spain, in the Basque country, he was a foot soldier stationed at a hot and humid military outpost in Culiacán in northwestern Mexico. A month after Coronado and his force left Compostela on the Mexican coast where they had assembled, they arrived at Culiacán. There de Castañeda left his wife and eight children to join the expedition. The journey was a pretty astounding adventure, as Coronado led his force through parts of Arizona, New Mexico, Oklahoma, Kansas, and Texas seven decades before English immigrants managed to gain a foothold on North America's Eastern Seaboard. De Castañeda waited twenty years after the expedition to formally write his journal. And then, he humbled himself before its readers, describing his "slight knowledge and small abilities" but assuring them of his ability to tell the truth. The mention of truthfulness was a passing slight against others on the expedition who had previously tried to relate its story. "Although not in a polished style," he wrote in a preface, "I write that which happened—that which I heard, experienced, saw, and did."[70]

Among the things de Castañeda saw roughly three hundred years before the onslaught against bison in North America began in earnest was a strange-looking beast that seemed to be an amalgamation of other animals. "[I]t is to be noticed first that there was not one of the horses that did not take flight when he saw them first, for they have a narrow, short face, the brow two palms across from eye to eye, the eyes sticking out on the side so that, when they are running, they can see who is following them," he noted. "They have very long beards, like goats, and when they are running they throw their heads back with the beard dragging on the ground." He told of a "girdle" around the middle of the body, woolly hair like that of sheep, and a hump on the back, "larger than a camel's." On the rump the animal had a short tail topped by a tufted pom-pom of hair. "When they run, they carry it erect like a scorpion," added de Castañeda. With this literary portrait the Spaniard vividly, and most creatively, likely became the first European to describe bison.[71]

So great were bison numbers, and so faithful were they to their migratory routes, that countless years of millions of trampling hooves had carved "traces" as much as fifty feet wide across the landscape during the herds' semi-annual hegira, driven by the seasons. Human travelers quickly embraced these paths for ease in travel across a landscape otherwise thick with pre-settlement vegetation. Native Americans, and later thousands of settlers, turned the traces into roads.[72] Lewis and Clark, George Rogers Clark, and even Abraham Lincoln walked the "buffalo trace" that runs between present-day Louisville, Kentucky, and Vincennes, Indiana. William McDonald, an enterprising settler, saw prosperity along this route. In 1812, at a place known as Sherritt's Graveyard in Dubois County, Indiana, he hung out his sign on what is believed to be the first tavern along the trace. Among his guests was William Henry Harrison, who later no doubt had more comfortable lodging in the White House during his term as president.[73]

Bison roamed the continent with no equal. There was a time when they were found as far east as present-day Washington, DC, north to Illinois, south into northern Florida and Mexico, and even as far west as Oregon. But it was on the Great Plains where bison grew their fame. These were the keystone animals. The locals knew what a good thing they had, and they didn't hesitate to take advantage of it. Along with stampeding herds off buffalo jumps to kill as many as possible at once, native hunters would don wolf skins, hoping bison would mistake them for coyotes and ignore them, and slowly crawl toward the animals at rest to shoot them with arrows. Other native hunters would encircle a small number of bison and then wield their bows. Still others would create a corral into which they funneled bison to their deaths. Bison were on the menu year-round for many Native American peoples, who found endless ways to roast, boil, broil, sear, and stew their flesh. They even pounded bison meat, with some fat and a handful of buffaloberries tossed in, into society's first power bar, pemmican. Ribs, the artist Catlin discovered during his years roaming the Plains, would be boiled down into "a delicious soup, which is universally used, and in vast quantities."[74] So dependent were native peoples on this protein that they perfected a way to give it shelf life, to dry it not with salt or smoking but simply by hanging thin strips in the sun for several days until the task was done.

Putting an exact number on just how many bison once grazed across the United States or the Northern Hemisphere is a task that has eluded many. It might be easier to count the snowflakes before your eyes. That's an exaggeration, but there were a lot of bison in North America, and estimates run the gamut, diverging by tens of millions. It's a numerical conundrum that shades a true understanding of the downfall of bison. Trying to fathom the collapse in forty years of a population of ten million bison is one thing, of sixty million or more is another. Today, the US Fish and Wildlife Service guesses that when Columbus reached the New World in 1492 there were as many as sixty million bison in North America. Others say there were thirty million, or maybe fifty million.[75] What everyone agrees on is that there were a lot. Lewis and Clark happened upon bison on a regular basis on their 1804–1806 journey to the Pacific Coast and back to St. Louis, and were astounded by the herds. "These last animals [buffaloes] are now so numerous that from an eminence we discovered more than we had ever seen before at one time; and if it be not impossible to calculate the moving multitude, which darkened the whole plains, we are convinced that twenty thousand would be no exaggerated number," they remarked of a herd encountered near the White River in present-day South Dakota.[76]

Whether native cultures kept similar track of the herds they saw is largely a mystery today.

Reports of enormous herds were typical immediately following the Civil War, when military forces were dispatched to the West (the region west of the Mississippi River) to conquer the frontier. When Richard Irving Dodge, a Civil War veteran transformed into a frontiersman for the US Army, and William Blackmore, a scout, captured their memories of their late-1800s escapades in the West, it sounded at times as if they were embellishing what they saw with their eyes. Blackmore tells of "an almost unbroken herd of buffalo" stretching for more than one hundred miles. Herds so long and broad that trains had no choice but to come to a halt to let them pass. Bison estimates not only rose into the tens of millions during their peak, but eclipsed even that staggering multitude. William Hornaday, who was so determined not to see bison go extinct that he wrote a voluminous treatise warning the nation of what it would lose if that happened, said trying to count the numbers of the mid-nineteenth century herds would be akin to estimating the number of leaves in a forest.

Hornaday was a hunter-turned-wildlife conservationist and naturalist, small in stature yet a dynamo of energy and commitment, obstinate when he found it necessary. His love of bison evolved from his efforts to kill some to display at the Smithsonian Institution in Washington, DC, during his time there as chief taxidermist. Before his encounter with bison, Hornaday traveled the world to kill animals for display in museums. But it was his experience with bison in the 1880s that not only developed in him a deep admiration for the animals, but also left him fearful for the future of bison and many other species. Late in that decade, assuming that the fate of bison had been determined, Hornaday wrote what amounted to a nearly three-hundred-page epitaph for the species, one he hoped would "cause the public to fully realize the folly of allowing all our most valuable and interesting American mammals to be wantonly destroyed."

Hornaday's book, *The Extermination of the American Bison*, written in 1889 when he was superintendent of the National Zoological Park in Washington, DC, might have included some exaggeration to forward his cause to lobby for the animals. Regardless, his esteem for bison showed through again and again. There was a time when herds were so massive in number and sheer bulk that they stopped river traffic when they would ford streams en masse, and even were blamed for derailing locomotives that tried to roll through herds.[77] It could take days for all the animals in a herd to pass a specific spot on the landscape. Dodge found it hard to grasp the enormity of the bison population. He recalled that on one outing he saw fewer than two dozen individuals occupying any one acre, yet the herd nevertheless was "not less than twenty-five miles wide, and from reports of hunters and others it was about five days in passing a given point, or not less than fifteen miles deep."

"From the top of Pawnee Rock I could see from six to ten miles in almost every direction. This whole vast space was covered with buffalo, looking at a distance like one compact mass, the visual angle not permitting the ground to be seen," recalled the colonel. "I have seen such a sight a great number of times, but never on so large a scale. That was the last of the great herds."[78]

It is a struggle today to comprehend herds so large. Imagine driving from Kansas City to Topeka along I-70 and seeing nothing but bison to the north and south as well as east and west, or from Cheyenne to Laramie in Wyoming on I-80, surrounded by bison. Or, better yet, from New York City to Princeton, New Jersey, on I-95, with bison to the left and to the right, slowly parting as you drive through them.

So numerous were the herds and adaptability of the animals, and so wide did they roam, that Hornaday speculated that bison would evolve various subspecies across North America. That's not inconceivable, given that bison migrated back and forth between North America and Asia and splintered off into various subspecies through the millennia as glacial periods ebbed and flowed. Pointing to the gaur in India and the African water buffalo, Hornaday presumed bison near the southern end of North America would evolve to have shorter hair due to the summer heat, and those near the northern end would be shaggier to cope with the cold. But they never had the chance. Bison were prey, and the human predators coming west after the Civil War proved ruthless, insatiable, and deadly. Their motives were multiple: deprive native cultures of food and shelter, feed the railroad workers laying the track for the steam locomotives, kill for sport, or earn a living by selling hides, tongues, and other parts of the bison to merchants in places such as Dodge City, where a heavy robe in good condition might bring the hunter fifty dollars.

So valuable were bison at market, Hornaday argued, that the federal government could have used that popularity to protect the species. He believed the government should have put an annual quota on bison kills so as to prevent the species from vanishing, while also providing an economic return to the nation. He figured that the total number of bison was so great in 1870 that five hundred thousand could have been killed on an annual basis without detriment to the overall population. They, in turn, would generate at least $2.5 million for the economy when sales of all goods and meats were tallied, a figure that translated to nearly $48 million in 2018. Placing a tax on buffalo robes, Hornaday maintained, would generate a revenue stream sufficient to employ "an army of competent men" to protect the herds from poachers.

Hornaday's transformation from hunter to conservationist came to completion as he worked on *The Extermination of the American Bison*. As he discussed the missed opportunity to both protect bison and generate a reasonable return for the country, he lamented that, "as yet, the American people have not learned to spend money for the protection of valuable game; and by the time they do learn it, there will be no game to protect."

The downfall of plains bison was underway long before Hornaday ran his calculations. It can be traced as far back as the 1830s, when the young United States of America began to expand constantly westward. Before settlement began, Native Americans trailed the great herds and killed what they needed for food and shelter. But as whites moved west and the eastern markets beckoned, the growing market for bison hides encouraged widespread killing, at least by the white hunters and mountain men. Those white expanding economies encouraged more native hunters to kill bison not for meat, but to sell their hides. Such was the demand that there came a point when it's been estimated that Native Americans turned ninety-six of every one hundred bison they killed into trade items. The American Fur Company proved a good market, buying forty-five thousand buffalo robes in 1839 and nearly seventy thousand the next year; French fur traders, meanwhile, exchanged muskets for robes.[79]

Catlin saw and understood what was happening. And as he saw the demise of bison coming, he voiced a crazy, patriarchal idea to protect the species, and their hunters, within the confines of a park. If nothing was done, he feared, both the bison and the native cultures would disappear. His solution was typical of the racism of the day: create "a magnificent park, where the world could see for ages to come, the native Indian in his classic attire, galloping his wild horse, with sinewy bow, and shield and lance, amid the fleeting herds of elks and buffaloes."[80]

Though Catlin's vision of a "nation's park" might have been intriguing, it was not realistic, and was certainly racist with its intent to subjugate native cultures to be on display. Of course, racism would continue to flourish in the West after the Civil War. Racism fueled the downfall of bison in the 1860s as the animals were killed not only to feed railroad workers and US Cavalry, but as a military strategy. General Sherman, in urging the Texas Legislature not to adopt a bill to protect bison, voiced his support for destroying "the Indian's commissary; and it is a well-known fact that an army losing its base of supplies is placed at a great disadvantage."

The attitudes of the military commanders, and even hunters such as Buffalo Bill, were condescending when it came to the native peoples. In a scenario repeated time and again through history, the "conquerors" asserted their will on other cultures. The Greeks practiced this, the Nazis did, and even present-day governments. As for bison, the soldiers and hunters were bent on their extermination, consciously and subconsciously. Though military commanders such as Sherman, fresh from the killing fields of the Civil War, found themselves in a different landscape, they approached their task in much the same way: leave death in their wake. In this case, the foes were the native cultures, and wiping out bison herds was a means to that end. The soldiers must have been taken aback by the seemingly constant presence of bison, but some if not most nevertheless took to the task of annihilating them. The military's ensuing campaign against the indigenous peoples of the Great Plains, coupled with efforts by those such as Buffalo Bill Cody, who killed thousands of bison to feed railroad workers, helped send bison populations on a swift and dizzying downward spiral. Sherman, whose reputation was built in part on the crippling march he led with Union troops through Georgia during the Civil War, wanted to have a similarly devastating and unnerving impact on the Plains peoples. In his view, "the quickest way to compel the Indians to settle down to civilized life was to send ten regiments of soldiers to the plains, with orders to shoot buffaloes until they became too scarce to support the redskins."[81]

Sherman's method was shared by other officers given the task of safely opening the West to white settlers. One disciple was Lieutenant General John M. Schofield, who commanded the Department of the Missouri that between 1862 and 1865 confronted Confederate troops in Missouri and Arkansas and also fought Native Americans. To Schofield, there was no better occupation than to "ward off the savage and kill off his food until there should no longer be an Indian frontier in our beautiful country."[82]

General P. H. Sheridan, in his autobiography, frequently mentioned his encounters with buffalo and the role the animals played for Native Americans. He came up with a strategy to focus on protecting settlers during the grazing and hunting seasons: when winter's cold and snow arrived "fall upon the savages relentlessly, for in that season their ponies would be thin, and weak from lack of food, and in the cold and snow, without strong ponies to transport their villages and plunder, their movements would be so much impeded that the troops could overtake them." To General Sherman, there was no shame it what they were doing. He looked back on his work driving native peoples onto reservations with pride, noting that it was accomplished in no small measure thanks to Civil War veterans who were looking for more warfare.

"These men flocked to the plains, and were rather stimulated than retarded by the danger of an Indian war," the general noted in his memoirs. "This was another potent agency in producing the result we enjoy to-day, in having in so short a time replaced the wild buffaloes by more numerous herds of tame cattle, and by substituting for the useless Indians the intelligent owners of productive farms and cattle-ranches."[83]

Buffalo Bill simply sensed that there were plenty of bison to go around, and so it didn't matter how many one killed. There were days out on the range when he couldn't count all the bison that he saw. During an eighteen-month stint supplying bison steaks, roasts, and tongues (a delicacy, due to its higher fat content) to the crews of the Kansas Pacific Railway, Cody figured he killed nearly 4,300 bison—roughly eight a day. Many fell from a shot from "Lucretia Borgia," a .50-caliber Springfield rifle he affectionately named after a fifteenth-century femme fatale. During this period of his life, Cody reinforced ownership of his nickname in a contest with "Medicine Bill" Comstock to see who was a better shot. The two were to spend eight hours killing bison, with five hundred dollars going to the one who claimed the most kills. This blood sport attracted a large audience. A referee was chosen to follow the two men out onto the prairie and tally their kills. Trailing these three were spectators by the wagonload and on horseback. By the end of the contest, Cody claimed sixty-nine kills, Comstock forty-six.[84]

Others also killed for the fun of it. Hornaday viewed the bloodlust as "the descent of civilization, with all its elements of destructiveness, upon the whole of the country inhabited by that animal."

Historians and onlookers of the day tell us that the great bison herds of the nineteenth century were divided and conquered by the expansion of the country. The move that began in 1863 to connect the Midwest to the West Coast by rail drove both a figurative and literal spike through the herds. Upon their completion at Promontory Point on the northern tip of the Great Salt Lake in what was then the Utah Territory, the tracks divided the massive bison herds into a northern and southern herd. Pursuing these herds was a growing number of buffalo hunters, who saw opportunity and came out in number to kill the animals. Some, like Cody, were hired by the railroads to provide meat for their workers, or worked independently to sell bison hides, tongues, and other merchandisable parts in Denver or Dodge City or elsewhere. In 1870, an estimated two million bison from the southern herd were killed. Much of the killing was done by teams of hunters and skinners. It wasn't just Buffalo Bill Cody and Medicine Bill Comstock who earned a living this way, but also Kit Carson, future lawman Pat Garrett, Charles "Buffalo" Jones, Frank Mayer, and many others. How they killed varied.

Cody preferred to ride his favorite horse, Brigham, to the head of a herd and shoot the lead animals while working to constantly turn the herd in a counterclockwise circle. The horse quickly learned his role. "He was a wonderful horse. If the buffalo did not fall at the first shot he would stop to give me a second chance; but if, on the second shot, I did not kill the game, he would go on impatiently as if to say: 'I can't fool away my time by giving you more than two shots!'" Cody said proudly.[85]

Some hunters killed by sneaking up on a herd, choosing a high vantage point, and methodically picking bison off one at a time with their Sharps or Remington rifles. The key was to make sure the first shot was deadly, so the bison would fall almost in place without startling the entire herd. Then the skinners would go to work. Mayer quickly saw the merits of hunting bison, which he referred to as "buffalo running."

"I got into it in 1872, when the rampage was at its height. The whole western country went buffalo-wild. It was like a gold rush or a uranium rush," he said. "Men left jobs, businesses, wives and children, and future prospects to get into buffalo running. They sold whatever they had and put the money into outfits, wagons, camp equipment, rifles and ammunition. I needn't talk. I did it myself. And why not? There were uncounted millions of the beasts—hundreds of millions, we forced ourselves to believe." At the time, bison hides sold for two or three dollars apiece, a sizable amount for a hunter in 1872. "And all we had to do was take these hides from their wearers. It was a harvest. We were the harvesters," recalled Mayer.[86]

Among the weapons of choice were the Hawken rifle and the Sharps 1874 sporting rifle. The Hawken, a .50-caliber muzzle loader, went west with mountain men and was accurate up to about four hundred yards. Robert Redford, in his portrayal of Jeremiah Johnson in the 1972 movie of the same name, could hardly believe his luck when he came upon one in the frozen grip of Hatchet Jack, a fellow mountain man killed by a grizzly.

"I, Hatchet Jack, being of sound mind and broke legs, do leaveth my bear rifle to whatever finds it," Redford's character read from a note pinned to Hatchet Jack's body. "Lord hope it be a white man. It is a good rifle, and kilt the bear that kilt me. Anyway, I am dead. Yours truly, Hatchet Jack."

Years later, the Sharps would replace the Hawken as the preferred killing tool. This .45- .50-caliber rifle was prized by buffalo hunters because of its long range, up to one thousand yards in the hands of someone like Buffalo Bill or Billy Comstock. A buffalo hunter by the name of Bill Tilghman was said to have killed more than 7,500 bison in his career. His rifle? A model 1874 Sharps—Serial No. 53858, .40-caliber with a thirty-two-inch barrel—that resides in the National Cowboy & Western Heritage Museum in Oklahoma City today.

Providing meat for railroad workers kept the buffalo hunters busy, as did a growing appetite for tanned leather. Technology made it easier to feed that appetite domestically and internationally. M. Scott Taylor, an economist in the Department of Economics at Calgary University, says there really is no mystery why bison were removed from the landscape. Economics, and technology, conspired against the animals. "What is surprising is the rate of killing and its variation over time: one half of the pre-contact buffalo population was killed in just ten years' time post 1870; the elimination of the other half took over one hundred years," he noted.[87]

The technological leap that helped hasten the downfall of bison was the perfection of a tanning process in England and Germany in the 1870s that enabled the quick conversion of hides into leather for shoes and factory machine belts. It drove up demand for hides while driving the southern herd down into extinction. With no motivation to dress out their kills and haul the meat to market, buffalo hunters simply needed to kill an animal, remove the hide, and move onto the next. "Historic accounts are clear that the introduction of the hide market vastly increased the return to buffalo hunting so that most meat was left to rot on the plains, and killing took place in regions where robes were of poor quality (much of the southern United States) and at times of the year when robes were worthless," the economist Taylor noted.

This new, more profitable demand for hides, not meat, came as a shock to some hunters. George "Hodoo" Brown learned of the change after lamenting warm weather that was spoiling the bison meat before he could get it to market. "They said to me, 'Why don't you skin them and just take the hides, and let the meat lay?'" said Brown. "I says, 'What the devil would I do with the hides?' One man said, 'Ship them to Leavenworth to W. C. Lobenstine. He'll buy your hides and send a check.'"[88]

William C. Lobenstine was a pelt dealer who in 1871 found a lucrative European market for bison hides. With a home office in Leavenworth, Kansas, he opened another to buy buffalo hides in the West Texas outpost of Fort Griffin. Hides dominated much of the town; at one point they were said to have been piled roughly six feet high the length of a block of the rowdy town. Hide hunters descended on the outpost from the surrounding grasslands and prairies.[89] And yet, lucrative demand notwithstanding, the Western frontier was not an easy place to master this profession. Hunters endured baking heat in summer, blizzards in winter, and pounding rainstorms the rest of the year. Buffalo Jones pointed out that skinning bison was neither quickly, nor always neatly, accomplished.

Some would take off the hide in excellent shape, leaving the head on the carcass, and then turn it over by main strength, while others cut off the head, and rolled the carcass on its back, using the decapitated mass to block up the carcass, thus facilitating the process of skinning. Some would drive a sharp steel rod through the neck of the animal and into the hard ground about eighteen inches, cut around the head back to the horns, split the skin on the belly, skin around the legs, then hitch a rope to the hide at the neck, and attach the rope to the doubletrees or to the rear of the wagon. To this the horses were fastened, and with a crack of the whip the team peeled off the hide as easily as taking off that of an onion.[90]

There was boredom at times for the hunters, but also stampedes that could land some in an early grave. And all the while they had to keep watch for native warriors. Mayer said they were a constant threat. But he understood their motivation; the white hunger for bison put their world at stake. "They sensed, if they weren't smart enough to know, and mostly they were, that we were taking away their birthright, and that with every boom of a buffalo rifle their tenure on their homeland became weakened and that eventually they would have no homeland and no buffalo," he said. "So they did what you and I would do if our existence were jeopardized: they fought. They fought with everything they had, in every way they knew."

Railroaders, always searching for ways to sell more tickets for their trains, turned the immense bison herds on the Plains into a target gallery. The "hunters" needed no flesh-and-blood horse, no long chase for their quarry. They simply bought a ticket on the "Iron Horse" and relaxed in a coach car until the engineer signaled that they were approaching a herd, as *Harper's Magazine* recounted in its December 14, 1867, edition.

Nearly every railroad train which leaves or arrives at Fort Hays on the Kansas Pacific Railroad has its race with these herds of buffalo; and a most interesting and exciting scene is the result. The train is "slowed" to a rate of speed about equal to that of the herd; the passengers get out fire-arms which are provided for the defense of the train against the Indians, and open from the windows and platforms of the cars a fire that resembles a brisk skirmish. Frequently a young bull will turn at bay for a moment. His exhibition of courage is generally his death-warrant, for the whole fire of the train is turned upon him, either killing him or some member of the herd in his immediate vicinity.

The railroad not only marketed the opportunity to shoot bison from its railcars, but opened a taxidermy shop in Kansas City where the kills could be mounted.[91]

We shouldn't be surprised that there are at least two views on which culture—Native American or Euro-American—better managed bison herds. The Plains cultures thought the military's approach to wiping out the great bison herds was wasteful, evidenced by the carcasses left rotting on the plains, a scene accelerated by the increasing market for hides, not meat, toward the end of the century. Hornaday, meanwhile, thought native peoples killed wastefully as well, sometimes taking five times as many bison as were necessary. But at day's end, Hornaday simply blamed mankind for the demise "of the most economically valuable wild animal that ever inhabited the American continent."[92]

Andrew Isenberg, a historian who wrote *The Destruction of the Bison*, blames both cultures for the animals' downfall. The horse and rifle benefited native hunters, making it easier for them to follow, chase down, and kill bison, while economic factors promoted bison hunting by both cultures. "Indian and Euro-American hunters pushed the species to the brink of extinction for commercial profit," concludes Isenberg. "Like other environmental catastrophes in the American West—the depletion of the California fisheries, the deforestation of the Great Lakes region and Pacific Northwest, and the 'dust bowl' of the southern plains in the 1930s—the destruction of the bison was, in part, the result of unsustainable exploitation of natural resources."[93]

There is no question that native peoples exploited bison. Why not? The animals provided for just about all their needs. But the end result of the exploitation differed between white and native cultures. For white people, the goal was to feed the markets, whether that meant literally nourishing railroad workers or providing hides that could be transformed into machinery belts. Native people sought to feed their own. They sought hides for shelter, clothing, and even for ceremonial purposes, some of which paid homage to bison. The Lakota people trace their existence to *Pte O-ya-te*, the Buffalo People. They had reason to see the herds remain, whereas the bottom-line desire of the military was to eradicate both the bison and the native peoples.

Philip Deloria instructs his Harvard students on these finer points. He himself had good teachers. His great-grandfather spent time as a minister on the Standing Rock Reservation in South Dakota, his grandfather answered the same calling for the Pine Ridge and Rosebud reservations, also in South Dakota, and his father, Vine Deloria Jr., was president of the National Congress of American Indians, as well as a historian who wrote *Custer Died for Your Sins: An Indian Manifesto*. A one-time musician proficient in clarinet, trombone, and mandolin who received a master's degree in journalism, Philip Deloria turned to history for his doctorate, which he received from Yale. With his PhD in hand, he went from New Haven, Connecticut, to Cambridge, Massachusetts, to become Harvard's first tenured professor of Native American studies. Portraying native peoples as environmentalists who constantly sought balance in their world is wrong, maintains Deloria. Native cultures of the nineteenth century viewed consumption, whether that involved bison or beaver or any other wildlife, much differently than did whites, he adds.

"Ideally, they tend to calculate their needs—and those are complex and do indeed go beyond simple subsistence—and have some rough index of how much beaver they need to take to meet those needs, more or less. One year, they may seriously over-hunt. The next year, they may not," the professor told me. "There's an unevenness and unpredictability about Indian trapping that makes white traders a little nutty—it's hard for them to interact with their own markets if their supply is uneven. One of the reasons for moving, in 1822, to a white trapper corps employed under conditions of debt peonage is because Indians are not producing enough fur for the markets, and not doing it predictably. White trappers immediately increase the output of fur to markets because they don't care at all about 'sustainability.' Indians might not have cared about it either, but the two groups did not approach their relationships with either markets or animals in the same way. It does not seem crazy to me to look carefully for something analogous with bison, given a slightly different time frame and different people."[94]

White people of the nineteenth century were known to kill just about anything just because they could. Englishmen visiting the West found it thrilling to hunt in general, but going after bison was a particular desire. "In the fall of that year [1872] three English gentlemen went out with me for a short hunt," recalled Colonel Dodge, "and in their excitement bagged more buffalo than would have supplied a brigade."[95] That had to be an astonishing number—or a tremendous exaggeration—when you consider that a Civil War brigade might have numbered 2,600 men. The colonel's hunting forays were profligate, multi-day affairs that put any and all sorts of wildlife in peril. One five-man hunting party arranged by Dodge tallied 1,262 kills over twenty days, a sum that included 127 bison, 11 pronghorn antelope, 223 teal, 57 wigeons, 187 quail, and, for good measure, 11 rattlesnakes and a bluebird.[96]

Such wanton killing did not go unnoticed. The time came when Buffalo Jones tried to warn Mayer that the herds were being wiped from the earth. Mayer wouldn't hear him, as he later recalled his conversation with Jones.

"Mayer," he began after the usual amenities and a stiff drink of corn whiskey, "Mayer, you and the other runners are a passel of dam' fools the way you are wiping out the buffalo. Don't you realize that in just a few years there won't be a dam' buff left in the world?"

I pooh-poohed at this kind of talk.

"Jones, you're clear off on the wrong side of the horse," I told him. "Why, there are as many buffalo now as there ever were. There are hundreds of millions of them."

"Are you getting as many as you used to?"

"Well, no. But that's my fault. I am hunting in the wrong place."

"Where's the right place?" Jones persisted.

"Damned if I know, but we are about to take off and find it tomorrow," I told him.

"You'll never find it," said he. "Because it just don't exist any longer. Unless we're mighty careful there won't even be a specimen to keep in a zoo."[97]

Two years later, an average of five thousand bison a day were being killed. Yellowstone was established that year, 1872, and its enabling legislation outlawed the wanton destruction of wildlife. But there was no one to enforce that regulation until the US Army arrived in 1886 to patrol the park. By 1876, the southern herd was judged to be wiped out. Six years later, the northern herd faced the same fate. Extinction for the species loomed in 1902, when, aside from some private herds such as the one Charles Goodnight had established on his Texas ranch, free-roaming bison numbers were thought to be as few as one hundred, with maybe two dozen in Yellowstone, hidden deep in the park's interior. Just as the passenger pigeon would soon go extinct in 1914, it appeared that bison were on the verge of beating them to that dubious distinction. And into that vacuum stampeded cattle. This domesticated livestock, not native to North America but brought to the New World with Spaniards, had crossed the Rio Grande from the south in the early 1800s with Mexican ranchers. When Texas became part of the United States, the ranchers went back south, leaving their longhorns behind to roam free. Free livestock appealed to Texans, who launched their own ranching industry.[98] By mid-century, domesticated cattle were gaining favor at the dinner table, and wild bison were being gunned down. As markets, and demand, continued to open for cattle, which were easier to raise than wild bison and also considered property, the native bovine was in decline. The Homestead Act tilted the balance even more in cattle's favor, as the prairie was sliced up into farms and ranches with cattle, not bison. As the Transcontinental Railroad moved closer to completion, ready transportation arrived to take cattle from growing herds to market, and more bison were killed to feed the rail workers. Though bison were much sturdier and designed to withstand killing cold like that which decimated the open range cattle industry in 1886-87, the Great Slaughter had left few bison to endure the winters.

Their disappearance from the landscape was noticed not only by naturalists of the day and hunters, but by those who tried to capture vestiges of Western landscapes before they were gone. Albert Bierstadt, one of the great landscape painters of the late nineteenth century, concluded his career with *The Last Buffalo*, a sprawling, six-foot by ten-foot painting that depicts a native hunter on horseback trying to drive his lance into a bull that is in the process of goring the horse. Lying in the foreground of the painting are several slain bison, while bleached bison skulls are scattered across the ground in the middle of the painting. The painting, wrote Linda S. Ferber for a 1991 retrospective of Bierstadt's career that opened in New York City, "is one of Bierstadt's most remarkable paintings, for like the 'wondrous inventions' of the 1860s, it is a masterfully conceived fiction that addressed contemporary issues."[99]

The painting captured a moment in history that was about to be altered.

Revival of a Precarious Species

The extermination of the buffalo has been a veritable tragedy of the animal world.

—Theodore Roosevelt

The latter half of the nineteenth century was the age of Manifest Destiny, and it officially brought to a close the American frontier as settlers swept into the West. It still was a challenging, albeit heady, time for immigrants moving west in search of succor from a still-young nation with not enough economic salve to go around. There still was a vast portion of wilderness and everything that meant: nurturing a homestead from the land, coping with wildlife that might eat your crops or your livestock, and encounters with Native American people angered by being forced from the land. It also became a time of concern for some who had thrived on the unbridled wildness of a western landscape that ranged from rolling prairie to snow-capped peaks. They had come of age in a countryside where you ate what you killed, slept beneath the stars, and marveled at the sheer immensity of not just the landscape but also its wildlife and, in particular, the plenitude of the latter.

Toward the end of the century, as the frontier was about to become sufficiently settled and no longer regarded as the "frontier," there was growing awareness that it was foolish to assume that an abundance of wildlife would forever define the West. It had been a grand time for adventurers, lusty men seeking to prove themselves while stretching the limits of the continent. It was as if they sensed the closing of the frontier, and wanted to go beyond its boundaries before it was erased by settlement. And yet, while they certainly sensed that they could not keep the wild pockets of America removed from settlement, there were those who were determined to save bison—and all wildlife—for the ensuing generations.

There was a need for action. Wildlife of all kinds was being killed for sport, for pot, just for the sake of killing. Bison numbers were dwindling. Not even the boundaries of the newly established Yellowstone National Park, which was off-limits to the "capture or destruction [of wildlife] for the purposes of merchandise or profit," could keep out the poachers. During a five-year period, from 1889 to 1894, 270 of the 300 bison known to reside in the park were killed.[100] The disappearance of bison from the landscape concerned a handful of men who had viewed nature and its resources as something to measure themselves against, and something to take as your right. One had explored the world early in life specifically to kill animals, another would one day become a world leader, a third traveled the world just to see what was out there, and the fourth left his name on an eight-hundred-mile-long cattle trail that stretched from Texas north into Wyoming and western Nebraska. They shared a love of the wilds, and of wildlife. How their intentions changed from killing wildlife to fighting for its preservation was both the beginning of the age of conservation and, perhaps, a recognition that there was a finite limit to wildlife.

Down from as many as sixty million head at the start of the eighteenth century, fewer than five hundred bison still stood in the wild at the passing of the 1800s. They were found in six herds scattered from Saskatchewan in the north to Texas in the south. These men were determined to keep the species alive.

That they largely succeeded was a testament to that determination, for they worked in what we would consider highly challenging times. Telephones were in their infancy, letters were the main form of communication but took time to reach their destination, and organizing widespread support and campaigns for wildlife, which had for the most part been viewed only as food, was a fledgling idea. And yet they were able to network and rally support from the halls of Congress to the White House to save bison.

CHARLES "BUFFALO" JONES

Charles Jesse Jones was a self-promoting, world-traveling cowboy, one fairly well-connected to the luminaries in the wildlife circles of the day. He lacked the acclaim of Buffalo Bill Cody, whom he knew, but he had moxie to go along with a hefty dose of narcissism. Jones had a passing relationship, at least, with Theodore Roosevelt, knew William T. Hornaday and Charles Goodnight, and made the acquaintance of George Bird Grinnell. All four were luminaries in the campaign to save bison from extinction. Jones thought more of himself than many others did, as evidenced by his patriarchal condescension of Native Americans and First Nations cultures, his disagreements with the military superintendent of Yellowstone over the handling of wildlife, and his trip to Africa in 1910 to lasso big game such as lions and rhinos that others—most notably Roosevelt—shot with rifles.

Born in a log cabin in Illinois on the last day of January 1844, Jones was the second of a dozen children brought into the world by Noah and Jane Jones. He was raised to farm, and by the time he was sixteen his father Noah put him in charge of hundreds of cattle, horses, sheep, and other livestock. Jones had always had a love of animals; he long told a story of how, when he was twelve, on a winter day while he was supposed to be sawing firewood he climbed a tree to grab a fox squirrel. As wild animals will do, the squirrel put up a fight, biting hard on one of Jones' fingers. But the youth held on and eventually tamed the squirrel to the point where it would rest on his shoulder as Jones walked about town. One day he was offered two dollars for the squirrel—an amount that "appeared like a colossal fortune to me"—and quickly parted ways with the animal. That payday anchored itself in Jones' mind: "From that time until this, I have never lost an opportunity in my power to capture every wild animal that runs on legs."[101]

Jones felt he was a natural for taming wild things. Farming, on the other hand, was boring. After a stint at Illinois Wesleyan University was cut short by a bout with typhoid fever, he moved to Kansas at twenty-two and soon turned to hunting bison, as did hundreds of others at the time. Another two decades passed before he realized the species couldn't survive all the killing, and he began to work on building his own herd. It was the historic March blizzard in 1886 that brought bison as a species worth saving into focus for Jones. Trains couldn't plow through drifts that rose to six feet and more that winter, and one locomotive froze to the tracks. Jones, riding across the prairie after the storm passed, saw dozens of cattle that had died in the storm. The only dead bison he saw were those that had been shot by hunters. So impressed was he by the ability of bison to survive the storm, that he later would gush when discussing the species, particularly its benefits at market. Bison had, he recited, meat superior to any livestock; a fine, warm pelt; hide that makes wonderful clothes; and milk "infinitely richer than that of the Jersey." [102]

"Why not domesticate this wonderful beast which can endure such a blizzard, defying a storm so destructive to our domestic species?" thought Jones. "Why not infuse this hardy blood into our native cattle, and have a perfect animal, one that will defy all these elements?"[103]

It seemed obvious to Jones: a fusion of cattle and bison could produce a hardier version of livestock that would be able to tolerate the roughest blizzard, make it to market in spring with promise of a good return, and have a disposition more amenable to being domesticated. But Jones' idea, which he would later in life put to the test, led to a soup of cattle and bison genes that contributed to today's relatively few pure-blooded bison. It also led to some odd-looking "bison" today on the North Rim of Grand Canyon National Park, animals that somewhat resemble both bison and cattle, and some bison-appearing animals that have white faces.

Jones—whose time in the saddle out on the plains left his face deeply tanned and creased above his bushy mustache and goatee, and his eyes in a perpetual squint—was a shrewd businessman. Early on he recognized the value of bison bones as a fertilizer. In 1879, along with three others, he founded Garden City, Kansas. Each received 160 acres as part of the deal, and that homestead served Jones well. It was in Garden City that he persuaded the Santa Fe Railroad to locate a station in the town, a move that helped bring Jones wealth through real estate sales. That wealth helped him build his bison herd, beginning in 1886 when he went down into Texas where he and some friends captured ten calves that would become the foundation of his herd. Over the next two years he added another thirty-nine, and by 1889 he had fifty-six. At the time the country's largest privately owned herd, it would prove to be a key to the survival of the species. In Garden City he was a celebrity. He was the town's first mayor, built the Buffalo Jones block in town, and would draw an audience when he drove a wagon pulled by two bison calves through town.

Jones' flamboyance rose again in 1897, when he decided he would be the savior of musk oxen as well as bison. His exploits in the Northwest Territories stemmed from an awareness that musk oxen, too, were threatened with extinction. From a distance, the resemblance of a musk ox to a bison isn't difficult to accept. As with bison, musk oxen are stocky animals. They have long, thick coats of brownish-black hair, sport horns on the sides of their heads, and tend to congregate. Their history on Earth seems to mirror bison, as well. They existed for hundreds of thousands of years, roamed from Asia into North America via the Bering Land Bridge during the Pleistocene, and learned how to evade Ice Age lions and other carnivores of the day.

In 1897 one of the last stands for musk oxen was in the Northwest Territories of the Canadian Arctic, and Jones was determined to hunt the animals and capture a few to raise along with other animals for display in museums and zoos. "My mission was to bring out from the Arctic regions musk oxen alive, if possible; also silver-gray fox, marten, and other valuable fur-bearing animals, to propagate on an island in the Pacific ocean," he let it be known.[104]

It was an audacious, if not ridiculous, scheme, by the logistics alone: capture the animals, keep them alive while transporting them thousands of miles to the coast, ship them to an island, and breed them. What Jones wasn't factoring in were the First Nations peoples who long had relied on musk oxen much the way Native Americans relied on bison. They were not on board with his scheme. Leaders of the Chipewyan, Cree, and Slave communities met with Jones to make clear he should go home to Oklahoma without firing a shot or lassoing any animals. Jones wasn't having any of it.

"An interpreter told me with great solemnity that these men had come a long way to meet me," recalled Jones, who adopted a "white man knows better" attitude with the native peoples.

They had heard of my advent into the country, and warned me not to take any animals out alive; they were nearly starved to death already, and if I took musk oxen away all other animals would follow and the people surely perish. I listened attentively until they had finished, then I told them that I had come three thousand miles, not to destroy, but to preserve the very animals they had been killing for subsistence. That they must learn to foster and propagate them or they certainly would perish of hunger.

With that quick dismissal, Jones continued into the Arctic wilderness with John Rea, a bull of a man with a face anchored by a sweeping handlebar mustache that curled past his cheeks. Born in Ontario, Rea had already spent one winter in the Northwest Territories, along the Mackenzie River, and was more familiar with the landscape than Jones. And he was a better shot, a skill that would come in handy, though not necessarily in hunting musk oxen. The animals, much to Jones' disappointment, offered no sport. "It was like slaughtering cattle in a corral," he said.

The two quickly discovered that musk oxen, when threatened, don't stampede off but bunch with their hindquarters tight together and their horned heads pointing out from the circle. When the men came upon two cow musk oxen and five yearlings, Jones told Rea to break the cows' hind legs with a shot, knowing that the yearlings would stay nearby. "True, this was cruel," he said later when self-righteously justifying the matter, "but such acts are always pardonable in the interest of science."[105]

They did succeed in capturing the yearlings, and stood back to assess the animals. "It was a very interesting hour of my life, when I could quietly stand and see every twinkle in their eyes," recalled Jones. "The long shaggy fleece that covered the little creatures was of a browner color than that of the old bulls. They looked more like doll animals than like real live musk oxen. Their short legs made me liken them to a little Shetland pony colt, as compared with a racehorse."

Proud of their catch and ready to head for home, the men tied the yearlings together with a length of rope, adding a loop about every dozen feet, and from each loop a short rope tied to a yearling's neck. All went reasonably well the first couple of days. Jones and Rea and their calves were able to cover fifteen to eighteen miles a day, with the animals rather quickly settling down into the daily march. But one day, awaking from a midday nap after covering ten miles, they found they were "ruined," as Rea put it. "Someone has killed all our musk oxen. They have cut their throats," he told Jones.

The killings were thought to have been done by a dozen or so native people, who had left behind a "peculiar-looking knife on the snow near the animals, having a handle about eighteen inches long, made of caribou or some other animal's rib or tusk, with a blade four inches long." The message was clear: "We had been warned time and time again by the Indians not to take any musk oxen alive," noted Jones. The two realized that had they tried to capture more musk oxen, they likely would have been the ones left dead in the snow. So they abandoned the hunt and headed for home.

It was highly questionable that Jones would have been able to breed the musk oxen to any great extent had he succeeded in bringing them back alive. While the species is alive and well today, there was a time early in the twentieth century when, like bison, its fate was in question. "One of the tragedies of our generation is the fate of the musk ox, once roaming by the hundreds of thousands through the Arctic North," Howard Mingos wrote in *The New York Times* on October 21, 1923. "A recent Canadian survey shows that less than one hundred musk ox are alive in Canada. . . . their slaughter has rivaled the massacre of the buffalo."[106]

When Jones returned to the United States, his attention turned back to bison and trying to save them if he could, particularly if he had a paying job to do so. Until the National Park Service was established by Congress in 1916, the US Army patrolled Yellowstone and enforced the laws intended to protect the park and its resources. Nevertheless, lawlessness prevailed in the park. Poachers, lured by black-market prices that soared to $300 for a bison head,[107] ravaged Yellowstone's bison herds. Poaching was illegal in the park, but the punishment meted out under the regulations only required that those caught poaching surrender their weapons and other gear.[108] It was no surprise that poachers soon returned to their sordid craft. Perhaps the most notorious poacher of the day, Ed Howell, was captured on March 12, 1893,[109] while in the act of skinning a bison he had killed near Pelican Creek deep in the park's interior. Nearby, six bison heads were hanging from a tree near the poacher's camp.[110] In a story that ran in *Forest and Stream*, a hunting magazine that George Bird Grinnell edited with a decidedly conservation-oriented bent (and which would merge with *Field and Stream* in the 1930s), the writer highlighted Howell's lackadaisical attitude at being captured. The poacher's great concern was not being fined, as it wouldn't amount to thirty dollars, but rather to being late for the spring sheep-shearing season in Arizona, the story noted.

There were efforts in the 1890s to safeguard the park's remaining bison from poachers, but those efforts—to build an enclosure in the Hayden Valley and to use undercover agents to track down poachers—failed. Jones, concerned for the future of bison and more than a little interested in landing a federal job, campaigned with a plan to accomplish both. He visited with Kansas's congressional delegation in 1887, but was unable to convince the politicians to take action to save bison. He had wanted their help to preserve lands in southeastern Colorado and in Texas for several thousand bison.[111] In 1890, the Kansas congressional delegation agreed to introduce legislation to set aside lands in Texas, as well as four islands in the Great Salt Lake in Utah, for Jones' bison, but the bills failed to gain approval.[112] In 1896 he approached the administration of President Grover Cleveland with a proposal to corral Yellowstone's bison, but again got nowhere. President William McKinley's Interior Department also could not be swayed.[113] Finally, in 1902, four months after the assassination of President McKinley elevated Vice President Theodore Roosevelt to the Oval Office, things began to tilt in Jones' favor. First, in January of 1902, the US Senate unanimously approved a resolution directing the secretaries of Agriculture and Interior to conduct a census of bison to inform the Senate "whether or not such animals are dying out or are on the increase; to what extent they are running wild or are being domesticated, and whether or not such as remain are of pure or mixed blood, and also informing the Senate whether or not any steps ought to be taken by the United States for the preservation from extinction of such animals."[114]

Not three weeks later, Agriculture Secretary James Wilson communicated to the Senate that the "American bison is on the verge of extinction. Scarcely a handful now remain of the millions which formerly roamed over the Plains of the West."[115] A more thorough response came from Interior Secretary E. A. Hitchcock, who corresponded with governors and various other officials, including the secretary of the Smithsonian Institution.

> From these reports it will be seen that the total number of buffalo or bison, both full and mixed blood, in the United States, is 1,143. Of these 72 are running wild, 50 being in the State of Colorado and 22 in the Yellowstone National Park. In my judgment, steps should be taken by the United States for the preservation from extinction of the buffalo or American bison, and with that end in view I have submitted to Congress an estimate of thirty thousand dollars for the purchase of buffalo and the corralling of them in the Yellowstone National Park. With these animals in a national reservation, under governmental supervision, it is believed that a herd of pure-blooded American bison may be domesticated, which will increase in numbers, and the herd now running wild in the park may be also benefited by the introduction therein of new blood.[116]

With determination in Congress and the Roosevelt administration not to let bison vanish, Jones' retention was not far off. US Army Major John Pitcher, Yellowstone's de facto superintendent, gained permission to search for bison he could add to Yellowstone's small herd, and in July 1902 the major summoned Jones to become Yellowstone's game warden, a job paying $1,800 per year.[117] When he arrived, Jones sized up the park's twenty-two- or twenty-three-head bison herd and went to work to build its numbers and diversify its genetics.

About a mile south of the military headquarters at Mammoth Hot Springs, there was a small area cut by a stream and covered with some trees. Here, Pitcher and Jones decided, would be a good spot for a fenced pasture. On that tract, the two men launched what today might be called a bison recovery initiative. To get some diversity into the bloodlines of the handful of Yellowstone bison, they obtained three bulls from Charles Goodnight for $1,380. Another eighteen cows were purchased from the Pablo-Allard herd[118] via Howard Eaton, a guide and dude rancher whom Roosevelt knew from his days in the Dakotas, for $8,800.[119] Somewhat ironically, and a reflection of the small group of bison ranchers at the time, Jones back in 1893 had sold twenty-six pureblood bison to Pablo and Allard, possibly in a move to address financial strain he was under at the time. Whether any of these bison were among the eighteen from the Pablo-Allard herd that went to Yellowstone is unknown.

Until the arrival of the twentieth-century, wildlife conservation—actively protecting and strengthening the numbers and genetic diversity of species—in the United States was largely unknown. Congress had in 1871 created the US Commission on Fish and Fisheries and assigned it a mission of studying fisheries and devising strategies to keep populations from declining. Fourteen years later, the Office of Economic Ornithology was added to the US Department of Agriculture and worked on, among other things, figuring out whether birds could be used to combat agricultural pests.[120] There were individual wildlife advocates, but few organizations with specific missions. Concerns over the plight of Yellowstone's wildlife gave life to the Boone and Crockett Club in 1887, when Roosevelt, Grinnell, General Sherman, Gifford Pinchot, and others came together to "promote the conservation and management of wildlife, especially big game, and its habitat," while also encouraging hunting of wildlife.[121] But there were few on-the-ground, human-driven manipulative efforts to conserve a vanishing species. Today, the efforts by Jones and Pitcher in Yellowstone, and those by Hornaday, Roosevelt, Grinnell, Goodnight, and a few others to prevent bison extinction, are viewed by some of the country's leading wildlife biologists as "among the first and best known conservation success stories."[122]

Jones had good success during his first year in Yellowstone. Not only did he catch three bison calves in the Pelican Valley to add to the corralled herd, but he increased the overall herd by twelve head in that time. However, his irascible demeanor and disdain for those who drank, smoked, and gambled got him crosswise with both the military leadership of the park and the rough-and-tumble crews he worked with. By the fall of 1905, he was gone.[123] But his work with bison in Yellowstone continued to pay benefits. By 1907, the herd that had been pastured south of Mammoth Hot Springs was moved to the Lamar Valley. There it grew so well that in 1936 not only were there nearly 650 bison on or around the Buffalo Ranch, as the location was known then and still is today, but 35 were set free in the park's Firehole Valley and another three dozen in the Hayden Valley.[124]

After leaving the park, Jones continued to experiment with crossing cattle with bison, ever hopeful he'd create an animal that could easily withstand the brutally cold winters on the Plains. While Hornaday urged caution about such crosses, rightfully concerned that they would sully pureblood bison genes, he also recognized Jones for his efforts. Grinnell, also, was intrigued by these "cattalos" that Jones was breeding.

"A half-breed cow of Mr. Jones' that I examined was fully as large as an ordinary work-ox, and in spring, while nursing a calf, was fat on grass," he noted after visiting Jones' ranch. "She lacked the buffalo hump, but her hide would have made a good robe . . . If continued, these attempts at cross-breeding may do much to improve our Western range cattle."[125]

Despite the praise for Jones' work at hybridization, it never succeeded in producing "hybrids with ease and certainty." The crosses had the defiant, ornery personality of a bison that made them difficult to handle, matured more slowly than cattle, and infertility became a problem. Today some of the results of Jones' efforts can be seen on the North Rim of the Grand Canyon, where the National Park Service is working to reduce their numbers to around two hundred through culling.

Theodore Roosevelt

Theodore Roosevelt's reputation as a conservationist has long outlived him. He continues today to be held up as the model of a conservation-oriented president. His transition from hunter to conservationist took hold during his years in the Dakota Territory, a place he explored as a young man early in the second-to-last decade of the nineteenth century. Statehood was still six years off for North Dakota, but the land was drawing farmers and ranchers thanks to the Homestead Act. By 1880, the territory's population had reached 135,177, with most in the southern half that would become South Dakota, and with most tied to farming.[126]

Roosevelt headed to the Dakota Territory from New York City for a three-week stay in September 1883 to find himself—

and, at the same time, live up to the traits of Theodore Sr., his father, who died too young, at forty-six. "My father, Theodore Roosevelt, was the best man I ever knew. He combined strength and courage with gentleness, tenderness, and great unselfishness. He would not tolerate in us children selfishness or cruelty, idleness, cowardice, or untruthfulness. As we grew older, he made us understand that the same standard of clean living was demanded for the boys as for the girls; that what was wrong in a woman could not be right in a man," the future president later recalled.

He also might have been driven to the Dakotas after hearing of the adventures his younger brother, Elliott, had in Texas. Six years before Theodore went to the Dakota Territory, Elliott, then just seventeen, found himself on a buffalo hunt in northern Texas. He was in search of adventure with one of his cousins and a half-dozen other men. It was an adventure that nearly killed Elliott. One day, while out hunting with a companion, the two found themselves in front of a bison stampede heading straight for them. "The two hunters knew that their only chance for life was to split the herd, which though with so broad a front was not very deep," wrote Theodore in an essay labeled quite simply, "Buffalo Hunting."

> If they failed they would surely be trampled to death. Waiting until the beasts were in close range, they opened a rapid fire from their heavy breech loading rifles, yelling at the top of their voices. For a moment the result seemed doubtful. The line thundered steadily down on them; then it swayed violently as two or three of the brutes immediately in their front fell beneath the bullets, while their neighbors made violent efforts to press off sideways. Then a narrow wedge-shaped rift appeared in the line, and widened as it came up closer, and the buffalo, shrinking from their foes in front, strove desperately to edge away from the dangerous neighborhood.[127]

In the Dakota Territory, Theodore Roosevelt wanted to experience the dust, storms, muscle aches, and hardships of the western frontier before it was overrun by settlement. He wanted to hunt for sustenance, to shed the perception of being a well-to-do New Yorker and greenhorn, and be acknowledged as a working cowboy. He was young, twenty-four years old and only two years into his marriage with Alice. He had never known want or hard, physical work. Roosevelt most certainly was a dandy when he arrived in the territory. He had been accustomed to playing lawn tennis in Bar Harbor, Maine, and exploring Europe with his newlywed wife,[128] not enduring a hardscrabble life in the badlands. In a letter to his mother, sent during a train stop in Chicago en route to the territory, he told her he had recovered from a recent bout of "cholera morbus" (possibly food poisoning or gastroenteritis), and was "feeling like a fighting cock; the cholera morbus seems like a dream of the past—or, to speak more definitely, a nightmare."[129]

The Northern Pacific passenger train made a beeline across the territory, with Medora near the very end of the line before the tracks crossed into the Montana Territory. This was a raw, demanding landscape, one with little authority other than nature to judge those drawn to it. There was very little north and south of Medora other than badlands, tribal reservations, and emptiness. Emptiness, at least, as one from New York City might view it. When Roosevelt arrived in town shortly after Labor Day at three a.m. one September morning, the weather was bitterly cold, the accommodations rough. The Pyramid Park Hotel he found was more like a cavalry barracks, with fourteen beds in a row. Come morning, all the men dipped their hands into the same washbowl. Roosevelt's first day in the landscape that now bears his name as a national park came as somewhat of a shock.

"It is a very desolate place, high, barren hills, scantily clad with coarse grass and here and there in sheltered places a few stunted cottonwood trees; 'wash-outs;' deepening at times into great canyons, and steep cliffs of most curious formation about everywhere, and it was a marvel to me to see how easily our mustangs scrambled over the frightful ground which we crossed, while trying to get up to the grassy plateaus, over which we could gallop," he wrote Alice in a letter carried by a hunter to the nearest post office. "There is very little water, and what there is, is so bitter as to be almost a poison, and nearly undrinkable; it is so alkaline that the very cows' milk tastes of it."[130]

Despite that view, Roosevelt immediately fell in love with the challenging landscape and bought the Maltese Cross Ranch before the end of his three-week stay. There's no doubt that the young Roosevelt felt out of his element. Understandably so, with the nearest town of any consequence being Bismarck with about three thousand residents some 130 miles east of Medora,[131] with its several dozen residents who lived seven miles north of the Maltese Cross Ranch. Here he was surrounded not by restaurants, groceries, and opera houses, but by a demanding landscape of friable soils, sparse vegetation, and little water in a region populated by ranchers, cowboys who would spend a day in the saddle, and animals that could kill and eat him. Cowboying alone nearly killed Roosevelt, as early in his stay his horse stepped into a badger hole and performed a somersault, tossing him "about twenty feet, but we were not hurt at all," he assured his wife.

The experience was bracing, stimulating to the young man. "I do not believe there ever was any life more attractive to a vigorous young fellow than life on a cattle ranch in those days," he wrote years later in his autobiography. "It was a fine, healthy life, too; it taught a man self-reliance, hardihood, and the value of instant decision—in short, the virtues that ought to come from life in the open country."

Roosevelt's life there, initially, was the stuff of dime-store novels. The Maltese Cross Ranch came with a cabin—small, but ready to move into—and he would return to New York City before winter. A well-circulated photo of the young Roosevelt clad in buckskins, with knife holstered in his belt and rifle in his hands, was taken not on one of his ranches, but in a New York studio.[132] Yet he wasn't too proud to hide his initial unease with the West, its wildlife, and its cowboys. "There were all kinds of things that I was afraid of at first, ranging from grizzly bears to mean horses and gunfighters," he jotted into his diary one day in 1883. "But by acting as if I was not afraid, I gradually ceased to be afraid."

Roosevelt's arrival in the Dakota Territory coincided with the slaughter of the bison herds. A cowboy who rode with the young New Yorker spoke of incessant gunfire all day from buffalo hunters, and the landscape "specked with buffalo carcasses." Bison robes bought from Indians, woolly fur on one side, the tanned side often bearing paintings, were being sold to train travelers for thirty-five dollars apiece.[133]

Little more than a week after arriving in the Dakota Territory, where he had come in part to kill a bison so he could hang its mounted head in his New York City home, Roosevelt thrilled at his killing shot. "Hurrah! The luck has turned at last. I will bring you home the head of a great buffalo bull, and the antlers of two superb stags," he joyously wrote Alice. The kill was made, he told her, from a ridge above a gully where the bison was grazing. "I crawled up to the edge, not thirty yards from the great, grim-looking beast, and sent a shot from the heavy rifle into him just behind his shoulder, the ball going clean through his body. He dropped dead before going a hundred yards."[134]

Though Roosevelt soon returned to New York City and Alice, it was a too-short reunion. The two hoped they would celebrate the fourth anniversary of their engagement—Valentine's Day—with the birth of their child, and so Roosevelt was in Albany attending to business as a member of the New York Assembly on February 12, 1884, when his wife gave birth at their New York City home. A telegram the following morning alerted him to the arrival, and was soon followed by another stating that Alice's life was in jeopardy. By the time he arrived home late February 13, Alice was fading. Roosevelt held her in his arms until she slipped away on Valentine's Day. A few hours earlier that same day, Roosevelt's mother, Mittie, had died of typhoid fever in the same house. She was forty-eight.

"The light has gone out of my life," Roosevelt wrote in his diary on February 14. An ensuing two-page entry briefly traced his few years with Alice, and noted that his wife and mother were buried together on February 16. The next day, his infant daughter was christened Alice Lee Roosevelt. "For joy or for sorrow, my life has now been lived out," the entry ended.

The deaths of the two most important women in his life no doubt factored into Roosevelt's decision to return to the Dakota Territory and his Maltese Cross Ranch that summer. Once there, his diary made no mention of his emptiness, with only short entries of days spent hunting. "On riding around a little knoll, I saw two antelope a long distance off, looking at me," he wrote on June 21, a Saturday. "I dismounted and fired off hand, with careful aim, holding a foot over him, and breaking his neck near the shoulder. By actual measurement the distance was three hundred yards, the best shot ever made with the rifle."

Soon he dipped again into his wealth, buying the Elkhorn Ranch farther north along the Little Missouri, for four hundred dollars. That became the headquarters for his Dakota operation. Today the low-slung log ranch house, which Roosevelt enlisted two friends from Maine to build, is gone, but the foundation stones remain, almost level with the grass. Still standing are some of the cottonwood trees that once shaded the house and the porch on which Roosevelt would escape the heat with a book or simply rock in his chair while taking in the wide, thin, and muddy Little Missouri and the badlands it had sculpted. This ranch not only gave the future president a place to mend after the loss of his wife and mother, but an opportunity to contemplate what was transpiring in the West. The wanton killing of wildlife concerned him, and he feared its outcome. Many refer to the Elkhorn Ranch as "the cradle of conservation," Tweed Roosevelt, the president's great-grandson, told me one day not long after I had visited the Elkhorn. "And it was indeed where TR developed many of his ideas that he was later able to implement when he became president."

One night over dinner, Valerie Naylor, at the time superintendent of Theodore Roosevelt National Park, told me that it was here in the badlands that Roosevelt saw "firsthand the decline of the bison, elk, pronghorn, overgrazing, and other issues. He saw that the wilderness was disappearing even then, in the 1880s." Indeed, it was during a bison hunt in 1889 that Roosevelt sensed what the future would dictate for bison.

"[F]or several minutes I watched the great beasts as they grazed . . . mixed with the eager excitement of the hunter was a certain half-melancholy feeling as I gazed on these bison, themselves part of the last remnant of a doomed and nearly vanished race," he wrote. "Few, indeed, are the men who now have, or evermore shall have, the chance of seeing the mightiest of American beasts, in all his wild vigor, surrounded by the tremendous desolation of his far-off mountain home."[135]

There at his Elkhorn Ranch the dandy-turned-roughrider formed and refined his thoughts on conservation. It became a passion that played out years later when, as president of the United States, he helped set aside 230 million acres of land, most as national forests, but also as some of the country's first national monuments. And all the while, he lamented the loss of bison. "The extermination of the buffalo has been a veritable tragedy of the animal world," he wrote. "Other races of animals have been destroyed within historic times, but these have been species of small size, local distribution, and limited numbers, usually found in some particular island or group of islands; while the huge buffalo, in countless myriads, ranged over the greater part of a continent."[136]

In his travels across his ranch and beyond in the Dakota Territory, Roosevelt was overcome by the disregard and indifference that had struck down bison. The killing was seemingly complete, he noted in 1885 in *Hunting Trips of a Ranchman*, a book that took form from the diaries he kept in the Dakota Territories.

"No sight is more common on the plains than that of a bleached buffalo skull; and their countless numbers attest the abundance of the animal at a time not so very long past," Roosevelt noted. "On those portions where the herds made their last stand, the carcasses, dried in the clear, high air, or the mouldering skeletons, abound."

A fellow rancher, who had ridden nearly one thousand miles following the Milk River as it swirls and cuts west to east across Montana to pour into the Missouri, told Roosevelt that "during the whole distance he was never out of sight of a dead buffalo, and never in sight of a live one." White encroachment westward was undoubtedly deadly to the species. Roosevelt came to blame not just the horses that made it easier for any and all hunters to quickly chase down bison, and the long rifles that made it easier to kill bison from a distance, but also the ranchers (as he once was; indeed, the bison he killed in 1883 is on display at his New York home, Sagamore Hill) for their demise.

As big as the frontier was in 1885, as sparsely settled as it was, it didn't seem big enough for bison to coexist with settlements. Even Roosevelt came to believe that bison were incompatible with the country's western expansion. They needed too much open space—exactly what the country needed if it was to grow. One had to go, Roosevelt knew, and it wasn't going to be Manifest Destiny. Ranching was thriving in the Dakotas. There was plenty of grass to fatten cattle, and the same train that Roosevelt rode to Medora stood ready to haul cattle back east to market. He saw the value of ranching, and helped organize a stockmen's association to lobby for their needs. His future role in the recovery of bison would come not as a rancher determined to breed their numbers larger, but as a politician deeply concerned about the animal's plight in the late 1800s.

"Less than a score of years ago the great herds, containing many millions of individuals, ranged over a vast expanse of country that stretched in an unbroken line from near Mexico to far into British America; in fact, over almost all the plains that are now known as the cattle region," Roosevelt noted in *Hunting Trips of a Ranchman*. "But since that time their destruction has gone on with appalling rapidity and thoroughness; and the main factors in bringing it about have been the railroads, which carried hordes of hunters into the land and gave them means to transport their spoils to market."

Hunting Trips of a Ranchman landed the young man a book contract with G. P. Putnam's Sons. It was a portrait of late-nineteenth-century western life that more than a century later would gain praise for the details and stories of frontier life and cowboying that Roosevelt laid out. But while Roosevelt's concern for bison was heartfelt, the thirty-five-year-old Grinnell found his writing skills weak and narrative unmoving. In dissecting the book for a review that ran in *Forest and Stream*, Grinnell pointed out that Roosevelt

is not well known as a sportsman, and his experience of the Western country is quite limited. . . . He has not become accustomed to all the various sights and sounds of the plains and the mountains, and for him all the difference which exists between the East and the West are still sharply defined. . . . We are sorry to see that a number of hunting myths are given fact, but it was after all scarcely to be expected that with the author's limited experience he could sift the wheat from the chaff and distinguish the true from the fall.[137]

Roosevelt stewed over the review, and soon found himself in Grinnell's New York City office to defend his book. While debating the merits of Roosevelt's writing, the two came around to find common cause in working to preserve bison. Together in 1887 they launched the Boone and Crockett Club, which produced outdoor publications and lobbied for wildlife conservation issues. One of its first actions was to adopt a resolution to work for "useful and proper legislation toward the enlargement and better management of the Yellowstone National Park."[138]

Later, when Roosevelt landed in the White House, Grinnell and Hornaday encouraged him to use his position to lobby for the protection of bison. He didn't disappoint them, at one point directing his interior secretary to purchase bison from private herds.

WILLIAM TEMPLE HORNADAY

Not long after Roosevelt finished his book, another easterner headed west. Not to find himself, but rather to find bison before they were gone. And once he found them, William Temple Hornaday did something unthinkable for a man who came to be viewed as the father of the American conservation movement: he killed them.

Hornaday was born in Indiana and grew up in Iowa during a time of national growing pains, including the prying open of the West through the Homestead Act and the national calamity of the Civil War. Though small in stature at five foot seven, he would grow up to have a large and profound impact on, and molding of, the national conscience when it came to conservation. As a young boy he was, much like Buffalo Jones, enthralled by wild things. During a trip to Indianapolis with relatives he happened into a gun and tackle shop where he saw his first mounted animals, some ducks. Here was wildlife he could study close up without having to chase across fields. He could see how the feathers all neatly layered together, how the webbed feet were good paddles, and how beaks dominated the faces. But here Hornaday faced a conundrum: while mounted exhibits had educational value, killing animals seemed wrong—their lifeless bodies were "of no use to anyone and would be wasted."[139]

He came to justify, for a number of years, at least, the hunting of wildlife by bringing these animals, as mounted specimens, into view of those who could not travel into the wilds. A professor at Iowa State, where Hornaday enrolled to study zoology and taxidermy, directed him after graduation to Henry Augustus Ward's Natural Science Establishment so he might improve his skills as an aspiring taxidermist. Ward's was in the business of preparing stuffed animals for scientific museums, and after graduating from college Hornaday joined the company's staff in Rochester, New York. Proving his abilities on what he described as "trial trips" to collect specimens in Florida, the Caribbean, and Venezuela, in 1876 he headed off on a two-year collecting assignment to Europe, North Africa, and Asia. Armed principally with a .40-caliber Maynard rifle, a breech-loading carbine commonly found in Confederate hands on the battlegrounds of the Civil War,[140] he trekked to Africa and India, Ceylon, Malaya, and Borneo. Later, during an expedition to the Orinoco River Delta in South America, he lamented the species he couldn't kill because of the difficulty in finding animals to take aim on.[141]

Many years later Hornaday would prove to be the most ardent defender of wildlife and proponent of a national consciousness for its preservation. His first encounter with bison, one that would transform him into an advocate for the species, came soon after he joined the United States National Museum (the forerunner to the Smithsonian Institution), in 1882 as chief taxidermist. He had been receiving more and more reports that bison were becoming scarce in the West. At one point, reflecting his concern for the future of the species, Hornaday noted that "it was the ability of a single hunter to destroy an entire bunch of buffalo in a single day that completely annihilated the remaining thousands of the northern herd before the people of the United States even learned what was going on."[142] By early 1886, the extermination of the species was at hand, believed Hornaday. At the museum, the only bison in the collections were in ragged condition. There were bits and pieces of skeletons, two mounted heads, and just two fully mounted bison. Contemplating this paltry collection, and concerned that bison would soon be gone, the secretary of the museum, Professor F. Baird, called on Hornaday to go west to find a few specimens.

Hornaday viewed this as the trip of a lifetime. Few other institutions had the wherewithal to underwrite such an expedition, he believed, and it needed to be done before there were no bison to collect. "For the benefit of the smaller scientific museums of the country, and for others which will come into existence during the next half century, it was resolved to collect at all hazards, in case buffalo could be found, between eighty and one hundred specimens of various kinds, of which twenty to thirty should be skins, and equal numbers should be complete skeletons, and of skulls at least fifty,"[143] Hornaday decided.

The taxidermist was overly optimistic. After learning in late April 1886 that there were small pockets of bison in Montana, Wyoming, and Texas, he decided to head to Miles City, Montana, the next month. Once there, however, he was told that he was too late: outside of Yellowstone, there were no more bison to be found.[144] But then came word that there might be some bison left in east-central Montana in the rolling shortgrass prairie between the Missouri and Yellowstone rivers, a region not far south from present-day Fort Peck, known as Big Dry Creek. At the invitation of the owner of the LU-Bar Ranch, one of Montana's largest cattle operations with some eighty thousand head by 1890,[145] Hornaday and his crew headed north of Miles City into the desolate, scattered sagebrush badlands in search of bison. And bison he found—a young calf and a bull. The calf had fallen behind its mother as she dashed across the plains, and Hornaday kept it with plans to take it back to the National Zoo. Several days later he again came upon the bull and this time succeeded in killing it. But it was late spring, and the bison was between its winter and summer coats; the robe lacked the luster normally displayed in winter. Hornaday decided he would return in autumn to resume his hunt.[146]

The irony of killing bison before they might go extinct wasn't lost on Hornaday. But as with Jones, he saw scientific merit and justification in it. "To all of us the idea of killing a score or more of the last survivors of the bison millions was exceedingly unpleasant, but we believed that our refraining from collecting the specimens we imperatively needed would not prolong the existence of the bison species by a single day," he wrote.[147] Late September found the thirty-one-year-old Hornaday back in the saddle heading for Big Dry Creek with Harvey Brown, a University of Kansas student who had met Hornaday during the summer while working at the zoo, and three cowboys who served as guides and hunters. Brown's terms were quite acceptable—he volunteered to join the expedition—though a natural history professor at the university provided one hundred dollars for Brown's participation with the expectation that the university would gain a bison skin and skeleton in return.[148] Two weeks into October, four bison were killed, two by Hornaday, but the few bison left did not make the hunters' task quick or easy. The hunt continued on through November and into December, with the men enduring a typically cold and snowy Montana season. Though Hornaday early in his career had been a world traveler, the conditions he confronted as he searched for bison had to stagger him. A late-November storm dropped not only the temperature—to negative sixteen degrees Fahrenheit in the canyon where they had camped—but a great amount of snow.[149] "We had hoped to kill at least five more buffaloes by the time Private West should arrive with the wagons; but when at the end of a week the storm had spent itself, the snow was so deep that hunting was totally impossible save in the vicinity of camp, where there was nothing to kill," noted Hornaday. By early December, Hornaday was able to obtain another specimen, a large bull, while another member of the expedition killed a bison cow. The kills brought their total to twenty-two. Hornaday marveled at the animal he killed. His initial shot passed through the bull's shoulder and broke its leg. When the bison fell to the ground, the taxidermist went in pursuit of a cow; failing to kill her, he returned to the bull. The animal tried to flee, but with a broken leg, it couldn't go far. Hornaday found himself with an incredible opportunity few others might encounter. Here was an adult bison bull in its prime, standing not far off, for him to observe. And so the taxidermist pulled out his sketchbook and quickly began drawing the animal and jotting notes that could help him back in the preparation studio.

> This was a truly magnificent specimen in every respect. He was a 'stub-horn' bull, about eleven years old, much larger every way than any of the others we collected. His height at the shoulder was 5 feet 8 inches perpendicular, or 2 inches more than the next largest of our collection. His hair was in remarkably fine condition, being long, fine, thick, and well colored. The hair in his frontlet is 16 inches in length, and the thick coat of shaggy, straw-colored tufts which covered his neck and shoulders measured 4 inches. His girth behind the fore leg was 8 feet 4 inches, and his weight was estimated at 1,600 pounds.

When he was done, he squeezed off the killing shot.[150]

By December 20, the men were back in Miles City, congratulating themselves on their success, which Hornaday reported to Secretary Baird in a dispatch the next day. They had taken nearly two dozen skins along with skeletons and skulls that could perfect the displays. They had accomplished what old hands in Montana thought couldn't be done. "Our 'outfit' has been pronounced by old buffalo hunters, 'The luckiest outfit that ever hunted buffalo in Montana,' and the opinion is quite generally held that our 'haul' of specimens could not be equaled again in Montana by anybody, no matter what their resources for the reason that the buffalo are not there," Hornaday practically beamed to his boss in a dispatch. "We killed very nearly all we saw and I am confident there are not over thirty-head remaining in Montana, all told."

Hornaday was a riddle. He had grown up with rifle in hand, and earned a living traveling the globe to kill wildlife. He was motivated to go in search of bison to kill because he feared he'd miss his chance to shoot some. It wasn't until after his western bison safari that further diminished the few remaining wild bison numbers that he mounted his fight to somehow save the species from vanishing. To shoulder such a challenge, almost single-handedly, was a defining moment for Hornaday, and he attacked it with determination and a familiar stubbornness that showed when facing such considerable odds. That battle evolved Hornaday into one of the country's most passionate defenders of not just bison but all wildlife. This is evident in *The Extermination of the American Bison*, followed by *Our Vanishing Wildlife: Its Extermination and Preservation*. In the first, published in 1889 when Hornaday was superintendent of the National Zoological Park in Washington, DC, he marveled at the once-unimaginable bison population.

Between the Rocky Mountains and the States lying along the Mississippi River on the west, from Minnesota to Louisiana, the whole country was one vast buffalo range, inhabited by millions of buffaloes. One could fill a volume with the records of plainsmen and pioneers who penetrated or crossed that vast region between 1800 and 1870, and were in turn surprised, astounded, and frequently dismayed by the tens of thousands of buffaloes they observed, avoided, or escaped from. They lived and moved as no other quadrupeds ever have, in great multitudes, like grand armies in review, covering scores of square miles at once. They were so numerous they frequently stopped boats in the rivers, threatened to overwhelm travelers on the plains, and in later years derailed locomotives and cars, until railway engineers learned by experience the wisdom of stopping their trains whenever there were buffaloes crossing the track.[151]

Hornaday's writings reflected his newfound respect for, and championing of, wildlife. But he still took pride in his hunting and taxidermy skills after returning to Washington, and created an exhibit of the animals he expected to soon go extinct. And he wanted later generations to appreciate those talents. "Dear Sir," he wrote on March 7, 1888, "[E]nclosed please find a brief and truthful account of the capture of the specimens which compose this group. The old bull, the young cow and the yearling calf were killed by yours truly." The note was found in 1957, when it surfaced at the Smithsonian from beneath the faux prairie setting on which six bison mounts had stood. Crews found it while taking down the exhibit and replacing it with new stuffed bison taken from the National Bison Range in Montana. Hornaday's bison mounts, procured during that fall 1886 expedition, were shipped west back to Montana in 1958. Today they can be found at Fort Benton in the Montana Agricultural Center and Museum.

During Hornaday's preparation of the bison exhibit, a young man entered his studio and inquired about the six bison. That young man was Theodore Roosevelt.[152] That initial meeting led to a lifelong friendship, one that Hornaday later would lean on to see bison protected.

The arrival of the twentieth century found Hornaday lobbying then-President Roosevelt and others to constantly press for better wildlife protections. He lobbied on behalf of all species, speaking for pronghorn antelope, elk, pheasants, woodpeckers, grosbeaks, plovers, white-tailed deer, chipmunks, chickadees, purple martins, and jacksnipe—a shorebird he applauded for feasting on insects such as mosquito larvae, cutworms, and boll weevils. And, of course, he was determined to prevent the extinction of bison. The scourge of wildlife, he wrote in his wildlife manifesto of 1913, *Our Vanishing Wildlife*, were hunters.

"The rage for wild-life slaughter is far more prevalent to-day throughout the world than it was in 1872, when the buffalo butchers paved the prairies of Texas and Colorado with festering carcasses. From one end of our continent to the other, there is a restless, resistless desire to '*kill, kill!*'" he wrote in the book's preface.

Pleading for national attention to the wanton destruction of wildlife by "sportsmen," Hornaday called on specific states to step up. He thought the two Dakotas, Montana, Wyoming, Kansas, and Texas, because of their history in the buffalo wars, should "do something for the perpetual preservation of the bison species and all other big game that needs help." He lobbied officials he didn't think had done enough to protect bison. In December 1887 he wrote to Professor George Brown Goode, then director of the National Museum, to urge him to help protect bison by calling for a fence to be built around Yellowstone. "In winter the [soldiers patrolling the park] all retreat to the hotels, which are the only winter quarters provided, and the best game districts of the park are thus left entirely without protection, and for quite a long period," Hornaday pointed out. "It would seem that a wire fence eight feet high is imperatively needed around the entire park."[153]

Hornaday certainly didn't expect an overnight reversal in how wildlife was viewed, and didn't expect it to come without a significant nudge. So it was that his greatest, and most lasting, effort to save bison would occur in 1905, when he agreed, along with Ernest Harold Baynes, a naturalist, to organize a society dedicated to the species' preservation. Lamenting the loss of "our national animal," Hornaday gathered about him academics, politicians, and editors who could lobby in print to embark on a campaign to save bison.

CHARLES GOODNIGHT

Not as self-promoting as Jones, nor as driven as Hornaday, Charles Goodnight (with a nudge from his wife, Mary Ann) nevertheless played a key role in preserving the species. Born on the family farm in Macoupin County, Illinois, on March 5, 1836, the day before the Alamo fell to Mexican troops, Goodnight drew his education from daily life. When he was nine years old his stepfather took the family on an eight-hundred-mile trek to Texas, a trip young Charles made atop a mare named Blaze.[154] Structured schooling was nonexistent where the family settled. For Goodnight that was fine, as he preferred to ramble the countryside around his home to see what else lived there. He watched alligators build their nests, and then, as the process of decaying vegetation generated enough heat to incubate the eggs, saw the newborn gators scoot off. As he grew, Goodnight accumulated a diverse, but not entirely compatible, skill set. He spent time working on neighboring farms, was a jockey for a bit, an overseer of slaves, and ran oxen-pulled freight trains hauling cotton to Houston.[155] All the while, he maintained a fascination with animals.

West Texas in Goodnight's early years was a rough and wild country that native communities still claimed as their own. There were, he recounted late in life, "the harassing bands of savage enemies, and with the consequent need of incessant watchfulness against their raids, the settlers enjoyed but few respites from privations and dangers." When Goodnight was twenty, he and his stepbrother decided to leave Texas for the West Coast. They hadn't even made it out of the young state when "we concluded that Texas was large enough to supply an ample field for our energy, so we turned back over the same route just traveled."[156] It was on that return that the two came upon a rancher looking for help managing a herd of more than four hundred cattle. They worked out a ten-year deal, which started out poorly, bringing Goodnight and his step-brother, John Sheek, just ninety-six dollars. But they were determined to be cattlemen, stuck to their agreement, and "the herd intrusted to us became one of the largest and finest in the country." At the end of the decade, the two claimed between eight and ten thousand head of cattle for their work. That experience convinced Goodnight that cattle could provide a lucrative income and that Texas held all he would need from life. Goodnight's lasting fame came after the Civil War—which he spent largely as an Indian fighter and scout for the Confederate army—when he partnered with others to build a cattle business. Along with Oliver Loving, whom he had helped drive a longhorn herd to Colorado to feed men in the gold camps shortly before the war, Goodnight blazed the Goodnight-Loving Trail. The route wound from Fort Belknap, Texas, to Fort Sumner in New Mexico and on north into Colorado. Eventually the trail was extended further north, to Cheyenne, Wyoming, where the Union Pacific line ran east and west.[157] Their story was captured by author Larry McMurtry in his Pulitzer Prize-winning *Lonesome Dove*, which was turned into a popular TV miniseries in 1989. But it wasn't all a grand time. In 1893, partners Goodnight and Sheek were among a number of ranchers who sued the federal government for the loss of cattle and horses they believed were stolen in the 1860s by Comanche people, who sold them to Mexican traders. In 1901, the US Senate passed a resolution to settle the claims. As partners, Goodnight and Sheek had claims of $66,275 and they received $14,176 total, while Goodnight and Loving as partners had a claim of $16,275, but Loving was dead so Goodnight received that $4,010 as well.[158]

Buffalo robes in the nineteenth century were used for a lot of things, but saving one's life might not make that list. However, Goodnight credits one with blocking an arrow on the third cattle drive he and Loving made north. "Very tired by our day's hard ride, I was sleeping on a buffalo robe by the fire and an arrow sent with all the force of a strong bow struck the edge of the robe, deflecting sufficiently to pass under me, barely missing my body," he recounted.[159]

By 1876, Goodnight reduced the risks, hardships, and dangers of running cattle on long trail drives by establishing a home ranch. That year, having reached agreement with a New Mexico rancher over their respective grazing territories, Goodnight headed for Palo Duro Canyon in the Texas Panhandle with 1,600 longhorn cattle. The canyon, cut by the Red River southeast of Amarillo, was in the heart of a landscape he had earlier encountered as a scout for the Texas Rangers during the Civil War. Six- to eight-hundred-feet deep in places, the canyon made a perfect headquarters for Goodnight's fledgling cattle operation. There was reliable water, the caprock topography provided a measure of shelter from winter storms, and abundant grasslands meant good grazing.[160] The following June, the forty-one-year-old Goodnight, whose confident demeanor showed through his thick, black beard and piercing gaze, agreed to a partnership with John G. Adair, a wealthy Englishman who owned estates in England and Ireland.[161] Adair provided the capital, $372,000,[162] and Goodnight the ranching knowledge, sweat, and muscle. The Texan soon began building their combined JA Ranch, buying out other ranchers within seventy-five miles of Palo Duro Canyon, usually for between twenty and thirty-five cents an acre.[163] He eventually created a 1.3-million-acre operation with one hundred thousand head. "I took all the good land and all the water I could get and under the contract they were to designate twelve thousand acres more that I was to take the next year at my option," he later said of his business dealings. "Well, I scattered that all over the Palo Duro Canyon; every good ranch in the country, every place a man was liable to look, I took."[164]

Goodnight embodied the American cowboy. He worked hard, used colorful language, and drank a bit, though he prohibited his ranch hands from doing likewise. He was creative, designing the chuckwagon prototype for long cattle drives. To the rear of a Studebaker wagon left over from the Civil War, he added a wooden box to serve as a pantry, holding odds and ends and ingredients that were then within arm's reach of the cook. The box's hinged lid doubled as a work surface. A box below held pots and pans, and two days' worth of water could be stored in a barrel lashed to the side of the wagon.[165]

There was one problem with Palo Duro Canyon, from a cattleman's perspective. Thousands of bison occupied it when Goodnight arrived in 1876. By his estimate, about ten thousand. And they had to be moved out so the cattle could move in and grow fat on its grasslands. Like the no-nonsense cattleman he was, Goodnight saddled up alongside two ranch hands and proceeded to round up and drive out the bison himself. "Such a sight was probably never seen before and certainly will never be seen again. The red dust arising in clouds, while the tramp of the buffalo made a great noise. The tremendous echo of the canyon, the uprooting and crashing of the scrub cedars made one of the grandest and most interesting sights that I have ever seen," Goodnight said, reliving the task years later. "These buffaloes were moved down the canyon some fifteen miles, giving ourselves room and grass for our sixteen hundred cattle."[166]

A year later Goodnight made his second trip into the canyon, bringing his wife, Mary, and Adair and his wife, along with building materials and supplies for six months. During this stay, Mrs. Goodnight got her first close-up look at bison. "The large park below us held some thousand or fifteen hundred buffaloes grazing at sundown. The night that followed, I shall never forget," Goodnight remembered.

> As you probably know, the volume of sound from a large herd of buffalo is very great, it being mating season, the sound was great indeed with numerous stampedes making it appear very close. Mrs. Goodnight, not being accustomed to such scenes, became greatly alarmed, saying they would run over the wagon. I utterly failed in convincing her that the herds were miles away. It began to rain: the downpour was terrific and the lightning a blaze of light, immense, with thousands of flashes on the wagon sheet. To pacify her, while knowing it would be useless, I got up and made a great fire with dry cedars, assuring her that buffaloes would be easier turned by a light than by a cavalry regiment.[167]

Mrs. Goodnight did eventually get used to bison, and even urged her husband to build a small herd.

> In the spring of 1879—to be exact, May 15th—at my wife's request, [I] started out to look for some young buffalo. At last I found a few younger ones in Palo Duro Canyon, and "roped" them from horseback. The month following W. W. Dyer, my wife's brother, caught two young females. From this start we have now a herd of forty-five purebred buffaloes. In 1884 I began to cross them with Polled Angus and Galloway cattle, and have a herd of sixty of these cross-breeds. This year we have been fortunate in getting fifteen buffalo calves.[168]

Goodnight had been a careful steward of his cattle genes, bringing new bloodlines down from the stockyards in Kansas City for desired traits. He opted for Hereford cattle over Durhams because they were hardier,[169] and eventually had more than one hundred thousand cattle in his operation.[170] At the same time, he built his bison herd, which would grow to 250 head, around a bull he called Old Sikes. As did Jones, Goodnight wondered if he might produce a line of hybrid livestock more resilient to winter's fierce weather by crossing buffalo with cattle. He even wrote a short entry for the *Journal of Heredity* on what he learned from his hybridization experiments.

> I take a male buffalo calf, put him with a native cow and let him suck her until weaning time. I let him run with common cattle until large enough to serve. He will then cross with any kind of domestic cattle. In making the first cross, no male calves have ever been born; cows conceiving them either suffer abortion or die, hence I only get heifer calves and a small percent of them.

There were benefits, however:

> the "cattelow" are much greater in weight, eat much less and hold their flesh better under more adverse conditions. They will easily cut about seventy percent net of their gross weight. They have a better meat, clear of fibre, and it never gets tough like beef. They have long and deep backs, enabling them to cut at least 150 pounds more meat than other cattle.[171]

While these "cattelow" never caught on, Goodnight's bison—he was said to be careful to keep the pureblood bison separate from the hybrids[172]—have come to be viewed by some as the only continuation of the southern bison herd, which was considered to be wiped out in 1876. From this herd, he sent animals to Hornaday at the New York Zoo, as well as a few to Yellowstone in 1902 to help diversify that small herd's genetics. What's left today of the Goodnight herd—the original animals of which were considered to have been one of just six "foundational" herds used to reverse the species' nineteenth-century downfall—is genetically preserved in the Texas State Bison Herd at Caprock Canyons State Park in Quitaque, Texas.[173] When the bison were offered to the state, veterinarians tested their genetics, and kept only those without cattle genes.

Those four men weren't alone in directly, or indirectly, working to improve the future for bison after the Great Slaughter. Overall, there were five or six foundation herds that prevented the animals' disappearance. Building these herds, along with Buffalo Jones and Charles Goodnight, were James McKay, a barrel-chested, bushy-bearded, 350-pound Canadian of mixed descent, two mixed-blood Montanans, and Frederic Dupree, a rancher and fur trader in the Dakota Territory. McKay's surname descended from his Scotch father, who worked for the Hudson's Bay Company, while his mother was thought to be of First Nations heritage, possibly Cree.[174] McKay followed his father's path to the HBC, working as a clerk overseeing some trading posts. His guiding and hunting abilities, as well as his fluency in several native languages, among them Cree and Ojibwa, made McKay well-respected and viewed as an asset by the day's politicians. But it also left him in a precarious position in the late 1860s when he was appointed to the body that governed the Red River settlement, where he lived.[175] In 1867 the eastern provinces of Canada came together in a confederation, and the new government looked to the west and cast its eyes on the lands claimed by the Hudson's Bay Company. Red River was the largest settlement in that wide expanse, but it was claimed by the Métis Nation, a group of people of mixed native and European blood.

The Métis people were concerned about the new country's designs on their lands, and objected to being swept up in it without consultation. This led to the Red River Resistance, a rebellion that pitted the Métis Nation against the Canadian government. They eventually reached an agreement: the Métis Nation would join the Canadian Confederation as the province of Manitoba. Before that happened, though, a pro-Canadian man who opposed the Métis peoples' position was tried, convicted, and executed by the Métis Nation for supposedly threatening their leader, Louis Riel. After Manitoba was added to Canada in 1870, the federal government sent a military force to the province to exert its authority. McKay, noting his own mixed heritage, was not about to take up sides. But after the conflict ended, his neutrality served McKay well, as he was appointed to the new government overseeing Manitoba and the Northwest Territories. During this tumultuous period, McKay found time to nurture a small herd of bison. By 1889, after the herd was traded a few times and had grown to nearly ninety head, it was sold to Buffalo Jones.[176]

Not long after McKay started his herd, Samuel Wells, a Pend d'Oreille man who also went by the name Walking Coyote, corralled four bison not far from present-day Glacier National Park that he in turn sold to Michel Pablo and Charles Allard, who had mixed Native American and European blood. Dupree started his herd in the early 1880s when he lassoed five or six bison calves he found along the Yellowstone River in eastern Montana and brought them back to his ranch in what was then the Dakota Territory. Hornaday's New York Zoological herd could qualify as a sixth foundation herd, as the bison came from various private herds and provided the nucleus for the Wichita Mountain and Wind Cave herds.

The American Bison Society

It was deep in New England in New Hampshire, the Granite State, that an unorganized campaign for the recovery of bison as a viable species was contemplated. It was there that a herd of about 160 privately owned bison resided. And it struck Ernest

Harold Baynes, who was born in Calcutta, India, to an English father and an Indian mother[177] and grew into a self-taught naturalist and "crusader" on behalf of wildlife,[178] that they should not be the last of their kind. In June 1904 he moved to a home next to the Corbin Game Preserve, which had at the time "one of the largest herds of Buffalo in the world."[179]

Austin Corbin II, a questionable character viewed by some as a robber baron who made his fortune in banking,[180] amassed the herd in the late 1800s on a twenty-six-thousand-acre preserve known as the Blue Mountain Forest Association at Croydon, New Hampshire,[181] in the west-central part of the state not far from the Vermont border. Corbin, much like Buffalo Jones before him, envisioned a hunting preserve where "all the animals of the world can live there harmoniously."[182] A noble goal, though just as audacious and unlikely to succeed as Jones' island proposal. Among the animals he arranged to populate this preserve were wild boar from Germany and Russia, white-tailed deer from Canada, elk from Minnesota, even beavers. And bison. Corbin had taken it upon himself to try to save bison, and arranged to obtain animals from Oklahoma, Montana, Wyoming, Manitoba, and Texas.[183] Their arrival, in a "bison drive," didn't go unnoticed by the locals, as Baynes later noted.

> It was on a bright morning in 1890, that the farmers working in the fields near the road between Newport and Croydon Flat, stopped their oxen for a minute to gaze in wonder at a passing herd of the strangest "cattle" they had ever seen. Great brown beasts they were, with burly, horned and bearded heads, short, powerful necks, high, rounded humps and short tails, ending in a tuft of hair. These creatures were pictures of prodigious strength. From their mighty forelimbs hung banners of long dark hair, which waved in the breeze as they marched along with a majestic stride befitting the

grandest animal which ever trod the soil of the American continent. They were the Corbin herd of bison, on their way to their new home in the Blue Mountain Forest. [184]

That herd, and Baynes' knowledge that wild bison were almost a thing of the past, prompted him to write a series of articles for a Boston newspaper in an attempt to build public interest in bison.[185] He discussed the idea with a friend, Professor Franklin W. Hooper, director of the Brooklyn Institute of Arts and Sciences, who encouraged him to embark on a letter-writing campaign to President Roosevelt, among others. Roosevelt was impressed by Baynes' letter, and promised to mention the plight of the bison in his annual message. He did, on December 6, 1904, urging the Congress to allow him to set aside lands in the national forest reserve system "as game refuges for the preservation of the bison."[186]

Baynes took to the lecture circuit in January 1905. On the eighteenth of the month he gave a lecture to the Boston Society of Natural History titled "The American Buffalo—A Plea for His Preservation," and that prompted a gathering the very next day of "several gentlemen who had become interested [and] met informally and discussed plans for the organization of a society which should have for its object the preservation of the Buffalo." A few days later the same talk was presented to the Camp-Fire Club of America, and afterwards Baynes discussed the idea of a bison society with Hornaday, who—after some reluctance because he thought this new organization might conflict with his efforts at the New York Zoological Park—agreed to serve as the society's president.[187]

Roosevelt further boosted the campaign to save bison by telling Congress in his fifth annual message, delivered December 5, 1905, that it was urgent that the country take action to preserve the species. That was not the crux of his wide-ranging annual message, which touched on issues as diverse as interstate commerce, labor laws, government reorganization, and a conference on nations. But he found the space to stick in a paragraph about bison.

> The most characteristic animal of the Western Plains was the great shaggy-maned wild ox, the bison, commonly known as the buffalo. Small fragments of herds exist in a domesticated state here and there, a few of them in Yellowstone Park. Such a herd as that on the Flathead Reservation should not be allowed to go out of existence. Either on some reservation or on some forest reserve like the Wichita Reserve or some refuge, provision should be made for the preservation of such a herd. I believe that the scheme would be of economic advantage, for the robe of the buffalo is of high market value, and the same is true of the robe of the crossbred animals.[188]

Three days later, an organizational meeting of the American Bison Society was held with thirteen men and one woman present. The gathering included Grinnell, the editor of *Forest and Stream*; Hornaday, director of the New York Zoological Park; the editor of *Woods and Waters*; and the director of the New York Aquarium. Hornaday was quickly elected president, and Roosevelt voted the society's honorary president, which he learned via a letter Baynes sent from New Hampshire on January 6, 1906. Hooper, aware that bison also roamed the Great Plains in Canada, suggested that an invitation to join the society be extended to that country.

The society's arrival did not provide the first push to preserve bison on public lands outside of Yellowstone. Earlier in 1905 the New York Zoological Society, which employed Hornaday as its director and general curator, gave him permission to approach the federal government about establishing a bison preserve. That initiative led in the fall of 1907 to fifteen bison from the zoo being sent to Oklahoma and the Wichita Mountains Wildlife Refuge, which had been created just four years earlier to preserve an intact patch of mixed-grass prairie and the native wildlife that went along with it.

The idea to rebuild the West's wild bison herds was espoused by a number of men, all who traveled in the same circles. Madison Grant, the secretary of the New York Zoological Society, used his friendship with President Roosevelt to see the Wichita Mountains Game Preserve created, and Congressman John F. Lacey, who had crafted the Lacey Act in 1894 to protect Yellowstone's bison, carried the requisite Wichita legislation through the House of Representatives.[189] Hornaday was in the background lobbying and explaining how he thought the preserve should be fenced to keep bison in and predators out. "We feel that it is the duty of individuals to do something toward the establishment of the series of buffalo herds that should be established very soon," he wrote Lacey in pushing for the Wichita preserve.[190]

When choosing the members of this small herd in southwestern Oklahoma, Hornaday combined young and old, including a female calf just six months old and a bull five-and-a-half years old. There were six males and nine females, and Hornaday sought diverse genetic lines in choosing them.

The Bison thus selected represent four distinct strains of blood. The large breeding bull is not related to any of the other members of the herd. It is the belief of the writer, based on recent studies of the development of wild animals derived from a small number of progenitors, but ranging free on large areas of territory, that on any range for animals as large as that of the Wichita Bison Range, the dangers of evil results from inbreeding are too small to be considered seriously, provided the original stock is sound and healthy.[191]

The decision to create a bison herd was welcomed by cowboys who, like Native Americans, feared their fate and that of the bison was linked.

"The cowboy is rapidly becoming as extinct as the buffalo," said Frank Rush, who traveled from Oklahoma to New York City to escort Hornaday's bison west. "Back there on the range these buffalo will be able to wander among the bones of their forebears and wallow to their heart's content in the holes made by buffalo of the olden days. They will be attended by some of the old cowboys who hunted buffalo on the plains in pioneer days, and who will now care for them with as much care and zeal as they once chased them with rifle and lariat."[192]

Hornaday's experience with that conservation project gave him a model to follow with the American Bison Society: offer the federal government bison for free in return for land and stout fencing.[193] At the same time, there was need for high-profile individuals whose lobbying on behalf of bison would be heard. Goodnight, Jones, Hornaday, Roosevelt, and Baynes weren't the only individuals working to save bison. Grinnell lobbied for the species editorially from his perch as the long-time editor of *Forest and Stream* and later at the Boone and Crockett Club. "Does the public wish to have America's largest land mammal pass wholly out of existence, or is it worthwhile for the Government to spend some money to preserve this species for future generations?" Grinnell asked his readers in the July 1, 1905, issue of *Forest and Stream*.

Grinnell's rebirth as a bison proponent was somewhat startling in that he previously had suggested that bison be exterminated for the good of the country.

"The Indian, the buffalo, the elk, deer and moose will disappear; from many sections they have already done so," he wrote in the December 14, 1882, edition of *Forest and Stream*.

This was to have been expected, and while it may be deplored, it cannot be avoided. The interests of civilization demand that the country be settled and improved, and sentiment cannot be permitted to stand in the way of such improvement. Lamentable as it is to see these superb animals swept off from the face of the earth, it is something to which we must submit. All we can do is to exert ourselves to render this extermination as gradual as possible.[194]

John Muir, the early twentieth century's environmental giant, did much the same, writing in 1897 that, "[I]n the nature of things they had to give place to better cattle, though the change might have been made without barbarous wickedness."[195]

Hornaday's success with the Wichita Mountains preserve was severely tempered by the sale of most of the Pablo-Allard herd to Canada. By 1907, with Allard eleven years dead, and homesteading coming to the West, Pablo offered to sell his bison to the US government.[196] When the United States showed no interest, he found a willing buyer in the Canadian government, which paid $245 per head. Seventeen railcars were used to ship 410 bison to Lamont, Alberta, where Elk Park, the forerunner of Elk Island National Park, had recently been established.[197] So proud was Canada of acquiring these bison that the country later would recognize the purchase and bison mission of Elk Island as a Canadian National Historic Event.[198]

The loss of the bison to Canada was a huge blow to the American Bison Society, which at the time was lobbying to create a National Bison Range in Montana. Hornaday shrewdly used that setback to persuade Congress to support the bison range. Again, he used the carrot of free bison to seal the deal. President Roosevelt signed the requisite legislation on May 23, 1908, and Hornaday went to work assembling a herd for the range. After a fundraising campaign, he purchased thirty-four bison from the estate of C. E. Conrad,[199] a wealthy Kalispell, Montana, business-man who had built his herd from animals purchased from the Pablo-Allard herd. The Conrad estate threw in two more bison, a seven-year-old bull and a six-year-old cow, and Goodnight the next year made a gift of two of his herd for the range.[200]

The American Bison Society was at the forefront of building federally owned herds of bison, but it was not the only protector. By January 1, 1908, hundreds of bison could be found in national parks, state parks, zoos, and private herds. Hornaday's own January 1 tally showed 136 in the Corbin herd, 240 remaining in the Pablo herd, nearly 400 at Elk Island National Park in Alberta (the bulk of the Pablo-Allard herd that the US government passed on), and 158 in Philip's herd in South Dakota. Another 125 were held in other countries, including four at the Zoological Gardens in Antwerp, Belgium, noted Hornaday.[201]

Though Hornaday later wrote that he believed the National Bison Range "alone would be sufficient to save the species from becoming extinct,"[202] the American Bison Society didn't rest on that project. Its work turned to establishing another satellite herd, which would end up at Wind Cave National Park.

Yellowstone's Stigma

Chipmunks in New York's Central Park get more consideration and protection than the bison in Yellowstone. The fact that Interior uses the bison as its official symbol adds the insult of misleading advertising to the injury of mass mayhem.

—Jeff Ruch, executive director of Public Employees for Environmental Responsibility, 2006

There are more than four hundred units of the National Park System in the United States, each with its own fan base. Yellowstone arguably stands above all others, and not simply because it was the first national park established by Congress. The park's collection of geothermal wonders, topped by the Old Faithful and Steamboat geysers, is second to none. But Yellowstone also is renowned for its reputation as North America's Serengeti, home to a rich and diverse wild kingdom that is believed to include all the mammalian species that wandered the landscape centuries ago. Stand before the thundering geysers, or a thundering herd of bison or a howling pack of wolves, and you won't go home disappointed. Having the good fortune to live within a half-day's drive of the park, I have been astounded again and again, year after year after year for more than three decades, by visits to the park. One trip, by canoe deep into the South Arm of Yellowstone Lake, brought me face to face with a paw print, bigger than a saucier pan, in the wet sand of the beach. Here was the home of *Ursus arctos horribilis*, aka grizzly bear. Practically overrunning the bear's imprint was a series of wolf tracks, *Canis lupus* in lope. And then there were dainty tracks possibly left by sandhill cranes. Following an evening cracked open at times by lightning bolts from thunderstorms passing to the north, the audio show resumed the next morning, as in the predawn murkiness a rich, melodious howl first broke the silence and then hung in the air. Perhaps it was the wolf's presence that silenced the elk and the cranes that had been so vocal the day before.

The National Park Service Organic Act of 1916 directed its namesake agency to "conserve the scenery and the natural and historic objects and the wild life therein and to provide for the enjoyment of the same in such manner and by such means as will leave them unimpaired for the enjoyment of future generations." It's only deep in the backcountry of a park, whether Yellowstone or Yosemite or Glacier or Great Smoky Mountains or Everglades, that you gain a good and sound appreciation of "the scenery and the natural . . . objects and the wild life therein." These backcountry locales have been preserved by the National Park System, and for that we're all fortunate. Unfortunately, what the Organic Act didn't take into consideration is the simple fact that some wildlife migrates. And that wildlife ignores park boundaries. Each year, pronghorn antelope from Grand Teton National Park and the Jackson Hole Valley in northwestern Wyoming make an annual migration of about two hundred miles to winter range south of Pinedale in Wyoming's Green River Basin. The route, purportedly the longest land mammal migration in the continental United States, has been dubbed the "Path of the Pronghorn." In 2008, this migratory corridor was formally recognized by the staff at Grand Teton, the US Forest Service, the US Fish and Wildlife Service, the US Bureau of Land Management, and private stakeholders.[203] There are many other migrations. Some overhead, as raptors come and go spring and fall through such national parks as Glacier and Shenandoah, while humpback whales swim in loops from Glacier Bay National Park in Alaska to Hawaii and back for breeding, calving, and feeding. Even monarch butterflies migrate, with hundreds heading to Muir Woods National Monument in California to winter.

Elk and bison also migrate, in and out of Grand Teton and Yellowstone, and they would, too, from Badlands and Wind Cave, if fences had not been erected to contain the bison there. The problems of managing wildlife that might spend only part of the year inside a national park are vexing to park-service staff. Parks are politically well-defined by their acreage and boundaries, and many species only spend part of the year in those landscapes. Yellowstone's ability in recent decades to maintain a bison population that fluctuates between three thousand and five thousand, depending on winter's severity, has not always been so clear and assuring. In the 1980s and 1990s, bison that migrated out of the park into Montana in winter were gunned down. In 1997 alone, more than one thousand of the park's bison were killed, either shot outright or taken to slaughterhouses, out of fear they might transmit brucellosis to livestock. Mike Finley, at the time Yellowstone's superintendent, charged that the killings "virtually decimated the northern bison herd in Yellowstone."[204]

There long has been talk about creating migratory corridors, such as the Yellowstone to Yukon initiative, a vision to establish a 2,200-mile-long swath of wilderness that, in theory at least, would enable bison, wolves, grizzlies, wolverines, bighorn sheep, mountain goats, and other animals to freely wander, migrate, and swap genes as they naturally would. But to accomplish such a corridor requires buy-in from federal, state, and local officials, not to mention private landowners. As the great reluctance from Montana officials and some landowners to allow bison from Yellowstone to leave the park demonstrates, collective support and approval of protecting migratory passages won't materialize without strong societal pushback. Further complicating the task are the impacts climate change is having on landscapes. As habitats change, some species will move out, some will move in, creating a transformative mosaic of wildlands and wildlife that will need to be managed. To that point, an expansive 2018 study by the National Park Service and the National Audubon Society found that, on average, there could be up to a 25 percent turnover of bird species in some national parks by 2050 because of the changing climate.

The challenge is not lost on National Park Service leadership. They have developed a webpage specific to migratory species, which reads:

> To preserve a species' migration, conservation efforts must target the species at a broad level that goes far beyond national park boundaries. Issues range from philosophical beliefs, to baseline needs, to biological unknowns, to social concerns and attitudes, with questions as basic as how such conservation could be achieved—and if it should even be attempted.[205]

Despite recognition of the problems tied to species' migrations, the park service is handicapped by local politics and political boundaries in its efforts to adequately conserve that wildlife as directed by the Organic Act. The boundaries drawn in 1872 when Yellowstone was established never took into consideration migrating animals such as bison, elk, and pronghorn, nor the predators that trailed them on their seasonal journeys. And nowhere in the National Park System are politics and wildlife more entwined than at Yellowstone. The intersection of the two-legged politicians and cloven-hooved bison has led to blindness to issues, spurred litigation, fueled the coffers of nonprofit conservation groups, and ended the career of a venerable National Park Service employee who spent his last years as the park's superintendent. Politics tied to the cattle industry held up efforts at least through 2018 to approve a quarantine program that would allow Yellowstone bison found to be free of the brucellosis bacteria to be sent to tribal lands, state agencies, and other organizations that want herds that carry the robust genetics of Yellowstone's herd. They also led, in the latter years of the twentieth century, to a killing ground on the park's northern border when park bison were determined to reach their historic, instinctual lower elevation wintering and calving grounds and ran into a firing line arranged by Montana officials to keep the animals away from cattle.

How to manage the migratory nature of bison is one of the thorniest wildlife issues confronting the park service. There are, across the National Park System, pocket herds of bison. You can find them at Tallgrass Prairie National Preserve in Kansas, Wind Cave and Badlands national parks in South Dakota, Theodore Roosevelt in North Dakota, Grand Teton in Wyoming, Denali in Alaska, and, of course, in Yellowstone, where the most esteemed herd of all resides. Viewed as conservation herds that carry the purest of bison genes, these are the animals that, largely, hold the future of bison as a sustainable and viable species on the Great Plains. Already their efforts are proving successful. Wind Cave, Badlands, and Theodore Roosevelt national parks through 2015 alone contributed nearly ten thousand bison to Native American tribes, state parks, and other entities seeking their own herds.[206]

The vision of bison roaming parts of the Midwest as they did in the nineteenth century is not new, but is constantly being refined as more is learned about bison biology, both internally and as it relates to their reliance on the landscape. As this knowledge is honed, it could be applied to other species that need large landscapes to survive and thrive. If you've ever driven across the country in the past half-century, you've seen the problem. Development has crisscrossed the nation, while the natural landscape has shriveled, been manipulated, transformed, eroded, and paved over. Elk have lost nearly three-quarters of their historic landscape, pronghorn antelope about 64 percent, and grizzly bears 53 percent. Bison, today, have access to less than 1 percent of their historic range.[207]

Concern over the paucity of lands available to bison led to a gathering of wildlife biologists and conservationists at the Vermejo Park Ranch in northern New Mexico for a series of three meetings spread out over 2005 and 2006. The nearly six-hundred-thousand-acre property owned by Ted Turner was an appropriate setting. Turner long has been a proponent of bison, and some 1,500 of the animals wander free across the ranch that spills north over the state border into southern Colorado. As they debated the future of bison in North America, the attendees painted an optimistic outcome in what has come to be known as the Vermejo Statement:

> Over the next century, the ecological recovery of the North American bison will occur when multiple large herds move freely across extensive landscapes within all major habitats of their historic range, interacting in ecologically significant ways with the fullest possible set of other native species, and inspiring, sustaining and connecting human cultures.

As much thought and effort they put into discussing the bison's plight, they also weren't presumptuous. They acknowledged that large herds of bison wouldn't move in freedom across their historic range within a decade. Or even five decades. But, they added, it wouldn't be unreasonable to see that goal attained in a century. From that paper, three overriding guidelines evolved: let wild bison be wild, maintain the genetic diversity of bison, and restore the bison ecosystem.[208] Those three tenets seem obvious enough. Who, being in favor of seeing more bison in their natural element, wouldn't agree that bison should be allowed to function as a wild species, to move unfettered, as they will? Those herds also need a robust range of ages and sexes, and human intervention should be minimized. Don't treat them as livestock. Don't cut their horns off for safety's sake, don't selectively breed them, don't aggressively manage their health, don't fence them in (too tightly).

But transforming words on paper into significant results, as the yet-to-succeed Yellowstone to Yukon initiative shows, is not easy and takes time. Since 1993, the Y2Y initiative has gained the support of some three hundred partners, groups ranging from outdoor clothing purveyors and hunting organizations to Native American governments, photographers, and even the National Park Service. During its first twenty-five years, Y2Y has increased the acreage of protected areas—national and provincial parks, wilderness areas, conservancies, and preserves—by 21 percent. It has worked collaboratively to purchase 550,000 acres of private lands to preserve migratory corridors. Much of the timeline envisioned with ecological recovery of bison requires creation of alliances with "as many stakeholders as possible." Perhaps the most difficult phase of that assemblage of collaborators is found within Montana, which traces about fifty-four miles of Yellowstone's northern border. Within the park in 2018 there were more than four thousand bison, a number that can quickly expand to nearly five thousand, depending on how hard a winter plays out.

Bison, fortunately, reproduce rapidly. In Yellowstone, the rate has ranged from 10 percent to 17 percent per year.[209] Once facing the oblivion that is extinction, bison have rebounded in number and prestige. They are disparaged by many Montana officials and ranchers, subjected to hunting, quarantine, or slaughter as methods of controlling a disease spread almost entirely by elk, and managed to unnaturally low population numbers. And yet, these bison are key to a successful future for the species. The park's bison are descended from a very small herd in the upper headwaters of the Yellowstone River that escaped the Great Slaughter of the late nineteenth century. Though prized for their pure genetic line that goes back centuries, half or more of these bison carry a cattle-introduced disease that, frankly, scares the hell out of ranchers. *Brucella abortus* is a bacterium thought to have reached the United States from European livestock. It can cause spontaneous abortions or stillbirths in bison, elk, and cattle. Until 2010, if two or more herds in a state contracted the disease, or if a single herd was found to carry the disease and was not sent to slaughter, all herds in that state were blacklisted from markets. Today that blacklisting applies only to the affected herd. Nevertheless, the risks of the disease infecting cattle have stigmatized Yellowstone bison and impeded their instincts to head outside the park to lower ground for calving. And it has stood in the way of distribution of their genes to other bison herds in the West.

By 1991, most cattle in US herds were free of the disease, but brucellosis was confirmed in nearly two dozen cattle or domestic bison herds in the Greater Yellowstone Ecosystem between 2002 and 2015, according to the US Animal Health Association, a nearly 125-year-old nonprofit organization that works with state and federal entities to control livestock diseases. The ever-present possibility that more herds could be infected with the disease has been the leading roadblock to Yellowstone bison being treated as wildlife, not livestock, and allowed to roam freely into Montana as do park elk. Cattle production is the largest agricultural industry in the state, generating nearly $1.5 billion in annual revenues. As such, there is understandable concern about how brucellosis could impact that industry. Yet the fact of the matter, according to the National Academy of Sciences, is that elk, not Yellowstone bison, are the culprit when it comes to spreading brucellosis. But, as Doug Smith, Yellowstone's senior wildlife biologist, points out, "elk are really gods around here."[210]

"Here" being Montana.

A century ago, in 1917, brucellosis was detected in the bison of Yellowstone. Exactly how the disease reached the park is unclear, but it has been largely accepted that either infected cattle, or elk that picked it up from cattle, brought it into the park. The disease spreads from bison to bison or, theoretically, bison to cattle, bison to elk, or elk to cattle, through oral contact with aborted fetuses, contaminated placentas, or related birth discharges. Although more than 90 percent of infected cow bison abort their first pregnancy, the percentages quickly drop to about 20 percent after the second pregnancy, and to near zero after the third, a phenomenon associated with naturally acquired immunity. Male bison can contract the disease, too, and it can lead to sterility. Both cows and bulls also can develop arthritis and/ or bursitis from a concentration of the bacteria in their joints, leading to lameness that increases the risk of being preyed upon.

Brucellosis can be an economically ravaging disease, one that justifies the battle to contain it, if not wipe it out. It's estimated to have cost the livestock industry and the state and federal governments billions of dollars between efforts to wipe out the disease and losses to ranchers, according to the US Department of Agriculture's Animal and Plant Health Inspection Service (APHIS), the federal agency tasked with protecting the nation's agricultural interests. Three decades after brucellosis was detected in Yellowstone bison, the federal government launched an eradication program in concert with state officials and the livestock industry. The disease had a good head start in evading eradication, and pretty assuredly from an overlooked source. In the Yellowstone region the arrival of brucellosis likely dates to 1912, when the Bureau of Biological Survey, the precursor to today's US Fish and Wildlife Service, started feeding elk on the National Elk Refuge in Jackson, Wyoming. This and other feedlot operations in Wyoming congregated hundreds and thousands of elk through the winters. Not only did these feedlots make it easy to transmit disease through the herds, but the forage led to unnaturally high elk populations. Some Montana officials grouse about the feedlots, especially the one in Jackson. They say genetic studies on strains of brucellosis have traced some Montana outbreaks back to that feedlot.[211]

The brucellosis eradication program in recent decades has centered on the Greater Yellowstone Ecosystem, a rugged, mountainous landscape that covers more than thirty-four thousand square miles and is one of the world's largest nearly intact temperate-zone ecosystems. It's a spectacularly beautiful and wild region shared by Idaho, Montana, and Wyoming that is covered by forests and peaks that climb to nearly fourteen thousand feet above sea level. Cupped in those mountains are the headwaters of rivers that stand out in western history: the Snake, Madison, Green, and Yellowstone. Wolves, grizzlies, and wolverines live there, as do moose, elk, bighorn sheep, mule deer, and bison.

Working with APHIS, officials from the three states can put in place control programs for animals that have been infected or exposed to brucellosis. The disease, on rare occasion, can spread to humans in the form of undulant fever, or Bang's disease. This illness is physically debilitating, causing deep pain and exhaustion that can come and go for years. Terry Jones knows that firsthand. As we sat in his south-central Wyoming backyard, the jagged profile of 10,274-foot Laramie Peak in the Laramie Range not far off to the west, the retired railroad worker told me he was pretty sure he contracted the disease during a November 2016 elk hunt in the Greater Yellowstone Ecosystem. While helping a friend field-dress an elk kill, Jones cut his hand on a sharp bone. Ten weeks later, he noticed the first symptoms: great pain in his joints, most noticeably his hips and back, fever, weight loss, weakness, and general exhaustion. He wasn't sure what he had. At first he considered it might be a cold or flu. The pain in his body seemed to move around, too, but was worst in his hips. Once an infectious-disease specialist made the diagnosis, Jones was put on a hefty regimen of intravenous antibiotics as well as oral antibiotics that eventually knocked out the disease.[212] But six months after he contracted the disease, Jones said, he still had not regained his strength. It would come back, his doctors told him, but it would take time.

In Yellowstone, upward of 60 percent of bison are thought to have been exposed to brucellosis; the herds are judged to be chronically infected with the disease. But while bison long have been viewed as the key players in carrying the disease to livestock, that's not the case at all. A National Academy of Sciences paper published early in 2017 said definitively that elk, not bison, are far and away most responsible for transmitting brucellosis to cattle in the Yellowstone region. The authors noted that while there has been no conclusive transmission of brucellosis from bison to cattle in the region since 1998, "the risk of transmission from elk to cattle may be increasing."[213] Part of the increase in the spread could be tied to the return of wolves to the ecosystem and growth in the grizzly population. Those predators have altered wildlife dynamics, in part by forcing elk outside of the park into the surrounding forests and countryside. Development of some private lands outside the park also has benefited elk by essentially creating hunt-free zones and so providing for de facto pools of brucella.

The National Academy of Sciences report raises an interesting question: Have Yellowstone bison been made a costly scapegoat for a problem created by elk? Montana officials, and the National Park Service, have been extremely vigilant in seeing that bison don't range too far from the park. The same can't be said about elk. But due to the threat elk pose to cattle herds, Montana wildlife biologists not only track elk herds—the state in January 2010 began outlining Designated Surveillance Areas so ranchers know where the greatest transmission threat exists—but also measure their infection rate. Ranchers are also required to vaccinate their cattle against the disease. (Idaho and Wyoming also created DSAs, and combined these districts cover nearly thirty-one thousand square miles in eastern Idaho, southwest Montana, and western Wyoming.) But the years of focus on Yellowstone bison as brucellosis carriers seem to have blinded Montana officials and ranchers to the risk from elk. In short, they underestimated the threat from elk. That realization led to the DSAs and relatively high-tech monitoring of elk for brucellosis. Elk travel fast, much faster than bison. In Montana, elk are turning up in places where they weren't seen five, six, and seven decades ago. To help track the movement of brucellosis, wildlife biologists for the state capture cow elk and fit them with radio collars. Five years later, they are recaptured, and those that test positive for brucellosis are culled.

But to trace the history and progression of wildlife disease in Yellowstone, you need to look back more than a century. Managing wildlife was not part of standard training for the US Army, which patrolled Yellowstone from 1886 until the National Park Service came into being in 1916. In 1902, concerned that bison were heading toward extinction, the army began to treat the animals like livestock. They would round up bison, provide feed in winter, and actively manage the age of the herds by culling old individuals. By the late 1920s, roughly six hundred acres of hay ranches were established within Yellowstone to grow forage for the wildlife. It was a husbandry practice that at the time carried many unforeseen ramifications, from the competition between wildlife and livestock for range on public lands to unnaturally high populations and the easy spread of disease. These management practices continued through the mid-1960s. By 1966, efforts to rid the Yellowstone herds of brucellosis led to a great slaughter that saw the population plummet from about 1,500 to perhaps 200.[214] Realizing that they could end up killing all the park bison to contain the disease, Yellowstone managers put an end to the culling.

It was one of those "what were we thinking?" moments. Today, Yellowstone's bison are widely regarded as the only herd in the country that has descended directly from animals that occupied this landscape from time immemorial. As a result, their genetic "knowledge" is rich and robust with wildness and instinctual behavior. As with their ancestors, these bison confront natural selection on a daily basis, whether the challenges come from predators, the weather, or breeding competition. Commercially raised bison, meanwhile, often live in fenced pastures and are rotated from pasture to pasture as the seasons turn; the lack of predators mute their instincts. Yellowstone bison are considered by many scientists to be the only ecologically viable population of plains bison in the United States: they have a wide swath of the park's 2.2 million acres to utilize.

Any story concerning the survivability of a species, plant or animal, requires a primer, at least, on biology and genetics. When you accept that there are an estimated five hundred thousand bison across the United States and Canada, you wouldn't think you'd need such a primer, that the species wouldn't be in any danger of extinction. But what if a vast majority, more than 98 percent, of those five hundred thousand animals had cattle genes in their genome? What if only Yellowstone bison, and maybe those at Wind Cave, were genetically pure? The argument that if it looks like a bison, walks like a bison, and smells like a bison then it must be a bison might not be entirely accurate.

The US Fish and Wildlife Service decides which terrestrial and freshwater species, plant and animal, receive Endangered Species Act protections. And it has ruled that Yellowstone bison don't merit the act's protection. But a federal judge isn't so sure. Early in 2018 he ruled that the Fish and Wildlife Service didn't sufficiently refute evidence provided by the Buffalo Field Campaign and Western Watersheds Project that the genetic purity of Yellowstone's bison is threatened by disease, hunting, habitat loss, mismanagement, and the risk of the introduction of cattle genes into their population. The Buffalo Field Campaign, or BFC, dates to the hard winter of 1996–97, when more than one thousand Yellowstone bison instinctually moved out of the park and into the lowlands to the north, where they were slaughtered due to the fear of brucellosis. To chronicle the killing that winter, a group called Buffalo Nations was formed to conduct daily patrols to monitor the bison and to advocate for the species and educate the public about speciesism, or discrimination, of bison by Montana officials. The organization, tagged the Buffalo Field Campaign in 1997, was formed by Rosalie Little Thunder (Lakota Sioux), and videographer Mike Mease. Though decidedly on the low end, financially, of conservation nonprofit organizations, BFC has maintained high visibility through its demonstrations around the park, email campaigns, and sheer tenacity. In campaigning for Yellowstone bison, the organization has developed a "Buffalo Bill of Rights," which mentions such things as allowing bison to remain wild and free in their native habitat; they should be honored and respected for their cultural and spiritual significance to the Plains cultures; they should be allowed to fully return to their natural and historical migration patterns; and they should be preserved as "the genetic wellspring for future wild, free-ranging buffalo populations."

The legal battle over whether the bison need ESA protection could eventually become moot, through growth of the Yellowstone herds. But for now the judge wants the Fish and Wildlife Service to show why BFC's petition "is unreliable, irrelevant, or otherwise unreasonable." That left the agency reevaluating the genetic studies the Buffalo Field Campaign introduced to justify an ESA listing.

To finish this genetic primer, you can trace the relevance of the case back to 1870, when an estimated two million bison from the southern herd, found south of the main east-west railroad line that crossed the Great Plains, were killed. Two years later, an average of five thousand bison a day were being killed. While Yellowstone was established that year, 1872, and its enabling legislation outlawed the wanton destruction of wildlife, there was no one to enforce that regulation until the US Army arrived in the park. By 1876, for all practical purposes, the southern herd was judged to be wiped out, and six years later the northern herd faced the same fate. Extinction for the species loomed in 1902, when free-roaming bison numbers were thought to be as few as one hundred, with maybe two dozen in Yellowstone. Today, bison in Yellowstone are believed to be free of domestic cattle genes, while most other bison in North America are thought to carry cattle genes, even some in conservation herds. The mix of cattle and bison genes can be traced to the well-intentioned efforts by Goodnight, Jones, and some others who experimented with crossing the two to produce a sturdier cow, one better-suited to the harsh winters on the open plains. "Introgression" of cattle genes into bison replaces bison DNA with some snippets of cattle DNA. Though such a swap impairs the genetic integrity of bison, there is evidence that cattle traits contained in these swaps aren't always exhibited by bison offspring, though those with cattle genes tend to be smaller in stature than purebred bison.

To better understand the genetic nuances, I called Jim Derr, an expert at deciphering bison DNA. Derr is an easygoing professor of veterinary medicine at Texas A&M University who has done decades of research, and has run tens of thousands of genetic tests, to profile bison as a species. He also has developed a primer on the best way to obtain bison genetic material to test (a typical pair of household pliers is great for pulling tail hairs). From his office, he explained that if the cattle genes are contained in mitochondrial DNA (mtDNA) and it is determined those genes are detrimental to bison, they're easy to cleanse from a herd. Both males and females contribute nuclear DNA to their offspring, he told me, but only females contribute mtDNA. So even if the mtDNA was passed on to a bull, the genes and their traits end with him. Any female offspring that inherit mtDNA can be slaughtered. "You can test for it easily, and the bulls can't pass it on, and the cows do pass it on to their sons and daughters but their sons can't pass it on, so it's a dead end," said Dr. Derr.

Through his research, the wildlife veterinarian has arrived at an explanation for how bison avoided a genetic bottleneck that very likely would have led to their extinction soon after the Great Slaughter. In short, the work of Goodnight, Jones, Hornaday, and others with private herds that remained after the slaughter were able to exchange enough animals to prevent or at least limit the detrimental effects of inbreeding. The depth and breadth of his bison research has Derr working to apply that knowledge in Africa to ensure genetic integrity in wildlife. Here in the United States, his research has left him with little concern that cattle genes could doom bison as a purebred species.

"Well, it depends," he replied when asked whether Yellowstone's bison deserve protection under the Endangered Species Act. "I suppose it hinges on what you consider an endangered species and how you define 'endangered.' There are different ways to determine why you would invoke endangered species status or threatened status on a species. And I think the overriding concern would be to protect that species from further harm. There's a threat and you're going to designate it as endangered or threatened in order to reduce or prevent or eliminate that threat."

Designation as a threatened species also would require the federal government to set population goals for bison to reach to be declared recovered. A key benefit to Endangered Species Act designation, whether as a threatened or endangered species, would be the requirement that habitat be protected for bison. Critical habitat, in this case, would include areas with vegetation that would support bison with space for them to roam, and would likely require management protection guidance. It also could include suitable areas that are not currently home to bison. Depending on the population number that would reflect recovery of the species, land beyond national park landscapes might need to be considered for habitat.

Put it all together—a small percentage of bison in conservation herds, some ranchers managing bison for specific traits, no protection under the Endangered Species Act, no rigid population goal to attain for purebred bison, and bison largely blocked from living across their historic habitat—and bison today can be viewed as a very conflicted species. Just the same, Derr doesn't see any threat that would doom them. The Yellowstone bison don't seem to have any cattle introgression, nor do those at Elk Island National Park in Canada. From those herds, bison have been transferred to establish sub-herds, such as the Henry Mountains herd in Utah that was started with Yellowstone bison. That Utah herd, in turn, was tapped to build another at the Book Cliffs in eastern Utah. So while the Yellowstone herd in the park is artificially restricted in population growth, its genotype has been distributed beyond the park.

Wildlife veterinarians who examined the animals' DNA to determine whether they were a sound pool from which to build new herds west of the Mississippi confirmed the genetic integrity of Yellowstone's bison in 2014. Taking samples from ear punches, hair, skin, blood, and muscle, the scientists concluded that the park's bison offer more genetic diversity to the national bison population than other federal herds. But the genetics of Yellowstone bison might be even more unique, and could point to a need for greater conservation of the animals. That was the point the Buffalo Field Campaign argued in 2014 when it petitioned the US Fish and Wildlife Service to extend threatened or endangered designation to all park bison. In a somewhat lengthy petition of more than sixty pages,[215] the group and the Western Watersheds Project argued that Yellowstone's bison represent the last, and largest, remnant population of plains bison that ranged across much of the country until they were almost entirely wiped out late in the nineteenth century. Citing a range of threats, from disease and habitat loss to climate change and accidental introgression of cattle genes, the groups maintained that ESA protection was needed in short, to prevent the species' extinction.

The Fish and Wildlife Service's counterargument, which was rejected by the court, was that Yellowstone bison herds have been growing in number and need no ESA protection. The agency, possibly channeling Hornaday, dismissed climate-change concerns by noting that bison historically ranged from Mexico to Canada and from the Rocky Mountains to Florida, and so could adapt to warmer conditions. Fish and Wildlife Service attorneys argued that Yellowstone's bison are not so genetically unique, pointing out that bison from the Goodnight and Jones herds augmented the twenty-three or twenty-four animals that evaded the Great Slaughter.

That point, that there might not be "subpopulation genetic differentiation," is the bone of contention, for the Buffalo Field Campaign and Western Watersheds Project found a study that suggests Yellowstone's central and northern bison herds are actually two genetically distinct herds and so should be preserved as separate gene pools. If the judge agrees, then the federal government's goal of three thousand bison total in Yellowstone to constitute a genetically viable population could be too low and so negatively affect genetic diversity. It might require that six thousand bison, at least, are needed to protect that diversity. Regardless of the outcome, the matter shows the great challenge facing groups that envision more bison on the public landscape. How many animals are necessary to protect the species' genetic purity and diversity, and how much habitat do they need? As with efforts to preserve the sage grouse, other land-use practices—fracking, coal mining, agriculture, even suburban sprawl—could stand in the way of habitat expansion for bison. Two-thousand-pound bison, of course, are a sturdier species, at least outwardly, than a four-pound bird. But, as with sage grouse, bison need wide expanses if they're to become ecologically viable on a large scale once again. Montana officials could very well be a political and agricultural microcosm of what bison would face on a larger scale across the Plains states.

Back at Yellowstone, Dan Wenk believed the focus on bison instead of elk as the brucellosis culprit stemmed from the disease in elk being "almost an unmanageable problem." Park bison have a well-defined space—Yellowstone—that they're allowed to be in. Elk largely roam where they want. "Whether it be the state of Montana, or APHIS, or anybody else, I think they look at the Yellowstone population of bison and say, 'This is a problem we can deal with,' without ever thinking that you can't just deal with this issue in one population," he said.

Wenk spent forty-three years working for the park service, rising from a fresh-out-of-college job as a landscape architect, to deputy director of the National Park Service and acting CEO of the National Park Foundation, to finally the job he wanted most, superintendent of arguably the world's premier national park. An amiable man with a quick smile that spreads out beneath his neatly trimmed gray mustache, Wenk is a mediator. At Yellowstone he brought a solution in 2013 to an issue that long had dogged park superintendents: how to appease environmentalists and snowmobilers with a winter-use plan for the park. It wasn't a perfect plan. It didn't completely ban snowmobiles from the park as some environmentalists wanted, but contained their numbers and required cleaner technology. Yet the park service also committed to spend more than one hundred thousand dollars a year to keep open Sylvan Pass near Yellowstone's east entrance. That money goes not just to grooming the snow-covered road for snowmobiles and snowcoaches, but also to lob 105 mm artillery shells onto hillsides rife with avalanche chutes that rise above the road. But overall, the final plan, after more than a decade of battles, was one both conservationists and the snowmobile community could live with, and which helped reduce noise and air pollution in the park.

Crafting an accepted plan to move bison out of Yellowstone to tribal governments and other organizations that want herds with the park's gene history would have capped Wenk's career with another once-thought-impossible achievement. But politics interfered as he was unceremoniously led to the door of retirement by then-Interior Secretary Ryan Zinke. Wenk had planned to retire in March 2019, after completing, he hoped, the effort to safely transfer Yellowstone bison that did not carry brucellosis to the Fort Peck Reservation. But that date was moved up to September 29, 2018, after Zinke told Wenk to move to Washington, DC, to oversee the National Capital Region or retire. Wenk saw little sense in taking the new job for a handful of months. Bitter for a while, he at one point said he felt "abused" by the Trump administration. Though he later would say he regretted using that word, Wenk nevertheless felt he was being punished.[216]

Hoping Wenk would succeed with his bison plan was Mike Mease. A stocky, bearded man who looks as comfortable as the park's bison in the cold, snowy winter months, Mease in 1997 cofounded the grassroots Buffalo Field Campaign to fight to see Yellowstone's bison treated as wildlife, not domestic livestock. He brought no small measure of tenacity and his skills as a documentary videographer with him to capture how bison were being maligned. Waging a relentless campaign on a meager budget, the nonprofit group has been creative with its tactics. The winter of 2007–08 was snowy—extremely snowy. By February, the drifts in West Yellowstone were reaching to the eaves, and residents stayed busy shoveling the fluff off their roofs. It was the sort of winter that tells bison they need to head to lower elevations than those inside the park, and as they move out Montana authorities and National Park Service personnel show up to stop them. In 2008, that could involve either corralling the bison to be hauled off to slaughter, or having a line of hunters shoot those that head north and out of the park beyond Mammoth Hot Springs. They try to haze bison back into the park with ATVs, horsemen, and even helicopters. With the heavy snows also luring snowmobilers into the park, Mease and his colleagues at the Buffalo Field Campaign figured a rally at the park entrance in West Yellowstone would garner attention. So on a crisp mid-February day, a week after about 130 park bison had been shipped to slaughter while another 112 were killed at Yellowstone's northern boundary, members of the group gathered among the deep drifts of snow at the park entrance to protest the ongoing hazing and killing of bison by the park service and the Montana Department of Livestock. They rallied and marched and greeted snowmobilers heading into the park with a puppet dressed as the grim reaper pinned with an identifying sign that simply said, "Park Service." The event was both a protest and a learning opportunity for some Yellowstone visitors, who weren't aware of the issue with park bison. Some visitors posed for photos with BFC protesters, while others questioned them about the purpose of the rally.

Two years earlier, in 2006, BFC and Public Employees for Environmental Responsibility, a nonprofit group that advocates for environmental justice for public lands and the agencies that manage them, suggested that the Interior Department remove the bison from its logo. "This year, more than one in five members of the nation's largest remaining 'free-roaming' herd, located in Yellowstone National Park, will be killed—by slaughter, hazing, and maiming—as a result of federal action," PEER officials said.

Until Wenk was led into retirement, Mease thought progress was being made on the quarantine and transfer plan that would eliminate the need to send Yellowstone bison to slaughter. Instead, the Interior secretary seemed intent on lowering the park's bison population below the three thousand targeted by the Interagency Bison Management Plan. "He wants to kill it down to two thousand, and of course we're suing the government right now for an endangered species listing over the three thousand number being way too low," said Mease.

All the years that the Buffalo Field Campaign has been fighting on behalf of bison, elk have been carrying brucellosis further and further into Montana. "And yet, there's no consequence for them," said Mease, who agrees with native peoples that the state's approach toward bison is nothing short of prejudice. "The cattle industry don't want the state of Montana to recognize wild buffalo as a wildlife species because we have some of the greatest wildlife protection laws of all the states," he maintains. "And if we started to allow them to come out [of the park], then they're competition for grass. At least that's how I feel. The cattle barons of the West are still pretty entrenched."[217]

For Montana officials, and those at Yellowstone, the BFC is the figurative wolf leaping at their hamstrings. Organizations such as the National Parks Conservation Association, Defenders of Wildlife, and the National Wildlife Federation are more traditional in how they advocate for the park's bison. Those groups write letters concerning planning documents, show up at meetings to make well-crafted statements, keep their websites and email distribution lists polished and fine-tuned. Mease and his colleagues, meanwhile, churn out a mix of at times graphic videos and photographs of the hazing operations. That imagery is supplemented with press releases critical of both the Montana livestock industry and the federal agencies, including the National Park Service, which developed the hazing plan. "A formidable threat awaits these buffalo. Not the natural predator of bear, wolf, or lion, but the beast of greed that takes human shape: government agents unjustly catering to livestock interests will soon arrive with harmful intentions to force these buffalo—with horse, ATV, truck, helicopter and law enforcement—off of their native habitat in Montana," reads one of the group's releases. On its website, BFC keeps a running tally of park bison killed due to the brucellosis scare. The tally for 2017–18 was 1,030. Since 1985, the group claims, more than 11,000 Yellowstone bison have been killed.

"All we're trying to do is get the same rights for the Yellowstone buffalo as we give to all other wildlife in our state,"

Mease told me. "And that's the bottom line. We're not going to go away until we achieve that. I might go to the grave before it's achieved, but nonetheless I'll at least know that I tried."

There are others trying to save bison from being sent to slaughter. Twice, early in 2018, someone broke into the Stephens Creek facility that Yellowstone uses to hold bison for quarantine or shipment to slaughter and freed dozens of the animals.

It's been nearly 150 years since Yellowstone became the world's first national park, more than a century since the National Park Service was established by Congress and tasked with preserving the park system's natural resources so future generations could enjoy them. Those two events were a testament to the nation's stewardship of precious natural resources. It was only later that we became aware of the intricacies of ecosystems and ecological functions and the precarious balance of nature. Bison, time and again, somehow have managed to regain their equilibrium, to evade extinction. But the world is a much, much more crowded and complicated place today, and Yellowstone bison face many more challenges than Blue Babe ever did.

Train Ride to the Future

In response to your inquiry as to the welfare of the bison, which were donated to the Government by your Society for this Reserve, and which were brought here last November, I would state that the winter was very much in their favor, there has been no loss and they are in the best of health.

—Wind Cave Warden Fred M. Dille to the
American Bison Society, May 30, 1914

Clattering through the plank-lined chute, the fourteen bison were leaving the big city for the high plains. Penned into individual wooden crates that were then loaded into two steel railroad cars, they rolled west late in 1913 on a two-thousand-mile journey that would prove more astonishing than anticipated. Plastered on the sides of the cars so all would know of the precious cargo within were oilcloth signs proclaiming, "Live Buffalo for the Wind Cave National Preserve, South Dakota. Presented to the Government by the American Bison Society and the New York Zoological Society."

The animals—seven bulls, seven cows—were personally selected by Dr. Hornaday, the driver behind the American Bison Society who pushed Congress again and again to create a national bison herd from the New York Zoological Society's forty-two-head herd. They were placed into their crates on November 24, and the next afternoon loaded into waiting railcars. A switching engine then pulled the two cars to Grand Central Station, where they were added to the express train. It could have been called the Thanksgiving Special, as the trip encompassed that holiday.

It was a cold, mostly cloudy evening in New York City the next day when the bison left the New York Zoological Society grounds and began their trek to South Dakota, relying on the New York Central, Chicago, Rock Island, and Pacific Railroads to get them to Hot Springs, South Dakota. The fee, by today's standards, was inexpensive, just $850, and the cargo so highly valued that at one point another train was held "for two hours in order that these bison might make connections without delay," those who attended the American Bison Society's eighth annual meeting, in January 1914, were told.

The bisons' mode of travel was slightly more upscale than years earlier when a collection of bison left the West for the National Zoological Park in Washington, DC. Those animals took a slow freight train. The fourteen bison that headed in reverse, from east to west, in 1913, were in two steel railcars coupled to a fourteen-passenger-car train. Three attendants—H. R. Mitchell, Hornaday's nephew who served as chief clerk of the New York Zoological Park and a representative of the American Bison Society, Fred M. Dille of Wind Cave National Park, and Frank Rush, supervisor of the Wichita National Bison Range— shared space with the animals in the cars. Bunks had been built on one end of the car for the three men's relative comfort, while the bison had little space but to lie down and soundly kick the side of their enclosures when agitated. It was a hard, jarring, and cold trip. Outfitted with an alcohol stove and a supply of canned goods, the attendants were definitely not traveling in first class. Fortunately, Thanksgiving Day found them in Missouri Valley, Iowa, where a layover of several hours allowed for a proper Thanksgiving dinner, complete with cranberry sauce, at a local hotel. The bison had their own feast, of sorts. Timothy hay, oats, and water were stocked aboard the cars to feed the animals, most of which quietly endured the trip. "All ate fairly well of hay and crushed oats after the first night," noted Mitchell, who chronicled the trip for the society. "The greater number of the animals remained quiet and laid down and got up in their crates at their pleasure after they were once loaded in the cars, but several continued to be 'scrappy' all the way, and would kick the crates violently on the slightest provocation."

As it rolled west, the train drew interest from onlookers. At many stops, crowds gathered to learn about the animals and their destination. Some of the curious were even given the chance to peek into the crates near the car doors.

Sixty-three hours after leaving New York City, the bison reached Hot Springs. Their crates were carefully hauled out of the freight cars and placed on a variety of wagons for the final eleven-mile jouncing excursion to the new game preserve, which covered not quite 4,200 acres on the northwestern corner of Wind Cave National Park.[218]

By the 1860s, the rabid approach of buffalo hunters and the military had erased bison from the future park's landscape.[219] The location for their return was selected in July 1911 by J. Alden Loring, a forty-year-old field naturalist[220] who worked with Hornaday at the New York Zoological Society as the curator of mammals. He had traveled to Oklahoma to scout out a location for the Wichita preserve, and Hornaday again sought his help in finding a suitable location in South Dakota that could hold not only bison but also elk, pronghorn antelope, and bighorn sheep. Loring was well prepared for his assignment. Trained as a mammologist and field naturalist, his career was similar to Hornaday's, as they both traveled the world to collect wildlife specimens for display. Before Hornaday hired him at the New York Zoological Park, Loring had held positions with the US Bureau of Biological Survey, the US Department of Agriculture, and the Smithsonian Institution. When Theodore Roosevelt traveled to Africa in 1909 for a yearlong expedition to collect specimens for a natural history museum, Loring accompanied him with orders to collect small mammals for the Smithsonian. Loring also returned with more than a few stories; he later wrote a book called *African Adventure Stories* and traveled the lecture circuit to discuss the continent's wildlife. His work for the American Bison Society didn't receive as much acclaim outside of the society, but it proved vital to the organization's efforts to establish herds of bison in the West. In 1905, Loring delivered a report recommending that a bison herd be established in Oklahoma and carefully detailing the physical landscape. He discussed specifics on the soils, elevations, trees, and water sources, and made mention of past wallows. The naturalist came away convinced that bison herds grazed this land before the Great Slaughter. His report was used to persuade Congress to fund the bison reserve there. Six years later, Loring again was retained by the society, for five hundred dollars, to explore South Dakota for possible locations to establish another bison herd. He started his search in late June that year with a visit to the Sioux Indian Reservation at Rosebud in the southern part of the state. A few days spent talking to the locals convinced Loring that the location was too far from a rail line, too small, and required too great of an investment to purchase land from the tribal and federal governments. From there he traveled to the western side of the state to inspect the Black Hills near Pactola. But Loring quickly scratched the site off his list, as well, noting that it lacked enough acreage with open grazing lands for bison. Plus, horses and cattle had overgrazed the landscape. Heading seventy-five miles south to Wind Cave National Park, he finally found what he wanted: a rolling, mostly open, grassy landscape cut here and there with creek beds and occasional springs as well as "ravines, gullies, and draws that afford protection from storms and are supplied with good grass of one kind or another." Another bonus was ample Jack pine and cedar timber that could be cut for fence posts. But he realized that land with water rights outside the park boundaries would need to be purchased to ensure water for the bison preserve during dry seasons.[221] In fact, Loring was adamant: if the water rights couldn't be obtained, the site wouldn't be suitable. Obtain water from those ranches to supplement the natural flows in Cold Springs and Beaver creeks, he said, and with nearly seventeen thousand acres available for the preserve, a herd of more than eight hundred bison could thrive there.[222]

One-hundred-and-five years after those fourteen bison arrived at Wind Cave, I walked the small, shallow, U-shaped valley in the park where they found their old home in their new home. It was a late May day, the sun was warm, and a gentle breeze kept the insects from settling on me. Rimmed by three vehicle pullouts along highways 395 and 87 that head north to Custer, South Dakota, the scene seemed ubiquitous among the countless other tiny valleys cupped by the Black Hills. Walking down the grassy slope into the vale, I found pieces of the past. The ranch house and barn, acquired with the purchase of eighty acres—along with water rights—from W. A. and Irene Rankin for part of the preserve, served for years as the game warden's home and headquarters.[223] They were now gone, as was the corral that held bison for a while. But here was a row of purple-flowering lilacs, and there was a hedgerow that once rimmed the main building that served as office and home for the preserve's overseer. Over there was the slightly submerged concrete pad that once bridged Beaver Creek. Fragmented strands of barbed wire appeared here and there, as did rusted cans, a Rapid City Bottleworks bottle from another century, and piping that funneled water somewhere once upon a time. Easy to spot as it rose about four feet above the dirt, the only intact manmade fixture of that long-ago operation to return bison to the West, was an American Foundry Co. water hydrant, manufactured in 1881. Its brass top, bright and shiny as if it were new, thanks to many others who had walked this landscape and rubbed their palm around it, captured my eye. The creek, as it did in 1914, still runs through the valley, which must have seemed like an ideal release point because of the ease with which the bison could have been kept within a corral, at least initially.

Farther out from this small valley ran the rolling plains that captured Loring's attention. The land, then adjacent to the national park, that Loring selected had significant cultural ties to Native Americans, primarily the Lakota and Cheyenne peoples. The Lakota hold deep respect for the site of present-day Wind Cave National Park because their origin narrative identifies the cave as the place in the world where they were given life.[224] The landscape also was a traditional Native American hunting ground, so it had nutritional value to them. Loring mentioned none of this in his report to the American Bison Society. To him, all that seemed to matter was that the Black Hills setting, with its accessible water and sweeping prairie, was ideal for bison.

After the American Bison Society accepted his report, on August 10, 1912, Congress passed the requisite legislation to both create the preserve and accept the society's gift of bison. The legislation provided twenty-six thousand dollars to surround the preserve "with a woven wire fence eighty-eight inches high."[225] Fifteen months later, on November 28, 1913, shortly after nine thirty in the morning, the train carrying the New York bison rolled into Hot Springs. Mitchell was beaming. "The day was bright and beautiful, and as we came in sight of the long string of slowly moving teams against the background of the clear-cut timbered outline of the distant Black Hills, we could not help but feel that this small group of captive animals were coming in to their own," he noted.[226]

It took all of the daylight to reach the compound, but a great bonfire was lit to welcome the bison and warm their handlers, who also had the aid of flickering lanterns to find their way. When it came to actually releasing the bison into the landscape, some of the animals moved almost nonchalantly.

"The first animal took its release very calmly and only when noisily urged disappeared into the surrounding darkness," reported Mitchell. "The unloading by the uncertain light of our lanterns and bonfire proved to be a more or less difficult task. Greatly to the surprise and disappointment of some of our spectators, we had a good deal of trouble in getting some of the bison out of their crates. In several cases the operation was more like removing the crate from the animal than the animal from the crate."

The release of the bison at Wind Cave made roughly 350 head, in six herds, that the federal government could claim that year. In June 1916 six more bison, two bulls and four cows, from Yellowstone joined the Wind Cave herd. Amazingly, from a genetics standpoint, these were the only bison imported to Wind Cave, yet down through the decades they have served as the progenitors of thousands of offspring that have remained free of inbreeding problems. Thanks were due to Hornaday for the careful choices he made in selecting the animals from his New York Zoological herd, which had received animals from a number of private herds. The genesis of the zoo's herd could be traced to 1888 and a pair of bison that had been captured near Oglala, Nebraska. Four more came from a Rapid City, South Dakota, ranch, noted D. F. Houston, the US Agriculture secretary, in a letter of thanks to the American Bison Society.

It happens that after the lapse of a quarter of a century the Government has re-established on National reservations a herd of buffalo in each of the States from which the original herd was secured. Since 1888 great changes have occurred, both in the condition of the buffalo and in public sentiment regarding their preservation. The future of the species now seems assured, and the reports of the past few years show a gratifying increase in the various public and private herds.[227]

At the New York Zoological Park, the bison had about twenty acres of open meadow, surrounded by trees, to roam. A "Bison House"—a barn running eighty feet along a hillside—served as shelter for the animals when needed. To provide visitors with a good view of the bison, the barn had a flat roof they could walk out onto.[228] Joining bison at the new preserve were elk from Yellowstone, and pronghorn antelope from Alberta were shipped there, too, to kindle populations of native wildlife that once called the Black Hills home.[229] Initially under the purview of the US Department of Agriculture, the preserve was transferred to the National Park Service in July 1935. It was then decided to let bison range over the entire park landscape, and Civilian Conservation Corps crews went to work fencing the park.[230] It was an auspicious start to what would prove to be a keystone for rebuilding the West's bison herds.

Prior to the establishment of the Wichita Mountains Wildlife Refuge and Wind Cave herds, just about all of the country's last remaining bison—some two thousand individuals—were held by a small number of ranchers and conservationists scattered across the country. There was Austin Corbin II's herd of about 160 in New Hampshire; Charles Goodnight's herd of almost 50 in Texas; the Charles Pablo-Michel Allard herd in Montana; James Philip's herd of nearly 75 in South Dakota; and Gordon W. Lillie, aka Pawnee Bill, with 55.[231] William C. Whitney, a politically well-connected financier who served a stint as the US Secretary of the Navy under President Cleveland, had personal game preserves in both Massachusetts and upstate New York on which he ran some bison. He made a gift of his thirty-two bison to the New York Zoological Society, and that constituted the bulk of the founding stock of the zoo's bison.[232] It was a herd with a rich, diverse genetic pool.

After walking the grounds of the Wind Cave National Game Preserve of 1914, I headed back to park headquarters to catch up with Greg Schroeder, Wind Cave's resource management chief, to talk bison. Having grown up in South Dakota, where time out of school usually meant time outdoors, Schroeder got his college degree in wildlife biology. With that, he found his way to Badlands National Park in the southwestern corner of the state, and then to Wind Cave. Large and muscular, no doubt from having to work regularly with elk and bison and mule deer, Schroeder is well-versed in bison and the genetic debates that can arise with them. As we sat in an office in the basement of the park's visitor center, he attributed the character of Wind Cave's bison herd to the uniqueness of its founding stock. Today it would be impossible to find bison as unrelated to one another as those that existed more than a century ago, he maintained. Hornaday was able to tap into a wide range of bloodlines, thanks to the donations to his herd at the New York Zoological Park. Four different bloodlines were said to have been represented in the fifteen bison that the zoo sent to the Wichita preserve. "When they were trying to gather up the last of the bison, basically out there on the prairie for this conservation herd, you couldn't replicate that today," Schroeder said. "There's no way you could replicate that today, how unique each of those individual animals were."

Interestingly, perhaps only from a wildlife biologist's perspective, both the Wichita and Wind Cave herds were started with bison from the New York zoo, yet those two herds aren't as genetically related as you'd think. The Wind Cave herd is more closely related to Yellowstone's bison. As just six bison from Yellowstone, and only two bulls, were added to the Wind Cave herd, that raises the question of whether those bulls proved to be more dominant than those sent from New York, or whether the cows were more fertile and for a longer period.

Wind Cave these days is a park known to the traveling public primarily for its "hidden world beneath the prairie."[233] But those in the bison business know it for its pure genetic strain of *Bison bison*. Since 1987, the park has sent bison to thirty Native

American tribes, including the Yakama Indian Reservation in Washington State, the Iowa Tribe in Oklahoma, and the Round Valley Indian Reservation in California. Wind Cave bison also have been shipped to Antelope Island State Park in Utah's Great Salt Lake, Tallgrass Prairie National Preserve in Kansas—where the Nature Conservancy works with the National Park Service to manage the herd—and to TNC's Rancho El Uno in Mexico, an ecological preserve.

Wind Cave and Yellowstone reportedly have the purest strains of bison genes, though 2008 genetic research that hasn't been formally published claimed to have found cattle introgression in the Wind Cave herds. Still, because of Yellowstone's issue with brucellosis, Wind Cave bison are sought out for starting or contributing to conservation herds. But are cattle genes muddying the purity of bison? Some question that possibility, and say that as analytic technologies become more refined, cattle genes likely could be found in all bison today. Does it matter if an animal contains 100 percent, or 98 percent, bison genes? To be on the safe side, to not risk problems down the road with cattle genes adversely impacting the known purebred bison, which number fewer than 7,500, purebreds could be carefully monitored and managed to increase their numbers—which is what Interior Department personnel have been working on and hope to have a roadmap for implementing in 2019.

So far, Schroeder explained to me, cattle genes that have turned up in bison DNA elsewhere in the country reflect "neutral markers, they don't 'code' for anything." Put another way, they don't seem to be kicking out traits that are affecting bison. But even if they were slightly affecting bison, if the herd was not targeted for conservation of the species' pure genetics, the animals with cattle introgression still can play a valuable role. "It's out there as a mover and a shaker on the landscape," the biologist explained, painting a prairie portrait of bison wallowing about. "It creates habitat for other animals and it does things that are far more important than whether there's a one-tenth of a percent of cattle genes in it."

Not all conservation herds are free of cattle genes. At least seven of the more than sixty herds of plains bison turned up cattle genes in past testing, and researchers thought it likely cattle genes would turn up in another seventeen herds, while it was unlikely in another eighteen herds.[234] But cattle genes can be removed over time by culling the animals that carry them.

Parks and Bison

There are many opportunities to chart a course for a robust bison conservation strategy over the next century. It will need to be based on developing innovative partnerships with land-owners, tribes, states, conservation groups, commercial bison producers and others.

—DOI Bison Report, "Looking Forward"

Spring green-up on the prairie is a fat, sassy time for bison. Winter's heavy snows and biting cold are forgotten as vegetation sprouts anew under a warm sun. The cows have calved, and the bison move across the landscape in a mob, stopping to browse the tender greenery. Though focused on replenishing weight lost during the winter months, the animals are still leery of intruders, though also inquisitive. At one point during my late May visit to Wind Cave, I found myself surrounded by bison on the move. Though the national park covers only about 35,000 acres, combine that with Custer State Park's 71,000 acres on the northern boundary, and you have fairly nice-sized bison range. The prairie was lush during my visit, thanks not only to the normal spring revival but also to the Rankin Wildfire that burned 2,100 acres in the park the previous fall. The flames had cleansed the prairie of older and dead vegetation, converting it into nutrients the soil stored through the winter until the new growth materialized. I gazed out across a veritable smorgasbord for the bulls and cows and their frisky "red dogs," calves just weeks old. The herd's contented baritone grunts filled the air, overridden at times by the crisp, perky song of western meadowlarks that also seemed glad to see spring. Pulling my car to the side of the park road, I jumped out and quickly mounted my video camera on a tripod. Slowly panning across the herd, I zoomed in on bounding calves and the nonchalant cows. Suddenly my viewfinder filled with one spike bison (a two- or three-year-old) that was eyeing me suspiciously, unsure whether I was simply an oddity or a more concerning predator. We gazed at each other intently, as if in a staring contest. Her head was low to the ground, as if she was mulling a charge. I checked several times to make sure my car door was between us. Her winter coat was frayed and tattered, most of it already deposited somewhere on the prairie and destined for a nest, while her lighter summer attire was coming in nicely. And then, no doubt bored and unconcerned with me, she moved on.

There are a handful of locations where you can watch bison in the wild. National parks, Native American reservations, and a few state parks and scatterings of public lands are the last best stands for wild bison. Surprisingly, and sadly, while it's been estimated that roughly half "of the Northern Great Plains ecoregion remains in largely native prairie," just 1.5 percent of that landscape is protected within national parks and "similar protected areas."[235]

Yellowstone claims North America's largest free-roaming herds of plains bison, and tourists flock to the park so they can tell friends and family they saw the big, shaggy animals in the wild. In early summer and again in fall, if you motor through the Hayden or Lamar valleys you'll find them there, as well, specks on the hillside from a distance or dotting the meadow in the foreground. Though many bison head to the park's high country for the summer months, in winter they descend to the river valleys, where they use their massive heads as snowplows to uncover the remains of summer's grasses. Visit Wind Cave, and if you drive north or south on Highway 87 or along NPS 5 through the park's interior, you'll often see bison lolling about the prairie. They project a dilatory nature on Antelope Flats above and just east of the Snake River that meanders through Grand Teton National Park in Wyoming, and add perspective to the tiny parcel of the once Great Plains that is harbored at Tallgrass Prairie National Preserve.

What would these places be without bison? Though they might appear doltish from a distance, they're anything but. Yes, they move slowly across the prairie, some grunting as they go as if it were a great inconvenience. Some drop to the ground to roll about, squirming in an effort to shed biting insects or winter coats. Whirling around in their wallows, they suddenly come to a stop and sit upright and still, as if checking to see if anyone was watching their contortions. They stare with their languid eyes, yet they could leap up in a sprint, run you down, and toss you skyward with their pointed horns or grind you into the ground beneath their hooves. And then they would immediately return to grazing. Today there are ongoing discussions about where else in the West bison might be returned to establish herds. Never again will the Great Plains support tens of millions of bison as the region did in the early nineteenth century. But there can be pocket herds of these incredible animals to protect their gene lines, restore ecological conditions to their natural state, support native peoples' cultural and dietary needs, and delight visitors who want to view the United States' national mammal in person. Whether you find yourself surrounded by bison at Wind Cave, or contemplating hundreds of the majestic animals in the sweep of prairie at Theodore Roosevelt, it can be hard to appreciate the plight of the species unless you realize that the hundreds of thousands of bison counted today are descendants of a core founder population of one hundred or fewer wild bison. That those hundred survived the Great Slaughter is a testament to the determination of a few who gathered private herds to preserve the species.[236]

The genealogical lines of the past 150 years are fairly well defined, starting with the McKay-Alloway herd from southern Saskatchewan in 1873 and ending with Hornaday's herd at the New York Zoological Park. Interspersed between those were a number of other herds, such as the Goodnight and Jones herds, the Corbin herd in New Hampshire, the Philip herd in South Dakota, and the Conrad herd in Montana. Today's conservation herds, and, by some views, all bison alive, can be traced to just six herds.[237]

Had the low number of bison around at the turn of the twentieth century remained low for thirty or forty years, then inbreeding likely would have been detrimental, Dr. Derr, back at Texas A&M, told me. But it didn't. Goodnight, Jones, Pablo-Allard, and Dupree, along with Hornaday to an extent, all succeeded in blending those remaining bison genes.

Thanks to the six foundational herds, bison avoided the pitfalls of inbreeding at the end of the nineteenth century when there were only several hundred bison still standing in the wild. Their squeeze into, and healthy exit out of, the bottleneck was an anomaly, as inbreeding frequently occurs when populations dwindle. That can be seen in the flaws found today in highly endangered Florida panthers, in the Channel Island fox on a small cluster of islands off the California coastline, and as a threat to recovery of both the red wolf and the Mexican wolf. One theory that explains how bison avoided the perils of inbreeding is that their longevity on the continent endured other genetic bottlenecks that, in effect, weeded out all the deleterious alleles from their genome—those that cause defects in an organism. Another is that the dispersed groups of bison that did survive the Great Slaughter, those in private herds around the country as well as the Yellowstone bison, carried great genetic variation. So when they did intermingle through the bison exchanges by Goodnight, Jones, Hornaday, and others, the outcome was a robust, much hardier purebred species than might have been expected.[238]

"They did have to inbreed their way out of that [bottleneck]," Dr. Derr told me. "They did. But inbreeding doesn't cause the loss of genetic diversity. Inbreeding causes an increase in homozygosity [identical pairs of genes]. But one generation of outbreeding wipes that away. So inbreeding is not—this is maybe a population genetics lecture—but inbreeding over a long period of time can cause significant problems in population. Inbreeding over a short period of time can be corrected by outbreeding."

In other words, flood those 1900-era animals with diverse genetic material by tapping the varied genetic strains held in the private herds. That's what happened, and the result is evident today. Whether you love bison, hate them, or couldn't care less about their fate, they have demonstrated themselves to be an incredibly resilient species.

"You think about all of the things that happened to North American bison in the last ten thousand or twenty thousand years. They really should have become extinct," Dr. Derr mused. "And there's not very many species out there that have endured the amount of insult that North American bison have. And now they are thriving. They should have probably become extinct in the last one or two major glaciation periods when all the other 'mega mammals' died. But they didn't, they survived."

Today the genetics of those foundation herds can be found clustered in groups. Strains of the Goodnight and Pablo-Allard herds graze the grass at the National Bison Range in Montana, while the Wichita Mountains National Wildlife Refuge and Wind Cave herds can be traced back to the efforts of Hornaday and the American Bison Society. Badlands and Theodore Roosevelt national parks' herds also are related, with genes from Fort Niobrara National Wildlife Refuge found in their bison. Yellowstone's bison are often described as directly descended from those that grazed there during Pleistocene days, but don't forget that they received a genetic jumpstart from the Goodnight and Pablo-Allard herds in 1902.

The future of bison as a viable species with pure genetic lines is held, largely, in the nineteen herds on Interior Department lands through the National Park Service, US Bureau of Land Management, and US Fish and Wildlife Service, but also in the herds growing under the guidance of Native American governments. In the National Park System, you can find herds roaming Badlands, Grand Teton, Theodore Roosevelt (both North and South units), Wind Cave, and Yellowstone national parks, plus those white-faced animals on the North Rim of Grand Canyon National Park. Tallgrass Prairie has bison, and in Alaska, at Wrangell-St. Elias National Park and Preserve, there is a relatively small, two-hundred-head herd of plains bison that were transplanted there in 1928 from the National Bison Range in Montana. They also can be found at Fort Niobrara National Wildlife Refuge in Nebraska, Sully's Hill (once a national park but now part of Fort Niobrara NWR), the National Bison Range in Montana, the Neal Smith National Wildlife Refuge in Iowa, the Rocky Mountain Arsenal in Colorado, and Wichita Mountains National Wildlife Refuge in Oklahoma. Such dispersed herds were envisioned by Hornaday more than a century ago. He realized that large megafauna such as bison can't be successfully bred "and perpetuated for centuries" if they're confined in zoos. "It seemed reasonably certain that the only way to insure the perpetuation of the Bison species for centuries to come lies in the creation of several national herds, maintained by the Government on large areas of grazing grounds,"[239] he wrote.

Extensions of these federal conservation herds can be found on the Blackfeet Nation lands near Glacier, the Fort Peck and Fort Belknap reservations in central Montana, and the Wind River Reservation in Wyoming.

* * *

One morning I awoke to some of Theodore Roosevelt National Park's bison in the Cottonwood Campground, not realizing at the time that their blood might contain genes from the long ago Yellowstone herds. The half-dozen or so animals were milling about, enjoying breakfast on the campground's patchy lawn and using its cottonwood trees as scratching posts. I learned later that this herd's lineage goes to 1956, when the park received twenty-nine bison from Fort Niobrara National Wildlife Refuge, which in turn had received some of its founder stock in 1913 from Yellowstone.[240] Though Yellowstone has not been as productive as Wind Cave in dispersing its bison, through the decades it has sent bison to quite a few areas:

- 1906: A number of bison were shipped to Arizona where Buffalo Jones crossed them with cattle.
- 1914: Six bison went to Wind Cave National Park, and six years later three Yellowstone bison were shipped to Chickasaw National Recreation Area in Oklahoma.
- 1941 and 1942: A total of twenty-three bison from the park went to start the Henry Mountains herd in southern Utah (which, sixty-seven years later, sent some Yellowstone bison genes to Book Cliffs to start a herd there).
- 1948: Twenty Yellowstone bison went to Grand Teton National Park as the genesis of that herd.
- 1953: Two Yellowstone bison were added to the National Bison Range in Montana.
- 1963: Three bison were shipped to Badlands National Park in South Dakota.
- 2000: Descendants of the 1906 experiment by Buffalo Jones to cross bison with cattle in Arizona wound up on the North Rim of Grand Canyon National Park when they broke through a fence.

Tracing the travels of genes from Wind Cave's bison herd down through the decades requires a much, much larger map of the country. Just as the Lakota Sioux people trace their ascendancy to that small crevice at Wind Cave, the park today can be viewed as a wellspring of bison genes. Since 1987, Wind Cave biologists have shipped bison to more than a dozen states from Tennessee to California, plus Mexico. All told, about two thousand of the park's bison have been distributed to thirty Native American tribes, four state parks, six conservation groups, and another national park.

It's not easy mapping the genetic blueprint of bison in Interior Department herds. Through the years, geneticists and zoologists have produced study after study after study peering into the herds' genetic vigor, searching both for genetic diversity as well as contamination from cattle genes. Yet another study was underway in 2018 in a bid to determine the extent of cattle introgression in the federal herds and to create a portrait of genetic lineages that could be used to ensure that new conservation herds are genetically robust.[241] While past studies have detected an extremely small percentage of cattle genes in some herds, as low as 1 percent, is that enough to pose a threat to the long-term health of the species? Bison naturally wind down their metabolisms in winter, a coping mechanism that enables them to endure the frigid, snowy winters on the Great Plains. Cattle genes might impede that. They also might impact bison growth, stamina, and even grazing behavior.[242]

Ranchers in the commercial sector who aggressively manage their bison with veterinary care, unnatural male-female ratios, and artificial selection to bring out certain characteristics could inadvertently be damaging the species by altering the herd's ancestral engineering in unpredictable ways.[243] Of the federal herds at the lead of bison conservation efforts, there are concerns that all but one—the Yellowstone herd—are too small to ensure genetic longevity of the species. The dangers of having too few bison in a single herd played out in the Texas State herd, which was formed in 1997 from three dozen bison descended from the herd Goodnight started in the 1880s. Not only did the herd given to the state have some individuals with cattle genes, but it had low reproductivity and low genetic diversity.[244]

To ensure the health of the federal conservation herds, wild-life biologists have been sampling each herd's genetics to check for diversity, look for any cattle introgression once again, and come up with a roadmap for use in distributing bison to other parcels of the public lands empire. When it comes to establishing herds, they'd want to avoid sending animals with similar genetic backgrounds to the new herds—no mixing of animals from Wind Cave and Wichita Wildlife Refuge, or Theodore Roosevelt and Badlands. They'd also want to ensure none of the bison carry brucellosis or other diseases. Key to expanding the federal bison herds is drawing genetic portraits of each. Geneticists say at least one thousand individuals in a herd are necessary to ensure genetic stability. Eight of the federal conservation herds had at least three hundred animals but only Yellowstone had more than one thousand. The short-term goal is to see that each of the herds contain at least one thousand individuals by 2020, either in one herd or with related satellite herds, to ensure that diversity. That goal likely won't be achieved. Aside from Yellowstone, only Wind Cave, which counted about 350 adults in the park proper in the spring of 2018, has effectively far surpassed the thousand-head count when its satellite herds are included in the count.

Rebounding across the West

Through the efforts of tribes, ranchers, conservationists and others, the species has survived and can once again be lifted as a literal and cultural example of productivity from which each of us can learn.

—Republican congresswoman Kristi Noem, South Dakota, in a press release April 27, 2016

If you were a bison wrangler charged with growing your herd, where would you look to put them? You'd need a pretty big expanse of land, that's for sure. Pull out Hornaday's 1889 map that charted the decline of bison and you might gain an idea of where bison might fit. Take a look at Wind Cave's chart of where they've shipped bison. Realize that back in 1828, bison could be found in Texas and even farther south in Mexico. There are millions of acres today that could sustain bison if the political and agricultural hurdles could be cleared. Big Bend National Park lies along the US-Mexico border with more than 800,000 federal acres. Valles Caldera National Preserve in New Mexico is considerably smaller, at just 89,216 acres, but that's more than twice the size of Wind Cave National Park. There are other federal landscapes and state parks that might be interested in bison, too. Don't forget the Native American reservations, where staff and officials are working to expand their herds. At Fort Belknap

Reservation just north of American Prairie, the Gros Ventre and Assiniboine tribes recently bought an 11,000-acre ranch that they intend to expand their conservation herd onto.

It will be a challenge, for the Great Plains today is a figurative creation when compared to that of a century or more ago. If we viewed it as we do animal or plant species, the region would very likely deserve endangered status under the Endangered Species Act. The Great Plains that once rolled from the boreal forestlands of Manitoba and Saskatchewan in Canada all the way south to Texas and east from the Rocky Mountains to Iowa and Missouri has been fragmented, disrespected, and in many areas literally destroyed. Areas of the Plains have been plowed under for agricultural purposes, streams have been diverted and drained, ecological processes interrupted by human settlement and the accompanying needs. The lack of wildfire has allowed shrubbier, woody vegetation to encroach where prairie grasses once flowed.[245] That growth in turn affected species composition, creating habitat that, while unsuitable for such birds as killdeer and lark sparrows associated with more frequently grazed and burned plains, lured in western meadowlarks and Henslow's sparrows.[246]

Can bison ever return here in ecologically measurable and significant numbers? Measured against the sheer number of animals in the commercial bison herds, purebred conservation herds are a tiny, fragile fragment of the overall bison population. That could change in the near term, in part because of former Interior secretaries, and in part because of the Native American bison herds. President George W. Bush's interior secretary, Dirk Kempthorne, in 2008 laid out the federal government's role and responsibility when it came to restoring bison to the landscape. His 2008 Bison Conservation Initiative "set the goal of restoring herds to their ecological and cultural role on appropriate landscapes within the species' historical range." Every secretary since then—Ken Salazar, Sally Jewell, and Ryan Zinke—shared that vision, though some more actively than others. In 2011, when then-park-service-director Jon Jarvis issued his "Call to Action" document that was to serve as a blueprint for leading the agency into its second century, one plank called for sustaining at least three bison herds in the central and western parts of the country.[247] That should be made possible, where necessary, through the assistance of tribal governments, private landowners, and other public land management agencies.

Secretary Salazar nudged the initiative further in May 2012 when he issued a directive calling for short- and long-term proposals to transfer bison from Yellowstone to other federal or tribal lands. That directive was followed two years later by an Interior Department report that further crystallized the vision. It included an inventory of where bison are found on the public domain, and lands where herds could be established.[248] Today there are many landscapes, privately owned as well as in the public domain, with bison—from Ted Turner's ranches that combined graze fifty-one thousand bison, to TNC operations at thirteen locations that together manage about six thousand bison.

The Wildlife Conservation Society, which descended from the American Bison Society, helps the Interior Department and park service spread bison into some of the species' historic landscapes. The organization has worked with the Blackfeet Nation to build its herd, and has consulted with Interior personnel on growing the federal conservation herds. Part of WCS's work with the Blackfeet Nation was helping to arrange shipment of bison from Elk Island National Park to the tribe's reservation. In 2016 the first shipment, of eighty-seven bison, reached the reservation. Their arrival, ironically, was a symbolic reunion with the past, as the animals were released on lands their ancestors grazed a little more than a century ago as part of the Pablo-Allard herd and, of course, for centuries before that herd's appearance. On the reservation, the bison represent cultural values to the Blackfeet, and provide meat, of course, and a measure of revenue through the sale of hunting permits.

Though the Blackfeet Nation in 2018 was in the process of expanding its herd, it also was working to preserve pure genetic lines of bison through a satellite herd at the Oakland Zoo in California. In the spring of 2018, the zoo received fourteen cow bison from the Blackfeet Nation. Released onto part of the zoo's fifty-six-acre California Trail Expansion project, the bison were expected to play a further role in growth of the Blackfeet herd. While the cow bison were descendants of the Pablo-Allard herd, the zoo planned to acquire two bulls from Yellowstone. If the bulls will share their genes, the offspring will head back to the Blackfeet reservation in Montana to further enhance the "Innii Initiative" there. At the Oakland Zoo, the bison have a dozen acres of grasslands that mimic the setting of more than a century ago when the animals roamed California.

Halfway across the country to the east and not far from Chicago, the US Forest Service is working with the National Forest Foundation and the Nature Conservancy, among others, to reestablish a tract of tallgrass prairie, complete with a small bison herd, at a place called Midewin, a once-upon-a-time part of the US Army arsenal in Joliet. Those behind the experiment realize the challenge they're up against, recognizing that the landscape the forest service acquired in 1996 once was defiled by rusting weapons factories and abandoned bunkers.[249] The National Forest Foundation and its partners at Midewin understand how bison can act as cultivators, their hooves digging into the soil to give seeds of native plants space to gain purchase, and play a role in improving habitat for other native wildlife species. Overall, the animals were seen as a key to restoring the natural ecological system of the tallgrass prairie. By the end of the ten-year development period, in 2021, the goal is to have one thousand bison with access to more than six thousand acres laced with clear-running streams and sprouting six hundred species of native prairie plants.

And bison can help accomplish that goal, given their naturally better grazing habits. Bison and cattle are both bovines, but they have different impacts on the lands they graze. Bison have different tastes for vegetation that favors vegetative biodiversity, and they move more often and so have a lighter effect on the land. But convincing today's traditional livestock operators, the cattlemen and sheep ranchers, of the benefits of bison over traditional livestock can be tough as well as costly if you're talking about converting a one-thousand-head cattle operation into one with one thousand bison. Still, on-the-ground examples demonstrate how bison can be integral parts of the landscape. The state of Utah manages three wild herds of bison: one in the Henry Mountains in the southern part of the state, another in the Book Cliffs on the eastern side, and a third in Antelope Island State Park in the Great Salt Lake not far from Salt Lake City. The first herd got its start in 1941 at the request of the Utah State Department of Fish and Game and the Carbon-Emery Wildlife Federation. Wranglers moved eighteen Yellowstone bison to the Colorado Plateau of southern Utah. Though the initial release point was near the famed Robbers Roost area, a notorious hideout for Butch Cassidy and his Wild Bunch, not all of the bison lingered there. Some headed north, some headed west. In 1942, a group crossed the Dirty Devil River and headed west out onto the Burr Desert, a landscape of sand washes, scrubs, and slot canyons. The bison wintered in the desert before heading into the Henrys for the summer. Since 1963, the animals have made the Henrys their year-round range. Until the bison arrived, the mountains' main distinction was that they were the last major range to be added to maps of the forty-eight coterminous states. With oversight given to the US Bureau of Land Management and the Utah Division of Wildlife Resources, the herd has grown to more than three hundred animals that have 300,205 acres to roam. The BLM manages the habitat that bison and cattle share, while Utah works as intermediary between ranchers with grazing permits in the Henrys and sportsmen. The unique arrangement shows how bison can thrive in the wild, coexist with cattle without transferring disease, and generate revenue through an annual public hunt. Through the hunts, which see permits issued for fifty or so animals, depending on the overall herd population, and the dual management between the state and the BLM, the public and area ranchers have long supported the herd.[250]

Bison might be most visualized as a Plains animal, but in the Henrys they have demonstrated their adaptability. They've frequented grasslands at an elevation of roughly five thousand feet, used piñon-juniper woodlands, and even climbed to more than eleven thousand feet to browse the sub-alpine meadows on Mount Ellen and nearby Mount Pennell.[251] The nearly eighty-year bison relocation program in the mountain range has been a remarkable success in showing that bison and cattle can share habitat, but more importantly demonstrates how additional conservation herds could be established. Especially noteworthy is that the bison don't seem to carry any cattle genes and are free of brucellosis. As such, they represent a valuable genetic pool of Yellowstone bison, with some genes linked back to bison brought to the national park from the National Bison Refuge in Montana before the Henry Mountains herd was started.[252]

In 2009, Utah's third bison herd was established, in the rugged Book Cliffs in the eastern part of the state. Here, along what's described as the world's longest continuous escarpment, the herd was started with thirty bison from the Henrys and another fourteen from the Ute Tribe, which is a member of the InterTribal Bison Cooperative. The Ute government in 1986 had returned bison to part of its reservation in Utah, and some of the six hundred animals migrated to the Book Cliffs. In 2009, the decision was made to actively relocate some tribal bison to the 1.2-million-acre region, and fourteen bison were moved there. A year later, forty more bison from the Henrys joined the herd, which numbers about 450 head. The bison not only serve a cultural role for the Ute Indian Tribe on the Uintah and Ouray Reservation, but represent a revenue stream. Excess bison are butchered and their meat sold, as are bison robes and even mounted skulls. In the Book Cliffs, the two herds are allowed to commingle.[253] As with the Henry Mountains herd, these bison, as of 2018, were believed to be free of cattle genes and disease.

To solidify the return of bison to the Book Cliffs, the state has been opening holes in some of the piñon-juniper habitat to create clearings for grasses for the bison and other wildlife and even livestock. Invasive cheatgrass was removed, and in its place native species such as Indian ricegrass, crested wheatgrass, and sand dropseed were seeded. So, too, was Wyoming big sagebrush, another native. Almost seven million dollars were spent between 2007 and 2015 on improvements to water sources and winter and summer ranges.[254] Though Utah might not immediately be viewed as traditional bison habitat, the state sees value in the ecological role bison fill, as well as their recreational importance as a big game species for hunters.[255] That they coexist with cattle in the Henrys should send a message to states such as Montana that fear transmission of brucellosis from bison. The Henrys bison herd runs side by side with cattle, to a degree. Cattle stay close to water sources, while bison head off across the land, grazing steeper terrain and eating vegetation cattle typically won't touch. And bison, as they sculpt their wallows, rub itches against trees and boulders, leverage their hooves, and munch on vegetation, turn over the soils as a farmer with a tractor might.

Just as vital as maintaining genetic diversity in bison is preserving the cultural significance of the animals. They are not simply meat on the hoof, but cultural figures that carry lessons of social structure.[256] In northern Montana, up against the eastern boundary of Glacier, the Blackfeet Nation is growing its herd near Chief Mountain, a prominent, tribally significant peak that straddles the Glacier-Blackfeet Nation border. Some bison theoretically could mosey into the national park, which is welcomed by the park staff. Restoring bison to the park would underscore the park service's conservation mission, support the Blackfeet Nation's cultural goals, and reflect the traditional presence of bison in the Crown of the Continent region.

Elsewhere on the federal landscape, one potential location for a bison herd is Great Sand Dunes National Park and Preserve in Colorado. The park service in 2018 was crafting an environmental impact statement to explore the feasibility, and desirability, of placing bison in the park. Some bison already are at home on part of Great Sand Dunes. The Nature Conservancy owns the Medano-Zapata Ranch that adjoins the park, and some of its bison head into the park. Through the environmental impact statement, the park is considering the purchase of the ranch from TNC. However, TNC bison carry cattle genes, and so any plan likely would involve culling out those animals and working to build and maintain a purebred herd. Badlands National Park, not far to the east of Wind Cave in South Dakota, in 2018 was considering opening more of the park to bison. At Valles Caldera National Preserve in New Mexico, a National Park System unit that doesn't have bison, managers were interested in establishing a herd that would be at home in the sprawling grasslands there. Then there's the American Prairie Reserve, an ambitious project in central Montana managed by a nonprofit that envisions a 3.5-million-acre wildlife preserve created through a checkerboard mix of private, federal, and state lands. If American Prairie can pull together those 3.5 million acres, it's anticipated that it will be able to accommodate ten thousand bison.

Key to all these conservation herds is letting bison be bison, not treating them like cattle. Fence bison in, feed them hay or grain, vaccinate them, cut off their horns, selectively breed them, and they begin to act like cattle, not bison. Choose one trait through breeding for commercial purposes and you could twist or lose another trait that evolved with the species for a reason.[257] There is land available for bison, land that would benefit from their presence. What must be kept in mind, however, is that managing them as if they were livestock, not wild animals, does not improve on natural genetic selection.

Conserving Bison Genes
on a Large-Scale Landscape

[T]here's still a lot of uncertainty and a little confusion about whether or not in the twenty-first century bison conservation at large scale, with large numbers and with large assemblages, is a high priority.

— Dr. Glenn Plumb, former National Park Service
chief wildlife biologist

Western romanticists dream of settings replete with bison herds drifting across the plains. But turning those dreams into reality won't be an easy task. It certainly isn't possible to fully recreate the visage of the high plains of the mid-nineteenth century. That said, the passion of conservationists who dream of such sights is vital to seeing bison regain a larger foothold than they claimed entering the twenty-first century, for conservation in general needs passionate advocates if goals are to be achieved. There also needs to be support from the federal land-management agencies, Native American communities, and others if a greater number of wild herds is to become a reality.

From the park service's viewpoint, the growth of bison herds is key to conserving the species and strengthening its genetic pool. If and when a decision is made to put bison at Great Sand Dunes National Park, Interior Department personnel would want to look at each of the conservation herds in their portfolio to make the best genetic choices in establishing a new herd. As work goes into expanding conservation herds, there also could be room for additional commercial herds, which could be just as good for the landscape in terms of improving the ecology. Plus, for ranchers, bison carry an economic advantage over cattle at market, and offer a healthier choice for consumers shopping for steaks and roasts because the meat is leaner, lower in calories, and higher in protein. A 2017 comparison of the costs and profits of running bison on the range versus cattle by St. John's University showed that a bison-calf operation would generate a profit of $265.86 per bison-calf, while a beef cow-calf operation would net just $20.83. The bulk of the difference stems from lower medical and feed costs for bison, the study showed. A possible impediment for ranchers hoping to make the switch is the cost of bison heifers, which are about three times the cost of cattle.[258] If you're running a herd of hundreds or even thousands of cattle, that's a significant reinvestment cost.

There are a growing number of commercial bison operations. South Dakota claims the most in the country, with nearly thirty-four thousand bison raised for commercial production.[259] For many ranchers, a largely hands-off approach to day-to-day management is best. Some, though, might still want to selectively breed for specific traits; for instance, there has been a "more rump, less hump" movement to breed out the hefty hump above a bison's shoulders in favor of more meat in the rear end. But as a rule, most bison operations don't selectively manage their herds as much as their cattle counterparts.[260] "The bison producer out there today could be raising cattle if he wanted to," veterinarian Derr believes. "Because they have the land, they have the facilities to raise bison, and they could be raising cattle if they wanted to, but they don't. They want to raise bison."[261]

Market incentives ensure the future of commercial bison operations. The same can't be said for conservation herds. Their future lies in the cooperation of federal, state, and tribal governments, and non-governmental organizations such as the Nature Conservancy, Defenders of Wildlife, and the Wildlife Conservation Society.[262] All these players are key to restoring bison on a large scale, to view them as more than just an ecological relic, and to move beyond a limited number of museum-quality open-air conservation herds. Perplexing as it might seem, the combined population of bison in commercial herds has grown into the hundreds of thousands while that of conservation herds hasn't grown significantly above the number counted in the 1930s.[263]

That disparity not only threatens the genetic integrity of the species, but also the ecological integrity of the Great Plains. Bison are the key missing element of the Plains ecosystem. Their removal has adversely affected black-tailed prairie dog towns, and been followed by the loss of grizzly bears and wolves, two other apex fauna that positively affected the landscape. To those species you can add black-footed ferrets, an endangered species, swift fox, and burrowing owls.

Once upon a time there were tens of millions of bison on the North American landscape, roaming from coast to coast and from the Northwest Territories all the way south to the Gulf of Mexico. They were a foundational species, one that had a significant, and beneficial, impact on the landscape and on the other species that occupied it. They can be brought back, and there is precedent. Not to tens of millions, but to tens of thousands, numbers that can help benefit the Great Plains ecosystem. The Utah successes with the Henrys and Book Cliffs herds prove bison can still fill their original niche. But crucial to their return in any substantial numbers is not only landscapes that can accommodate them, but also public opinion. There was public applause in 2016 when the bison was designated the national mammal. The underlying legislation explained the strong ties bison have with the country, the reliance Native American peoples had on the herds, the benefits grazing bison bring to the prairie, and the economic value they hold.

A bison has been on the Interior Department's official seal since 1912, and is on the National Park Service's emblem, the arrowhead. The Wyoming state flag is dominated by the profile of a bison. The largest mammal in the United States now joins such other national emblems as the oak tree (the national tree since 2004), the bald eagle (the national emblem since 1782), and the rose (the national floral emblem since 1998) as official symbols of the United States. But those are two-dimensional emblems that live on forever. The hundreds of thousands of bison in commercial herds just might create a false sense that the pure genetic lines in conservation herds are not that important and not at risk from cattle introgression or disease. There are significant ecological losses occurring as long as bison can't roam freely on at least a portion of their historic habitat. That entire habitat likely will never see free-roaming bison again, but a surprising amount could be available to them. Roughly half of the original Northern Great Plains ecoregion still exists in largely native prairie. There are nearly 2.5 million acres of public lands covered by native prairie. Add to that total private lands with prairie and you have a fairly substantial landscape that could provide habitat for upward of thirty thousand bison.[264]

The Henry Mountains and Book Cliffs herds in Utah demonstrate that acreage can be made available to hold four hundred to five hundred bison. The recurring question to answer is whether the nation has the desire for and appreciates the value of accommodating tens of thousands of bison. Land-use patterns have cut and sliced and parceled out the Great Plains that bison once called their own. Today, cattle ranching occupies more than 95 percent of Plains grasslands,[265] a staggering number when you begin to wonder where bison might be returned. And yet, as the American Prairie Preserve in Montana is demonstrating, piecing lands together like a jigsaw puzzle can connect large tracts of land to furnish capacity for herds in the thousands, if not tens of thousands. With some creativity, open minds, and funding, private land between Wind Cave and Badlands national parks could provide tens of thousands of acres to allow bison from those two parks to form one continuous herd. Central to success is bringing the stakeholders together in support of bison. In its 2014 Bison Report, the Interior Department pointed to thirteen locations managed either by the National Park Service, Fish and Wildlife Service, or BLM where bison that pass through a quarantine program theoretically could be returned. They range from Valentine National Wildlife Refuge and Agate Fossil Beds National Monument in Nebraska to Great Sand Dunes National Park in Colorado and Chickasaw National Recreation Area in Oklahoma. Not all offer sprawling landscapes that could support thousands of bison. But then, that doesn't always have to be the focus. Small herds that serve as genetic subdivisions of larger herds are just as valuable. A National Park Service report that evaluated Agate Fossil Beds—a 3,058-acre park in western Nebraska once home for a working cattle ranch—promoted the monument as "one of the best sites to receive Yellowstone NP bison."[266] The report concluded that 129–219 bison could be sustained in the park, depending on how much moisture falls in a given year. That's not a huge herd, but it could serve as a genetic reservoir and boost the area economy as well through tourism.[267]

Technological creativity also is being used to preserve genetics. In Minnesota, the genes of Yellowstone bison are being harbored in a herd at Blue Mounds State Park. Yellowstone bulls and cows didn't travel to Minnesota, but their genetic material did. A Colorado State University animal reproduction professor, in the fall of 2016, artificially implanted embryos from Yellowstone cows into four cows at the Minnesota Zoo. Together, the zoo and Minnesota staff manage a conservation herd of bison. The genetic infusion from Yellowstone further diversified the lineage of the Blue Mounds State Park herd, which also counts bison genes from the National Bison Range (28 percent), Wind Cave National Park (32 percent), Fort Niobrara National Wildlife

Refuge (17 percent), Wichita Mountains National Wildlife Refuge (11 percent), Badlands National Park (7 percent), and Theodore Roosevelt National Park, both North and South herds (2 percent each). The Yellowstone contribution was measured at 1 percent.[268]

Yellowstone itself could boost the wellspring of bison genetics, if only politics would allow. Modeling done in 2009 indicated that summer range in and near the park could handle upward of ten thousand bison—more than three times the three-thousand-head goal for winter cited in the Interagency Bison Management Plan.[269] But national parks shouldn't be the only settings for bison. The mass appeal of bison makes them attractive for tourism. Photographic wildlife safaris already visit Grand Teton and Yellowstone, and tours are offered at many of the private preserves. At American Prairie in Montana, there are campgrounds you can use as base camps to spend your days watching bison. Back in the 1980s, two Rutgers University professors, Deborah E. Popper and Frank J. Popper, dreamed on a larger scale. Much larger. They proposed turning a great swath of the Plains into one large "Buffalo Commons." The idea was not solely to recreate the nineteenth-century landscape heavy with bison. Rather, it was viewed as a large-scale restoration program that would rehabilitate the Plains as its human population dwindled, moving out not because the region had turned back into the dust bowl it was during the 1930s, but rather to find better-paying jobs. The out-migration is not speculation, but a practice at work. Between 1900 and 2010, many rural counties in Texas, Oklahoma, Kansas, the Dakotas, Montana, Wyoming, Colorado, and New Mexico watched as more than 60 percent of their residents fled in search of a better life.[270]

The Poppers envisioned bison roaming the Plains where small-scale farming was turning into hardscrabble operations that held little allure for either younger generations growing up there or for newcomers. The professors didn't envision all human habitation leaving the region, instead believing there could be an economically viable middle ground between heavy agricultural or mineral extraction usage and wilderness settings.[271] At the time, the Poppers' proposal brought them no small amount of derision when it was unveiled. But what they predicted in terms of out-migration and economic doldrums has held true. Restoring bison could bring some jobs, and a measure of economic vitality, back to the region and contribute to grasslands restoration.[272]

But how far can bison expansion in the West go? The landscape is nowhere near as wide open as it was 150 years ago. And a lot of the original Great Plains prairie is no more. It's been estimated that 85–90 percent, maybe even as much as 95 percent, of the original tallgrass prairie has been lost to development, and 26–45 percent of the shortgrass prairie has been overtaken as well. (Put another way, though, 55–75 percent of the original shortgrass prairie remains largely intact).[273] Wetlands losses have ranged from 27–52 percent, with greater losses in Canada, while dams and diversions have affected many rivers and streams in the region, and pumping for irrigation has greatly drained the Oglala aquifer.[274] To restore bison to the Plains on a large scale, there would need to be active rehabilitation of some areas. Grazing systems would have to be developed for Plains ecosystems, and fire regimes would have to be managed, with an eye on historical patterns as well for human protection. And, of course, those approaches would have to take into consideration the altered landscape, and involve willing private landowners and other stakeholders.[275]

Pulling out maps—road maps, Google Earth maps, US Forest Service maps—I quickly spot pockets of public lands that could serve as quality bison habitat. Across Wyoming, the Dakotas, Nebraska, Colorado, Kansas, and Oklahoma there are vast spaces held in the public domain, places where bison would be at home. The national grasslands are federal landscapes that, by and large, encompass prairie ecosystems that bison once roamed in force. Combined, they hold nearly four million acres.[276] Of the twenty grasslands, seventeen touch the Great Plains and some come tantalizingly close to national park lands. Buffalo Gap National Grassland in South Dakota borders Oglala National Grassland in Nebraska, wraps much of Badlands National Park, and isn't far from both Wind Cave National Park and Black Hills National Forest, which also is adjacent to Custer State Park. Together those areas contain 2.25-million acres. Look to North Dakota and you'll find that the million-acre Little Missouri National Grassland, the largest of the national grasslands, actually encircles Theodore Roosevelt National Park. Stitching some of these grasslands to national park lands could provide a lot of potential bison habitat.

The debate over whether the public would support large-scale landscape conservation isn't newly voiced, but has been around for a surprisingly long time, Dr. Glenn Plumb tells me. The wildlife biologist retired from the National Park Service in 2018 only to pick up the title of bison specialist for the International Union for Conservation of Nature. As such, he works to promote conservation of bison as well as ecological restoration of the animals on their historic range, where possible. He realizes the challenge he faces. He knows there are those who believe the era of large-scale conservation initiatives has bypassed society. Even when Roosevelt and Hornaday were working to prevent the extinction of bison, there were those who opposed their efforts, points out Dr. Plumb.

"Some of the things that people were saying in those first couple decades were that the time of buffalo had come and gone and it was foolish and it was aesthetic and it was self-serving, falderal, for people to be keeping bison alive and then bringing them back out to the West, and that there was no place for bison in the West," he told me. "And these weren't just spurious people in corners. These were organized voices, at state and industry levels. So, has that changed? A little bit. But there's still a lot of uncertainty and a little confusion about whether or not in the twenty-first century bison conservation at large scale, with large numbers and with large assemblages, is a high priority."

At the Wildlife Conservation Society, the belief is that large-scale conservation can be ongoing, it just needs to be more creative than it was in the past. No longer are there enormous landscapes that easily can be plucked up and preserved. But there are contiguous lands, federal, tribal, state, and private, that can be unified under a common goal to provide the necessary landscape. Going that route is necessary today because the small protected landscapes that are within the federal lands kingdom cannot support all the biodiversity needed to maintain proper ecological function. But when you look across the landscape, you can see how different pieces of public and private lands, like a massive quilt, can be pieced together to provide the habitat necessary for migratory wildlife, such as elk and bison and even wolves and grizzly bears. The Blackfeet Reservation and Glacier National Park is one example. Another is the American Prairie Reserve, the Charles M. Russell National Wildlife Refuge, the Upper Missouri River Breaks National Monument, BLM lands, and private acreage. National parks, forests, and wildlife refuges currently are the nation's core areas for wildlife habitat, but that wildlife needs much, much more land to roam to be genetically diverse. Hence the drive to complete the Yellowstone to Yukon initiative.

The trick is coming up with the correct assortment, and breadth, of lands that don't require wildlife to be managed like an open-air zoo. That, unfortunately, was the case at Isle Royale National Park, which occupies an island in Lake Superior. The park service in 2018 decided to physically transport wolves to the island because the existing packs had dwindled to just two animals, in large part due to inbreeding. Without more wolves, the park's moose would overwhelm the available vegetation.

At Yellowstone, before he retired, Superintendent Wenk expressed hope that the era of large-scale conservation is not in the past. And he just needed to look at the lands surrounding his park to savor some optimism that it is not. "Yellowstone enjoys the fact that it is the heart of an ecosystem that's about sixteen, eighteen, twenty million acres, depending on who is counting the acres. And we are surrounded by five national forests, and that's not usual for many parks in the West," he told me. "But certainly some of the major migration routes for any animal take them through private lands and so that makes it more difficult. I think the days of conservation are not behind, but I think the days of really great collaboration and cooperation with state agencies are becoming more and more necessary."

Bring these initiatives to fruition and as a society we'll have learned how to coexist with wildlife for the long term. We'll be able to preserve species, provide for hunting and ecotourism that will benefit communities that need diversification themselves, and strengthen cultural ties of Native Americans to bison and the land—and they perhaps can teach other cultures some things about those connections. The key, especially with an animal the size of a bison, is finding a landscape large enough to accommodate them. As Montana illustrates with its bison bias, not everyone in today's society is okay with that. We either figure out how to make it work, or bison will be left "behind a fence as a relic, at an evolutionary dead end," Plumb told me.

In Utah, bison and cattle share rather large swathes of state and federal lands. In the Henry Mountains, there are about 800,000 acres available, of which 350,000 acres have been used by the state's bison herd, which numbers about 450. At the Book Cliffs, there are nearly 1.2 million acres available for bison. Those examples prove that there can be room, if there is tolerance.

With national parks, the preservation of nature, not the practice of multiple use, offers the safest home for conservation herds of bison. That's why conservationists have suggested that, along with putting bison on landscapes such as those at Great Sand Dunes and Agate Fossil Beds, the animals need to return to tribal reservations, and that there even is a need for more national park landscapes. Imagine, a national park covering 175,000 acres in the heart of Nebraska, a place once brimming with bison. The shortgrass prairie could not only nurture this species again, but also herds of elk and pronghorn. It could be home to jackrabbits and coyotes and, maybe, even wolves. Doubt that? Already wolves have crossed American Prairie's lands in Montana, and grizzly bears aren't too far away as they expand from the Rocky Mountain Front. In the heart of Nebraska there could be a unit of the National Park System that captures the quintessential North American landscape. This is not a new concept. Indeed, it's more than a century old, dating at least to 1882 when the "national park" concept was still in its formative stages. By the mid-1930s the National Park Service was intrigued by the idea of a plains park and began collecting information for a Great Plains National Monument. There was a need, then and now, for a park that preserved the Great Plains as it existed before settlement. Park-service planners kicked around the idea of a grasslands park, either in South Dakota or in Nebraska, but World War II intervened and the study was mothballed. It wasn't until 1960 that the US Senate was urged by the delegation from Kansas to create a prairie national park in the state. Such a park would be home to herds of bison and antelope and could prove well as breeding grounds for prairie chicken and quail, the Senate was told.[277] But, as happens with politics, the locals in Kansas that would be affected rose up against the proposal, in part over concerns of surrendering land to the federal government. When Western members of the Senate Public Lands Subcommittee aligned with the opponents, the legislation's future was sealed.

More recently, the idea for such a park in Nebraska resurfaced. In 1995, the National Park Service wrote a study for a Niobrara Buffalo-Prairie National Park. The study found that the region in northern Nebraska offered a wonderful plains river (the Niobrara), mixed-grass prairie, tallgrass prairie, and hardwood and pine forests. Here, the park-service planners concluded, was a wonderful landscape for a 138,000-acre park that would benefit recreation, science, and preservation.[278] But reality often is a complicating factor, and in this case the fact that a portion of the land envisioned for the national park was in private hands was a significant impediment. When the feasibility study was presented to Congress in July 1995, the park service took no position on it while awaiting the outcome of a proposal to enlarge the Niobrara National Scenic River in the same area of Nebraska. And even once that expansion was completed, the agency was silent on the larger question of a new national park, one that could preserve both a section of the Great Plains and bison.[279]

The idea of such a park received a nudge eighteen years into the twenty-first century when a Nebraska man tried to push a slightly larger "Great Plains National Park" vision. Stretching from Valentine, Nebraska, through the Fort Niobrara National Wildlife Refuge and another twenty-nine miles downstream, this proposal would embrace a portion of the national scenic river and tie into a fifty-six-thousand-acre bison preserve managed by the Nature Conservancy. But without funding to mount a campaign, and no congressional backers, the proposal was nothing more than a dream.

Still, there already are large tracts of federal lands that could hold bison without the need to create a new national park. I drove across part of it on my way home from Wind Cave. Driving south from Newcastle, Wyoming, I found myself surrounded by a landscape that seemed little changed by the past 150 years. My Subaru Outback bounced along the dirt road through a shortgrass prairie setting where you still find buffalo grass, bluegrass, and wheatgrass. I slowed for a snake—was it a Wyoming milksnake, or a prairie rattlesnake?—and carefully skirted it, preferring to keep my distance rather than stop for an introduction. Every now and again a single-track road even smaller than the one I followed skittered off to the left or right, many likely ending at a ranch house, others simply cutting across the prairie to somewhere else. Several times I pulled over to take in this time-honored landscape, to smell the prairie, and to listen for its residents. Rain clouds scudded past overhead, but held their moisture. Meadowlarks and fox sparrows sent their songs across the sweep of grasslands, burrowing owls bobbed up and down as if their heads were mounted on springs, and the wet springtime attracted chortling sandhill cranes and white-faced ibis, as well. No doubt there were badgers and fox out there, the occasional bobcat and itinerant black bear. Around me vegetation was green and lush, with wildflowers beginning to paint the prairie. Insects buzzed, pestering humans and most wildlife, serving up meals to birds.

More than 130 years ago this landscape was traveled by thousands of longhorn cattle. They were driven north from Texas, to stop in either Wyoming or Montana, to be fattened on the ample grasslands such as those that spread out before me. Sold at the end of the drive to mining camps or the cavalry. This rolling, grassy tableau today is part of the Thunder Basin National Grassland, one of the US Forest Service's twenty national grasslands. These grasslands for thousands of years provided for bison, but they're not for everyone. They formally were opened for human settlement in the late 1800s through the Homestead Act, but most of the lands reverted to the federal government after the Dust Bowl of the 1930s convinced many homesteaders their future was somewhere else. The settlers were driven out by relentless gusting winds, baking summers, frigid winters, and the lonesomeness of living miles from your neighbor. The National Industrial Recovery Act of 1933 and Emergency Relief Appropriations Act of 1935 allowed for the buyback of these lands, with the belief that the forest service could heal them. On June 23, 1960, the Department of Agriculture set aside 3.8 million acres of these lands as national grasslands. The hope was that these landscapes could be restored to near-native conditions that would provide for wildlife habitat, protect watersheds, and support both grazing and recreation. Five decades later, that possibility was voiced again. The National Grasslands Interpretive Master Plan, which the forest service adopted in 2013, maintained that many native species, including those considered threatened or endangered, would thrive in these areas. Place, time, and culture would thrive, too. The grasslands are more than just a setting for wildlife. They hold pieces of the recent past in broken down, slumping homesteads. They have rich topography and geology for those who see more than mountains as they look about. And they still embrace cultures that long have been synonymous with the Plains.

The Sioux, Apache, Arapaho, Arikara, Bannock, Cheyenne, Comanche, Crow, Mandan, and many other native cultures know the Great Plains as their homelands. Heal the lands, return native wildlife, and these cultural ties are rekindled and reinforced. Native peoples on the Plains long have associated the vitality of the world with bison. The Sioux even connected the appearance of bison with moral character when their daughters reached puberty.

> Walk the good road, my daughter, and the buffalo herds wide and dark as cloud shadows moving over the prairie will follow you. . . . Be dutiful, respectful, gentle and modest, my daughter. And proud walking. If the pride and the virtue of the women are lost, the spring will come but the buffalo trails will turn to grass. Be strong, with the warm, strong heart of the earth. No people goes down until their women are weak and dishonored.[280]

Today tribal governments are playing a large role in bison conservation. Not only do many of them have the desire to see bison back on the land, but they have the land to accommodate the bison. Fifteen tribal governments in the United States and Canada that were signatories to a Buffalo Treaty adopted in 2014 oversee more than eighty-four million acres, much suitable for bison. The Blackfeet Nation, the Assiniboine and Sioux tribes on the Fort Peck Reservation, and the Eastern Shoshone on the Wind River Reservation are just some of the native communities working to build their bison herds. There's no need to settle with putting bison back on one slice of the federal domain, the national grasslands. There are millions of public acres held by the US Bureau of Land Management, the US Fish and Wildlife Service, and elsewhere in the national parks and forests that would be suitable. These places seem perfect for bison.

Returning bison to the landscape sounds simple: find enough unbroken acreage that can support at least one thousand bison. The end result, once the logistical complexity is overcome, can be improved ecological function for both the animals and the prairie.[281] Achieving that elusive result won't be so simple, since intermingled within this landscape are state and private lands, and rangelands that are home to cattle herds. There are grazing allotments that go back decades, if not a century. There are traditions tied to cattle, not bison. Then, too, the landscapes of the national grasslands are not exactly the landscapes that settlers came upon when the Homestead Act of 1862 encouraged millions, eventually, to claim a piece of home for themselves. The sod was quickly busted to be turned into farmlands. And while the topsoil was suitable enough, the annual precipitation was iffy and the winds blustery. When that topsoil was blown into clouds that at times rose nearly four miles above the Great Plains states during the Dust Bowl,[282] it drove home how inhospitable the landscape could be. Bob Mountain knows well the history. He grew up on his grandparents' homestead in northeastern Colorado, where he helped the family tend to a dozen or so cattle. When I tracked him down in 2018, he was the national grasslands coordinator for the US Forest Service. He gave me an abbreviated history of the grasslands, and pointed out some of the barriers to putting bison back on them.

"A number of the grasslands were originally, obviously, busted out of the Great Plains," he told me. "And farmed. Most of them were, not all. And certainly not all parcels were in every grasslands, but in some of them virtually every acre was farmed at some point. The Fort Pierre Grassland in the middle of South Dakota was virtually all cultivated for a number of decades."

From his headquarters in Laramie, Wyoming, Mountain has headed out across the grasslands to check in on the operations, big and small, that have permits to run cattle, and even some bison, on those landscapes. His experience, and interactions with the permittees, has him convinced that it would not be an easy thing to replace cattle with bison. Take the Thunder Basin National Grassland for example, he says. There are nearly two hundred cattle producers that hold permits to run their livestock on parcels there. Those allotments are partitioned into a handful of pastures, perhaps eight or more, that cattle are rotated through throughout the year. There are spring pastures, summer pastures, and even fall and winter pastures. Nine hundred thousand or so acres of private and state lands are interspersed with Thunder Basin, which encompasses nearly 550,000 acres. And some of those acres are occupied by bison. One northern Wyoming rancher in particular who runs bison on his allotment prefers the easygoing calving season, something that can't be said of cattle.

"He says, 'I kinda like getting up at six o'clock and staring out the kitchen window and having a cup of coffee or two and seeing what happened last night,'" Mountain told me. "Rather than being out there every two hours," as cattle ranchers can be during calving season.

As with Greg Schroeder at Wind Cave National Park, Mountain at the forest service doesn't say it would be impossible for bison to roam all those acres if someone came up with enough money and could get all the various stakeholders in agreement. But it would require quite the paradigm shift for generations that ran cattle on the grasslands and which operate under grazing associations that have requirements as far as base property ownership and livestock ownership. Making the possibility of placing more bison on the grasslands more than a little intriguing, though, is the close proximity of other big expanses of public lands. And bison are comfortable on these lands. The aptly named Buffalo Gap National Grassland in southwestern South Dakota includes the original "Buffalo Gap" where bison would cross from their summer grounds to their winter grounds. That gap, and the town of Buffalo Gap, are about eleven miles northeast of Hot Springs, South Dakota, not far from Wind Cave National Park.

Jonathan Proctor has been working to move bison restoration forward for years in his role with Defenders of Wildlife. He's thought hard about bison roaming national grasslands, and agrees with Mountain that it would require a pretty big paradigm shift to become a reality. But it's not impossible. Though some grasslands are interlaced with private and state lands in a checkerboard fashion, there are others where that's not such a high hurdle to overcome. The connectivity of Badlands National Park, Buffalo Gap National Grassland, and Pine Ridge Reservation make that area more feasible than others for bison. Then, too, there's the example of American Prairie Reserve creating an area of 3.5 million public and private acres dedicated to biodiversity conservation.[283]

APR chose to develop its vision in central Montana because the grasslands of the Great Plains are the "least protected biome on Earth" and because that region has been identified as one of just four areas left in the world where landscape-scale conservation of grasslands is possible. It's not the only landscape where such conservation can be accomplished. Another promising venture that could mirror, albeit on a much smaller scale, what APR is working to accomplish is the Southern Plains Land Trust in southeast Colorado. That project might one day involve the Comanche National Grassland. Defenders of Wildlife is working to see such initiatives succeed. It has a goal of establishing ten conservation herds of bison within their historic landscapes by 2030, if not sooner. These herds would not be small, either, if Defenders succeeds. It would like to see two conservation herds of five thousand or more bison, with the potential to reach ten thousand animals. Another eight herds would have at least four hundred head, with the potential to grow to one thousand animals.

Key to achieving such successes, in addition to having suitable landscapes, is dealing with existing livestock permittees, habitat fragmentation, and the bias of federal agencies to favor cattle and sheep over bison.[284] Hurdles to regaining a functioning ecosystem include consolidation of federal and private lands, possibly through an initiative similar to land swap programs that have been used by the government in the past. Prairie dogs, considered a bane to some ranchers, should be valued as highly as elk and pronghorn. Then, too, there's the issue of allowing wolves, grizzly bears, mountain lions, and other predators to return. A return of bison would coincide with a phase-out of livestock grazing in certain areas.

The ecological benefits of such ambitious projects could be intriguing. A modern return-to-the-past experiment is being tested in Siberia, where Russian scientists are working to remake fifty square miles into a Pleistocene epoch appearance, complete with woolly mammoths (if they can genetically engineer them in test tubes), musk oxen, and bison. They believe they can stave off climate change by restoring highly productive grasslands with their native flora and fauna.[285] The Russians believe the steppe ecosystem they hope to recreate would serve both as a carbon sink and a mirror of sorts that would reflect the heat of sunlight back into the atmosphere, preventing the ground from absorbing it.[286]

While their success remains to be seen, studies in the United States indicate that putting more bison on the landscape would be beneficial to the grassland ecosystems. Improving the health of these ecosystems could go a long way, benefiting bird species that rely on them. The decline in health of the grasslands has been tied to a staggering decline of nearly 40 percent of grassland bird species between 1969 and 2009.[287] Feathered species that rely on this type of landscape that have been listed as endangered under the federal Endangered Species Act include the greater prairie-chicken, northern bobwhite, and aplomado falcon. Driving the decline has been the loss of perhaps as much as 95 percent of tallgrass prairie.[288] With the popularity of bison growing in parts of the West and Midwest, and efforts to establish bison on landscapes that historically were home to these iconic herbivores, more and more attention is being given to their effect on the land.

Epilogue

Opportunities to restore wild plains bison exist in several areas where public land is abundant and relatively contiguous. Over time, grassland reserves could be assembled by purchasing inholdings from willing sellers. South of Canada, this is the only strategy for preserving wild plains bison. It will require difficult, long-term political commitments. These commitments will not begin without a broad public understanding of the meaning and values of "wildness."

—James A. Bailey, author of *American Plains Bison:*
Rewilding an Icon

Fall is here, winter not far behind. I know this because of the flurry of white coming down as I drive north through the slippery twists and turns of Gallatin Canyon that is Yellowstone's western border and then head east over Bozeman Pass on I-90. American Prairie Reserve is still roughly five hours away, depending on the condition of the dirt and gravel roads that my map shows await me, but the scenery I'm driving through is a preview of where I'm heading. The golden-yellow stubble of grasses slipping past me on the right rises above a skiff of snow, swaying in the wind. Low-slung clouds clutch both the Bridger Range and Crazy Mountains on my left as well as the Absaroka Range farther off to my right.

There is precious little open range left in the nation, which makes American Prairie unique. A vision of conservation launched in 2001 with help from the World Wildlife Fund, the initiative strives to create the largest nature reserve in the United States on the northern plains of Montana. Under the preserve's management plan, small plots of private lands, located next to public lands, are strategically acquired. Then American Prairie works to obtain the grazing rights, either outright or through leases. On the preserve's Sun Prairie allotment, about 450 bison roam the thirty thousand acres, free to cross from private land onto state land then onto US Bureau of Land Management acreage. No opening of gates needed. If it one day threads together the 3.5 million acres its designers hope for, the reserve would cover a land mass about equal in size to the state of Connecticut. It is a grand twenty-first-century experiment in large-scale conservation, one centered on a sweep of shortgrass prairie that is one of the world's most endangered temperate ecosystems. Little water, loss of land to agriculture and development, and climate change threaten this place. The plan at the American Prairie Reserve is to counter the threats by establishing a rich, biodiverse mix of native plants and animals. Long range, APR's footprint would knit together private, state, and federal lands, including the Charles M. Russell National Wildlife Refuge and the Upper Missouri Breaks National Monument. On this landscape, about 10,000 bison would be free to roam. As of 2018, the preserve had nearly four hundred thousand deeded and leased acres in hand and 800–850 bison.

Turning off I-90 at Big Timber onto US-191, I find myself on a curious highway that since 1926 has tried to link Canada and Mexico. It probably does that, but not in one continuous run. It's severed in places here and there, and moved dozens of miles east and west as need be by progress that has shifted the road about. My journey up through Gallatin Canyon to Bozeman on 191 is proof of that, as it deposited me on the interstate a bit more than sixty miles west of Big Timber and my reconnection with the old road.

The farther north I head from Big Timber, the farther away I get from the transcontinental rush of traffic. I'm traveling a two-lane strip of pavement with more ravens passing by than other vehicles. The rigs that do pass me are 250s, Rams, and Silverados, the pickups that are the limousines of ranchers. Through Sweet Grass, Wheatland, and Fergus counties I drive, with Phillips County my final destination. A combination of Google Maps, Montana's official highway map, and the Avenza map app guide me. It's a good thing, too, as you don't happen upon American Prairie Reserve by accident. My initial task was to make it to Lewistown, Montana, a community of about six thousand residents that dates to an 1880s gold rush. The rush, centered in the nearby Judith Mountains, didn't last long, but Lewistown has forever marked its significance by being the geographic center of Montana. Beyond that, it's also the southern gateway to APR, if there is to be one.

The large chunks of lands here that are fenced for livestock require a maze-like approach to reaching APR. From Lewistown, my directions seem straightforward: head 40 miles north of town on US-191 to a *T* intersection known as Bohemian Corner, where I turn left. After crossing the Missouri River on a bridge with a sprawling view of this slice of the Charles M. Russell National Wildlife Refuge (the CMR, to locals), I keep on for 21 miles until, my sheet of directions state, I will arrive at "DY Junction" (at mile marker 109). I know I've reached that junction by signs on the left that point to the town of Portman. Dutifully following my directions, I turn right onto a gravel road. The single-track immediately offers two options, and as directed I veer left onto the Dry Fork Road and continue for 26 more miles to another *T* intersection, where I turn left. Another 3.5 miles takes me to a fork in the road, and I follow the right fork for another 12.7 miles to yet another *T* intersection. Turn right, my directions tell me, and continue on to APR's Enrico Science Center. My route takes me across Beauchamp Creek via a wooden bridge under the gaze of a half-dozen grazing cattle, and another bridge over Dry Fork Creek which, of course, is dry. Fortunately there is no rain or snow on this last leg of my journey, for that would have transformed sections of these miles into a muddy, wheel-sucking gumbo of bentonite clay that would bog down and tightly clench my Outback for days, if not weeks, on end.

Here in the Judith Basin, I am about 125 miles west of where Hornaday shot his bison 132 years earlier. It doesn't take much to imagine the herds of black angus I pass as herds of woolly brown bison. But the bison long have been replaced by cattle, and here in Phillips County—population of roughly 4,200 people scattered across 5,212 square miles—they take pride in their beef: "Phillips County Ag feeds 2.3 million per year," a sign tells me as I jounce by. Cattle are indeed king in Phillips County, with more than 65,500 head compared with about 2,000 sheep, 50 swine, 8 llamas, and 3 emus. Not many of these ranchers take kindly to the prospect of losing their range. President Barack Obama's Interior Department for a time considered having the president designate a "Northern Prairie National Monument" in this zip code. Had I kept on heading north on that crooked highway, US-191, to the border of Phillips County and Saskatchewan, I very likely would have passed through some of the prairie said to have been considered for the monument. Part of the vision was for a 2.5-million-acre monument that "would provide an opportunity to restore prairie wildlife and the possibility of establishing a new national bison range."

Not all of those 4,200 or so souls in Phillips County took kindly to seeing their BLM acres turned into either a national monument or a bison range, national or otherwise, as another sign I pass makes clear:

Don't Buffalo Me, No Federal Land Grab!
Save the Cowboy STOP American Prairie Reserve.

I'm so far north in the shortgrass prairie of north-central Montana that French-Canadian radio stations funnel through my car's speakers. Trees are scarce here, clustered along the water holes, ranch ponds, and creeks that drain what little water the prairie manages to claim.

The next morning I meet Damien Austin. He had started out his adult life thinking he wanted to major in art in college, only to venture into biology. Before he was done at Washington State University with a bachelor's degree in that field, he also picked up minors in ecology, chemistry, and psychology. That last area is proving helpful in his role at American Prairie, as he's in almost daily contact with ranchers who believe cattle, not bison, are the better bovines for the landscape. While working at the zoo in Billings, Montana, he learned about American Prairie from the resident veterinarian, who helped out at the preserve. Soon Austin was helping out, too, first as a volunteer, then as a paid general laborer, installing or mending fences and doing whatever other odd jobs the reserve needed done. Now, not too far from his fortieth birthday, he's the reserve superintendent.

As we gather in the cool, blustery morning air outside the reserve's Enrico Education and Science Center, I learn that, despite the lack of trees, bison can be hard to find on the rolling prairie of APR. Along with Austin and Lars Anderson, the resident bison wrangler, a small group of us are set to head out across the preserve to find two cow bison with failing radio collars, tranquilize them a bit, replace the collars with updated versions, and maybe take some biological samples. Anderson gives a few pointers about being around tranquilized bison: speak softly, if at all, no shuffling of feet in the grass, and stand twenty yards downwind of the animal. "They are not unconscious," Austin points out, explaining the effort to not startle the darted animals. "This is not a true anesthetic."

Four of us pile into a Dodge Ram pickup, while three others cram into a UTV, a rugged utility vehicle with a knobby tread design that is beefier than an ATV. Heading out across the reserve, our goal is impeded by the rolling prairie that conceals arroyos where a band of bison could get out of the wind. The growing breeze worries Anderson, who fears the wind is too strong to enable him to dart the bison. Sealing our fate is the fact that the failing radio collars upload their GPS data only every eighteen hours. That gives those cows wearing the collars a heckuva lot of time to vanish into the landscape. As we bounce across the prairie, small groups of bison close to the dirt track watch us roll by, while two bands of elk stare at us from a distance. Meandering along in search of the two bison cows, Austin talks of seeing the landscape restored to its pre-nineteenth-century vigor. He prefers not to use the word "experiment" for what APR is working on. Though Austin acknowledges that it's "definitely a big project, quite ambitious," he adds that it's been successful so far. That success, he continues, has come while working entirely within the system. "The things that we're doing with bison and the idea behind acquiring the land is something that happens on a daily basis in the state of Montana," he tells me over the low throb of the pickup. "We're not asking to change the rules or for special exceptions. We're operating within private property rights and with the BLM grazing system."

The desire to pull together 3.5 million acres stems from input from scientists who say that this much land is necessary to ensure the reserve is functioning on an ecological scale and so resilient to droughts, severe winters, wildfire, and whatever the climate might toss its way. "Because the environment is really arid and not that productive, some of those events can be long-lasting, so you need a really big landscape in order to build in enough resiliency," Austin tells me as we drive on in search of the two bison with the failing radio collars. Off in the distance a few pronghorn antelope dart across the prairie. Big swathes of those 3.5 million acres are in federal hands: the 1.1-million-acre Charles M. Russell National Wildlife Refuge, and the

495,500-acre Upper Missouri River Breaks National Monument, a picturesque vision of the past that President Bill Clinton designated in 2001. Long before the Homestead Act, before Lewis and Clark came up the Missouri River on their way west in 1805, and before the fur trade arrived in the late eighteenth century, this land was home to a diverse mix of native peoples known today as the Crow, Plains Cree, Plains Ojibwa, Blackfoot, Northern Cheyenne, Sioux, Assiniboine, and Gros Ventre. Today the landscape has been described by some as appearing much as it did when Lewis and Clark passed through more than two centuries ago. It is incredibly bucolic in mid-October during my visit. My stop on the US-191 bridge spanning the Missouri not far from where the national monument meets the wildlife refuge gave me sumptuous views of the river, lined by banks of cottonwood trees shimmering in the gold of fall. The stream flowed lazily beneath me and along a gentle curve in the prairie. Today the river, through the national monument, offers 149 miles of paddling bliss, something that can be greatly extended if you continue on downstream into the wildlife refuge. I made a mental note to begin planning my own canoe trip.

American Prairie brought its first bison to this setting in 2005, when it acquired not quite two dozen from Wind Cave National Park, followed by ninety-three more from Elk Island National Park. Those acquisitions created a genetic cocktail that flows back to the twenty-three animals found in Yellowstone after the Great Slaughter and the Pablo-Allard herd in northern Montana that was sold to Canada in 1907. Austin hopes to gain more Yellowstone genes by obtaining park bison, but that is up in the air until the brucellosis issue gets resolved.

Pairing the Charles M. Russell Wildlife Refuge and the Upper Missouri River Breaks National Monument with the APR vision brings more than one million acres and reliable water to the equation, but also a vexing conundrum that remains to be solved. In Montana, bison such as those now free on APR's land are considered livestock, not wildlife. At the wildlife refuge, the guiding mission is to manage the land to benefit native wildlife. It would seem that bison would be a good fit on the refuge, but their current classification as livestock is problematic. "Right now we're working on this cooperative blended landscape," Austin answers when I ask about the livestock-wildlife issue. "We've managed to work with the BLM and the state of Montana in order to get bison to graze on the land. And to date we have not had that on the CMR. So it definitely is something a little trickier, with the classification of the bison right now and the wildlife refuge's mandate for managing for wildlife." Another twist to this seeming roadblock is that many units of the National Wildlife Refuge System are home to bison. A bit more than three hundred miles west of Lewistown stands the National Bison Refuge, which was established in 1908 to help recover bison. "The refuge system has lots of bison on other refuges," agrees Austin, "and yeah, I think Montana's classification of bison is definitely complicating, for all kinds of things."

The dual classification of bison, as both wildlife and livestock, is an enigma. Moose aren't viewed as livestock, nor are elk, or deer, or, for that matter, grizzlies. To Jason Baldes at the Wind River Reservation, lumping bison alongside sheep and cattle as livestock is wrong; there needs to be a paradigm shift away from that notion. "That is a pretty big barrier that we often forget about, because so often we've been ingrained in thinking about treating buffalo like cattle, fencing them in, doing roundups, ear tagging, vaccinations, but there's no other wildlife species that we do that with," he pointed out. "So why is it that we treat buffalo like that? We're trying to move past that and create a newer vision of treating these animals with the utmost respect, and if we have such a profound cultural appreciation and history with this animal, then why would we treat them any other way?"

While Austin is left with resolving these issues, researchers continue to descend upon American Prairie to see whether the twenty-first-century prairie can be turned back into the nineteenth-century prairie. They are looking at native vs. nonnative vegetation, how riparian areas are, or are not, being affected by bison, and what birds think about the habitat.

Nearly two states and almost nine hundred miles south of American Prairie Reserve is another effort to restore the native prairie, and bison. The Southern Plains Land Trust describes its role succinctly: "Habitat is vanishing, leaving wildlife with no place to go. Here's our solution: Buy the land." So far, the trust that organized in 1998 has purchased 23,000 of the 25,000 acres it has in its portfolio and holds conservation easements on the rest, with most located in extreme southeastern Colorado, in Bent County. Guided in part by *American Serengeti: The Last Big Animals of the Great Plains*, a 2017 book Dan Flores wrote to recall the mammalian species that populated the Great Plains, the land trust hopes to recreate the nineteenth-century plains setting. As with American Prairie, the Southern Plains Land Trust is helped in its mission by declining human populations and low land prices. In 2018, property in the county was selling for two hundred to three hundred dollars an acre, while population density had dipped to two to six people per square mile. Southeastern Colorado holds about six million acres of state and federal lands, including the nearly 444,000-acre Comanche National Grassland (which is fewer than one hundred miles from the 108,000-acre Cimarron National Grassland to the east in Kansas). Twining the opposing emotions of melancholy and celebration, the trust's founders believe they can use both to forward their dream. Melancholy stemming from the realization of what has been lost from the landscape in the past 175 years, and the celebration that will be had when their mission is accomplished. A much, much smaller operation—both in acreage and funding—than American Prairie, the nonprofit land trust had about ninety bison in 2018. But it nevertheless is an example of how small herds can help protect genetic diversity.

The American Prairie initiative is a unique model to expand bison and preserve the temperate grassland ecosystem. The Interior Department has millions of acres at its disposal to further the future of bison, and Native American governments have millions more acres. But American Prairie, and the Southern Plains Land Trust to a lesser degree, is demonstrating how, in a nation with few large expanses of strictly public lands, public and private acres can be pieced together for both wildlife and the Great Plains ecosystem. Beyond the United States, similar examples of that ecosystem exist in the Patagonia region of Argentina, the Kazakh Steppe of Asia, and the Daurian Steppe/Amur River Basin of Eastern Mongolia, Russia, and China. American Prairie is not designed to be a nonprofit national park with all the requisite infrastructure. At the end of 2018 it had one campground on the preserve with another in planning, and a hut accommodation designed around thirty-foot-diameter yurts. But the hope is that as more and more people head to American Prairie to see bison, birdwatch, hike, and mountain bike, entrepreneurs in surrounding communities will furnish the hotels and restaurants to support those visitors. Economically, the preserve could provide a much-needed boost for this slice of Montana. A 2017 economic study, funded by the National Wildlife Foundation, found that the Missouri River Country travel region of the state, in which American Prairie exists, brought in just $113 million in nonresident spending in 2015, the smallest dollar amount of the state's six travel regions. While Glacier Country brought in the most, at $1.2 billion, the second-lowest region in terms of visitor spending was Southwest Montana, at $402 million, or nearly four times that of Missouri River Country. The study was somewhat bullish that American Prairie could improve the region's fortunes by educating visitors and in-state residents as to what can be seen at the preserve. "The whole reason we're putting this together is for the enjoyment of the public," Austin tells me. "So we've added key infrastructure in our early years now to try to get some facilities out on the ground for people to come out. But it's not our intention to provide all the opportunities, like a national-park-type setting."

The demise of bison in the nineteenth century has been equated with the loss of the nation's true wilderness. As the herds were lost, so, too, was the frontier, a large measure of the untamed wilderness. Countless species have disappeared since the arrival of the Anthropocene, the most recent geologic period that ushered in humankind. Our species has mastered the conquering and elimination of other species. But we also have prevented many from vanishing. Restoring bison, and the various Plains species that flourish along with them, can be done in a way that brings benefits across the human-nature spectrum. E. O. Wilson, the famed biologist who rose to acclaim exploring the world of ants but since has been outspoken about the need to protect Earth and its many ecosystems, points out that the current species extinction rate "is between one hundred and one thousand times greater than what it was before 1800." To help slow that loss of life, he has proposed the "Half-Earth Project," which aspires to protect half of the planet, land and water, to "reverse the species extinction crisis and ensure the long-term health of our planet."[289]

What seems astonishing, but shouldn't be, is that with relatively little effort the conservation herds can be rather quickly multiplied at least fivefold in number. Since they brought bison back to their landscapes, Wind Cave, Badlands, and Theodore Roosevelt National Parks alone have sent roughly 9,000 bison to native communities and other organizations determined to start their own herds. Assuming an annual reproductive rate of 16 percent, those 9,000 bison could have grown a population of nearly 100,000 in sixteen years.[290] Parks themselves could hold much greater numbers of bison than they currently do, as managers tend to be conservative in how they calculate carrying capacity. Badlands National Park had about 1,200 bison in

2017, but the carrying capacity could handle nearly twice that many during a normal year of precipitation. Wind Cave, which had a population goal of 425 bison, could provide for more than three times that number under normal conditions. Theodore Roosevelt biologists have set a target population of maybe 800 bison combined in the park's North and South units, but those areas could handle more than 2,600 during a year of normal precipitation.[291] In Yellowstone, where the bison are maligned in Montana and have limited wintering habitat to access, the animals historically claimed nearly five million acres around the headwaters of the Madison and Yellowstone rivers. The current range is less than eight hundred thousand acres.[292]

There is great desire to increase the number of conservation herds. The land is there. The commitment is there, as evidenced by the efforts of the Interior Department, Native Americans, land conservancies and other nonprofit organizations, zoos and states, and the National Bison Association to grow the numbers. Preserving more habitat for bison would send shudders, positive ones, through the temperate grasslands ecosystem. Species that could benefit range from swift fox and black-footed ferrets to greater sage-grouse and mountain plover. Allowing predators, the wolves and the grizzlies, to follow the bison also must be a serious consideration, for predation is a key element of nature. It culls the sick and the old and fires instinctual responses in both prey and predator.

Economically, a bison revival could create a tourism economy in areas struggling with out-migration due to the fading prospects for small agricultural operations. There are also the cultural benefits of bringing more bison to public and Native American lands. Benefits not just to Native American peoples who have struggled without them, but to other cultures who are curious about these big, impressive animals and can learn something about bison, and perhaps even themselves, in watching herds move across the landscape. "I think tribes can really have an influence in setting that precedent for what it can look like," Baldes told me. "And maybe encouraging the general public to have some idea of what could be."

Austin and I never did find those two cow bison. They were wild and free, able to roam where they wanted on this north-central Montanan slice of the Great Plains. And they're not alone. Thanks to the efforts at American Prairie, those of the Blackfoot, Fort Peck, and Wind River reservations, and at the Department of the Interior, along with many others, we are not about to lose the bison as most of us know it: the woolly animal with furry legs, black horns, and, if you agree with Pedro de Castañeda de Nájera, a tail carried high like a scorpion, ready to attack.

But there's a collective decision to be made when it comes to conservation herds. Can we spare this unique, ancient species a few million acres or so? Give it space to behave as bison do, to reinvigorate the Great Plains and assist in protecting the other species that were intertwined with it in the nineteenth century? It's hard to imagine these landscapes without bison. True, these animals are relics; they shouldn't be here. But they are, and while they probably would continue on without much more assistance, they certainly deserve the opportunity to regain a more solid footing, to leave some wallows on the open plains.

When Jason Baldes was working on his master's thesis, he went to the northern reach of the Wind River Indian Reservation, into Wyoming's Owl Creek Mountains, to study plant biodiversity and relic wallows. Once his eye captured the knack for discerning those shallow depressions in the soil, he slowly began to realize just how many there were. "Probably in a twenty-square-mile radius I found more than 150 wallows," he told me. "I think that when there were millions of buffalo on the landscape, there were millions of wallows. Most of them have been plowed up and paved over." Those before Baldes' eyes were pre-1885 wallows, the last year that bison were found on the reservation. Elsewhere on the Wind River Reservation, he has found buffalo jumps, bones still scattered beneath them, at elevations up to eleven thousand feet. With fewer than two dozen bison on just three hundred acres today, it will be a while before many more new wallows are ground into the prairie there. But they're coming. "We're in a new era of bringing back a species to its former landscape and having to relearn some of the ecological benefits of having buffalo on a landscape that hasn't seen them in 130 years," he said.

As that learning process is renewed and advances, those bison and their wallows will be out on the Plains for native vegetation and wildlife to benefit from, and for future generations of humans to marvel at, as we've been doing for millennia.

Endnotes

Prologue

1. "Accession card 1984 P-5," University of Alaska Museum of Earth Sciences, https://web.corral.tacc.utexas.edu/UAF/es/2011_07_27/jpegs /ES21661.jpg.

2. "Blue Babe: A Messenger from the Ice," UA Journey, University of Alaska, September 10, 2015, https://www.alaska.edu/uajourney/history -and-trivia/blue-babe-a-messenger-fro/.

3. "American Lion," *Wikipedia*, https://en.wikipedia.org/wiki /American_lion.

4. R. Dale Guthrie, *The Nature of Paleolithic Art* (Chicago: University of Chicago Press, 2005), vii–x.

5. R. Dale Guthrie, *Frozen Fauna of the Mammoth Steppe: The Story of Blue Babe* (Chicago: University of Chicago Press, 1990), 91.

6. Ibid., 92, 99.

7. Ibid., 83.

8. R. Dale Guthrie, "36,000-Year-Old Bison 'Comes to Life,'" *Alaska Mines & Geology* 30, no. 4 (October 1981): 11.

9. Guthrie, *Frozen Fauna of the Mammoth Steppe*, ix.

10. "Extinct Long-Horned Bison & Ancient Bison (*Bison latifrons* and *B. antiquus*) Fact Sheet: Summary," San Diego Zoo Global, 2009, http:// ielc.libguides.com/sdzg/factsheets/extinctlonghorned-ancientbison; C. Cormack Gates et al., *American Bison Status Survey and Conservation Guidelines* (Gland, Switzerland: International Union for Conservation of Nature, 2010), 5–6.

11. Guthrie, *Frozen Fauna of the Mammoth Steppe*, ix–x.

12. "Altimara Cave Paintings," Encyclopedia of Art, http://www.visual -arts-cork.com/prehistoric/altamira-cave-paintings.htm.

13. Black Elk and John G. Neihardt, *Black Elk Speaks: Being the Life Story of a Holy Man of the Oglala Sioux* (New York: State University of New York Press, 1932), 33.

14. Valerius Geist, *Buffalo Nation: History and Legend of the North American Bison* (Minneapolis: Voyageur Press, 1996), 17.

15. Ibid., 104.

16. Robert D. Brown, "The History of Wildlife Conservation and

Research in the United States—and Implications for the Future" (North Carolina State University, 2007), 6.

17. "FAQs," Turner Enterprises, Inc., https://www.tedturner.com /turner-ranches/turner-ranches-faq/.

18. Curtis H. Freese et al., "Second Chance for the Plains Bison," *Biological Conservation* 136, no. 2 (2007): 4, doi:10.1016/j.biocon.2006 .11.019.

19. "Loss of Great Plains Grasslands Puts Critical Ecosystems at Risk," World Wildlife Fund, October 24, 2017, https://3blmedia.com/News /Loss-Great-Plains-Grasslands-Puts-Critical-Ecosystems-Risk.

20. "The Biggest Land Mammal in Europe Returns to the Southern Carpathian Wilderness," LIFE Bison, https://life-bison.com/wp-content /uploads/2018/07/Bison-exhibition_digital-version_2016.pdf.

The Landscape

21. William T. Barker and Warren C. Whitman, "Vegetation of the Northern Great Plains," *Rangelands* 10, no. 6 (December 1988): 266.

22. Carolyn Hull Sieg, Curtis H. Flather, and Stephan McCanny, "Recent Biodiversity Patterns in the Great Plains: Implications for Restoration and Management," *Great Plains Research* 9, no. 2 (1999): 279.

23. Allen Steuter and Lori Hidinger, "Comparative Ecology of Bison and Cattle on Mixed-Grass Prairie," *Great Plains Research* 9 (Fall 1999): 339, http://digitalcommons.unl.edu/greatplainsresearch/467.

24. P.J. White, Rick L. Wallen, and David E. Hallac, eds., *Yellowstone Bison: Conserving an American Icon in Modern Society* (Yellowstone Association, 2015), 110.

25. Ibid., 7.

26. Doug Smith, personal communication, February 2010.

27. George Catlin, *North American Indians*, ed. Peter Matthiessen, (New York: Viking, 1989).

28. Robert S. Pfannenstiel and Mark G. Ruder, "Colonization of Bison (*Bison bison*) Wallows in a Tallgrass Prairie by *Culicoides spp.* (Diptera: Ceratopogonidae)," *Journal of Vector Ecology* 40, no. 1 (June 2015): 187.

29. "Bison Bellows: What's Wallowing All About?" National Park Service, 2016, https://www.nps.gov/articles/bison-bellow-1-28-16.htm.

30. L. David Mech, Rick T. McIntyre, and Douglas W. Smith, "Unusual Behavior by Bison, *Bison bison*, Toward Elk, *Cervus elaphus*, and Wolves, *Canis lupus*," *Canadian Field-Naturalist* 118, no. 1 (2004), doi:10.22621 /cfn.v118i1.892.

31. "Baby Bison Takes on Wolf and Wins" National Geographic Society, May 8, 2016, https://youtu.be/K6TnWW1s4hE.

32. "Grassland Birds," Wildlife Consevation Society North America, https://northamerica.wcs.org/Wildlife/Grassland-Birds.aspx.

33. White, Wallen, and Hallac, *Yellowstone Bison*, 108.

34. Ibid., 90–91.

35. "Swift Fox (*Vulpes velox*)," U.S. Fish and Wildlife Service, https://www.fws.gov/northdakotafieldoffice/endspecies/species/swift_fox.htm.

36. Sieg, Flather, and McCanny, "Recent Biodiversity Patterns," 293.

37. "What Part of the Bison Was Used?" All About Bison, https://allaboutbison.com/what-part-of-the-bison-was-used/.

38. Catlin, *North American Indians*, 264.

39. Ibid., 125.

40. Robert Utley, *The Indian Frontier 1846–1890* (Albuquerque: University of New Mexico Press, 2002), 226.

41. "The Earthlodge," National Park Service, https://www.nps.gov/knri/planyourvisit/upload/earthlodge%20Site%20Bulletin.pdf.

Tatanka

42. "American Indian Perspectives on Thanksgiving," National Museum of the American Indian, https://americanindian.si.edu/sites/1/files/pdf/education/thanksgiving_poster.pdf.

43. Ibid.

44. "The Home of the Bison—The Cultural Foundations of Tribal Affiliations to WCNP," National Park Service, https://www.nps.gov/wica/learn/historyculture/the-home-of-the-bison-the-cultural-foundations-of-tribal-affiliations-to-wcnp.htm.

45. Geist, *Buffalo Nation*, 23.

46. Ibid., 23.

47. Ibid., 26.

48. Ibid., 107.

49. Catlin, *North American Indians*, 256.

50. Philip Henry Sheridan, *Philip Henry Sheridan Papers: Autograph Letters, 1865–1887; Sherman, William T., to Sheridan,; 1868–1877* (manuscript and mixed material, Library of Congress, 1868), https://www.loc.gov/item/mss397680396/.

51. David D. Smits, "The Frontier Army and the Destruction of the Buffalo: 1865–1883," *Western Historical Quarterly* 25, no. 3 (1994): 315; James T. King, "Fort McPherson in 1870: A Note by an Army Wife,"

Nebraska History 41 (1964): 105.

52. Utley, *The Indian Frontier 1846–1890*, 221.

53. Ibid.

54. John Lame Deer and Richard Erdoes, *Lame Deer, Seeker of Visions* (New York: Simon & Schuster, 1972), 270.

55. Ibid., 131.

56. Donna Feir, Rob Gillezeau, and Maggie E.C. Jones, "The Slaughter of the North American Bison and Reversal of Fortunes on the Great Plains," Department Discussion Papers 1701, Department of Economics, (University of Victoria, 2017).

57. William T. Hornaday, *Annual Report of the American Bison Society 1905–1907* (Boston: American Bison Society, 1908), 77, https://archive .org/details/annualreportofambs00amer/page/n5.

58. Ted Steinberg, *Down to Earth: Nature's Role in American History* (Oxford University Press, 2002), 128.

59. "Badlands, Theodore Roosevelt National Parks Send Bison to Cherokee Nation," National Parks Traveler, October 20, 2014, https:// www.nationalparkstraveler.org/2014/10/badlands-theodore-roosevelt -national-parks-send-bison-cherokee-nation25783.

60. "Reduction in Wind Cave National Park's Bison Herd Benefits Other Herds," National Parks Traveler, October 26, 2017, https://www .nationalparkstraveler.org/2017/10/reduction-wind-cave-national-parks -bison-herd-benefits-other-herds.

61. Intertribal Buffalo Council, http://www.itbcbuffalonation.org/.

62. Lucy Tompkins, "International Bison Conference Announces Goal of 1 Million Bison," *The Missoulian*, July 5, 2017, https://missoulian.com /news/state-and-regional/international-bison-conference-announces -goal-of-million-bison/article_7868966d-f07c-56d7-a1d8-82ef0e17d66b .html.

63. "Farm to School Efforts Positively Impact Tribal Communities," USDA, November 21, 2016, https://www.usda.gov/media /blog/2016/11/21/farm-school-efforts-positively-impact-tribal- communities.

64. Brenna Ramsden, "Future of Pe Sla Is for Native American Youth," KOTA-TV, October 23, 2017, https://www.kotatv.com/content/news /Future-of-Pe-Sla-is-for-Native-American-youth-452590173.html.

65. Richard B. Williams, "History of the Relationship of the Buffalo and the Indian," Tanka Bar, http://www.tankabar.com/cgi-bin/nanf/public /viewStory.cvw?sessionid=%3C%3Csessionid%3E%3E&sectionname= Buffalo%20Nation&storyid=61954&commentbox=.

66. Sarah Anne Tarka, "My Brother the Buffalo: An Ethnohistorical Documentation of the 1999 Buffalo Walk and the Cultural Significance of Yellowstone Buffalo to the Lakota Sioux and Nez Perce Peoples," (MA thesis, University of Montana, 2007), 115, https://scholarworks.umt.edu/etd/692.

67. Ibid., 83.

68. Jason Baldes, "'It's Not Just an Animal to Us': The Significance of Buffalo Returning to Wind River Indian Reservation," interview by Wyoming Migration Initiative, Facebook, January 6, 2017, https://www.facebook.com/migrationinitiative/posts/1836716536546946.

69. National Academies of Sciences, Engineering, and Medicine, *Revisiting Brucellosis in the Greater Yellowstone Area* (Washington, DC: National Academies Press, 2017), 2, https://doi.org/10.17226/24750.

THE GREAT SLAUGHTER

70. Pedro de Castañeda de Nájera, *The Journey of Coronado, 1540–1542*, trans. and ed. George Parker Winship (A. S. Barnes & Co., 1904), xxxii.

71. Ibid., 141.

72. Samuel P. Snell, Ryan L. Jackson, and Angie R. Krieger, "Lost and Forgotten Historic Roads: The Buffalo Trace," (U.S. Forest Service, 2014), 2.

73. "A Noble Tree (And Some Not-So-Very Nobles): Information about William McDonald," Genealogy.com, https://www.genealogy.com/ftm/j/a/c/Frances-Jacklin-OR/WEBSITE-0001/UHP-0122.html.

74. Catlin, *North American Indians*, 125.

75. "Time Line of American Bison," U.S. Fish and Wildlife Service National Bison Range, https://www.fws.gov/bisonrange/timeline.htm.

76. William T. Hornaday, *The Extermination of the American Bison* (Washington, DC: Government Printing Office, 1889), 389.

77. Ibid.

78. Ibid., 389.

79. "Bison, a Plains Supermarket," Nebraska Studies, NET Foundation for Television, http://www.nebraskastudies.org/1500-1799/emergence-of-historic-tribes/bison-a-plains-supermarket/.

80. Catlin, *North American Indians*, 263.

81. Smits, "The Frontier Army and the Destruction of the Buffalo," 317.

82. John M. Schofield, *Forty-Six Years in the Army* (New York: Century Co., 1897), 428.

83. William T. Sherman, *Memoirs of General W.T. Sherman, Volume 1,*

rev. 2nd ed. (New York: D. Appleton and Co., 1889), chap. 26.

84. William F. Cody, *An Autobiography of Buffalo Bill* (Cosmopolitan Book Corp., 1920), 87.

85. Ibid., 79.

86. Frank H. Mayer, and Charles B. Roth, *The Buffalo Harvest* (Denver: Sage Books, 1958), PBS, https://www.pbs.org/weta/thewest/resources /archives/five/buffalo.htm.

87. M.S. Taylor, "Buffalo Hunt: International Trade and the Virtual Extinction of the North American Bison," *American Economic Review* 101, no. 7 (2011): 3165.

88. Ibid., 3169.

89. Smits, "The Frontier Army and the Destruction of the Buffalo," 332.

90. Charles C. Jones, *Buffalo Jones' Forty Years of Adventure: A Volume of Facts Gathered from Experience*, compiled by Col. Henry Inman (Crane & Company, 1899), 256.

91. Herman J. Viola, *Trail to Wounded Knee: The Last Stand of the Plains Indians, 1860–1890*, (Washington, DC: National Geographic Society, 2003), 44.

92. Hornaday, *The Extermination of the American Bison*, 465.

93. Andrew C. Isenberg, *The Destruction of the Bison* (Cambridge: Cambridge University Press, 2001), 2.

94. Philip Deloria, personal communication, 2018.

95. Smithsonian Institution, *Annual Report of the Board of Regents of the Smithsonian Institution for the Year Ending June 30, 1887* (Washington, DC: Government Printing Office, 1889), 498.

96. Stefan Bechtel, *Mr. Hornaday's War: How a Peculiar Victorian Zookeeper Waged a Lonely Crusade for Wildlife that Changed the World* (Boston: Beacon Press, 2012), 70.

97. Mayer and Roth, *The Buffalo Harvest*.

98. "American West: The Cattle Industry," History on the Net, https:// www.historyonthenet.com/american-west-the-cattle-industry.

99. Igor Volsky, "Bierstadt and Nationalism," Hudson River Valley Institute, February 28, 2007, http://www.hudsonrivervalley.org/library /pdfs/bierstadt1_igor_volsky.pdf.

REVIVAL OF A PRECARIOUS SPECIES

100. William T. Hornaday, *Our Vanishing Wild Life: Its Extermination and Preservation* (New York: Charles Scribner's Sons, 1913), 302.

Charles "Buffalo" Jones

101. Jones, *Buffalo Jones' Forty Years of Adventure.*

102. Ibid.

103. Robert Easton and MacKenzie Brown, *Lord of Beasts: The Saga of Buffalo Jones* (Tucson: University of Arizona Press, 1961), 38.

104. Jones, *Buffalo Jones' Forty Years of Adventure*, 287.

105. Ibid., 384.

106. Howard Mingos, "World's Wild Life Is Fast Vanishing," *The New York Times*, October 21, 1923, https://www.nytimes.com/1923/10/21 /archives/worlds-wild-life-is-fast-vanishing-my-species-extinct-civilized. html.

107. Aubrey L. Haines, *The Yellowstone Story, Volume Two* (Boulder: Yellowstone Library and Museum Association in cooperation with Colorado Associated University Press, 1977), 62.

108. U.S. Department of the Interior, *Rules and Regulations of the Yellowstone National Park* (Washington, DC: U.S. Government Printing Office, 1887), 154.

109. George D. Coder, "The National Movement to Preserve the American Buffalo in the United States and Canada Between 1880 and 1920," (PhD dissertation, Ohio State University, 1975), 75.

110. Ibid., 77.

111. Coder, "The National Movement," 91; Jones, *Buffalo Jones' Forty Years of Adventure*, chap. 15.

112. Coder, "The National Movement," 91.

113. Ibid., 90.

114. U.S. Congress, Senator Redfield Proctor's resolution, 57th Cong., 1st sess., *Congressional Record* 35, part 2 (January 30, 1902), 1109.

115. Secretary of Agriculture James Wilson to the Senate, regarding "Facts in Relation to the Preservation of the American Bison in the United States and Canada," Senate Document no. 208, 57th Cong., 1st sess. (1902).

116. Secretary of the Interior E.A. Hitchcock to the Senate, "Facts in Relation to the Preservation of the American Bison in the United States and Canada," Senate Document no. 445, 57th Cong., 1st sess. (July 1, 1902), https://archive.org/details/americanbisoninu00unit.

117. Haines, *The Yellowstone Story*, 68–72.

118. U.S. Department of the Interior Bison Leadership Team and Working Group, *DOI Bison Report: Looking Forward*, Natural Resource

Report NPS/NRSS/BRMD/NRR—2014/821 (Fort Collins: National Park Service, 2014), 73.

119. Coder, "The National Movement," 104.

120. "USFWS History: A Timeline for Fish and Wildlife Conservation," U.S. Fish and Wildlife Service National Conservation Training Center, https://training.fws.gov/history/usfws-history.html.

121. "History of the Boone and Crockett Club," Boone and Crockett Club, https://www.boone-crockett.org/about/about_history.asp?area =about.

122. Natalie D. Halbert et al., "Where the Buffalo Roam: The Role of History and Genetics in the Conservation of Bison on U.S. Federal Lands," *Park Science* 24, no. 2 (2007): 28.

123. Haines, *The Yellowstone Story*, 72–74.

124. W. Andrew Marcus, "Bison," in *Atlas of Yellowstone* (Berkeley: University of California Press, 2012), 154.

125. George Bird Grinnell, "The Last of the Buffalo," *Scribner's Magazine* 12, no. 3 (September 1892): 276.

Theodore Roosevelt

126. "Guide to State and Local Census Geography: North Dakota," United States Census Bureau, https://www2.census.gov/geo/pdfs /reference/guidestloc/nd_gslcg.pdf; "Dakota Territory Growth," Fargo, North Dakota: Its History and Images, North Dakota State University, https://library.ndsu.edu/fargo-history/?q=content/dakota-territory -growth.

127. Theodore Roosevelt, *Buffalo Hunting* (MS Am 1454.51[2], Theodore Roosevelt Collection, Harvard College Library), Theodore Roosevelt Digital Library, https://www.theodorerooseveltcenter.org /Research/Digital-Library/Record?libID=o285665.

128. Theodore Roosevelt to Martha Bulloch Roosevelt (letter, MS Am 1540 [37], Theodore Roosevelt Collection, Harvard College Library), Theodore Roosevelt Digital Library, https://www.theodorerooseveltcenter .org/Research/Digital-Library/Record?libID=o278505.

129. Theodore Roosevelt to Martha Bulloch Roosevelt (postcard, MS Am 1540 [6], Theodore Roosevelt Collection, Harvard College Library), Theodore Roosevelt Digital Library, https://www.theodorerooseveltcenter .org/Research/Digital-Library/Record?libID=o278351.

130. Theodore Roosevelt to Alice Lee Roosevelt (letter, MS Am 1541.9 [100], Theodore Roosevelt Collection, Harvard College Library), Theodore Roosevelt Digital Library, http://www.theodorerooseveltcenter

.org/Research/Digital-Library/Record?libID=o283352.

131. Elwyn B. Robinson, "The Great Dakota Boom," in *History of North Dakota* (Lincoln: University of Nebraska Press, 1966).

132. James Bradley, *The Imperial Cruise: A Secret History of Empire and War* (New York: Little, Brown and Co., 2009), 50–55, https://delanceyplace.com/view-archives.php?p=1604

133. "American Bison in the Badlands" (newspaper article, Daughters of the American Revolution, MSS 20578, SEE 10152), Theodore Roosevelt Digital Library, https://www.theodorerooseveltcenter.org/Research/Digital-Library/Record?libID=o292541.

134. Theodore Roosevelt to Alice Lee Roosevelt (letter, MS Am 1541.9 [103], Theodore Roosevelt Collection, Harvard College Library), Theodore Roosevelt Digital Library, http://www.theodorerooseveltcenter.org/Research/Digital-Library/Record?libID=o283355.

135. "Bison Bellows: Theodore Roosevelt," National Park Service, August 25, 2016, https://www.nps.gov/articles/bison-bellows-8-25-16.htm.

136. Theodore Roosevelt, "The Lordly Buffalo," in *Hunting Trips of a Ranchman* (New York: G.P. Putnam's Sons, 1885), chap. 8, https://www.bartleby.com/52/8.html.

137. Michael Punke, *Last Stand: George Bird Grinnell, the Battle to Save the Buffalo, and the Birth of the New West* (Lincoln: University of Nebraska Press, 2007), 163–64.

138. Coder, "The National Movement," 70.

William Temple Hornaday

139. Gregory J. Dehler, *The Most Defiant Devil: William Temple Hornaday and His Controversial Crusade to Save American Wildlife* (Charlottesville: University of Virginia Press, 2013), 16.

140. "Maynard Carbine," *Wikipedia*, https://en.wikipedia.org/wiki/Maynard_carbine.

141. Dehler, *The Most Defiant Devil*, 28.

142. Hornaday, *The Extermination of the American Bison*, 511.

143. Ibid., 530.

144. Ibid., 531.

145. Tom Stout, *Montana, Its Story and Biography: A History of Aboriginal and Territorial Montana and Three Decades of Statehood*, vol. 3, ed. Tom Stout (Chicago: American Historical Society, 1921), 776–77.

146. Hornaday, *The Extermination of the American Bison*, 534.

147. Bechtel, *Mr. Hornaday's War*, 6.

148. Harvey W. Brown, "Buffalo Hunting in Montana in 1886: The

Diary of W. Harvey Brown," ed. John M Peterson, *Montana* 31 (1981): 5.

149. Hornaday, *The Extermination of the American Bison*, 542.

150. Ibid.

151. Ibid., 389.

152. Bechtel, *Mr. Hornaday's War*, 50.

153. William T. Hornaday to G. Brown Goode (Director of the National Museum), December 2, 1887, https://siarchives.si.edu/history/ featured-topics/stories/letter-dated-december-2-1887-professor-george -brown-goode-director-national.

Charles Goodnight

154. H. Allen Anderson, "Goodnight, Charles," Handbook of Texas Online, http://www.tshaonline.org/handbook/online/articles/fgo11.

155. Ibid.

156. Charles Goodnight, Emanuel Dubbs, and John A. Hart, *Pioneer Days in the Southwest from 1850 to 1879: Thrilling Descriptions of Buffalo Hunting, Indian Fighting and Massacres, Cowboy Life and Home Building* (Guthrie, OK: The State Capital Co., 1909), 11, https://babel.hathitrust .org/cgi/pt?id=mdp.39015026728769;view=1up;seq=21.

157. T. C. Richardson, "Goodnight-Loving Trail," Handbook of Texas Online, http://www.tshaonline.org/handbook/online/articles/ayg02.

158. "Indian depredation case no. 9133: Charles Goodnight and John W. Sheek vs. The United States and the Comanche Indians" (microfilm), Southwest Collection, Texas Tech University, https://swco-ir.tdl.org /handle/10605/228931.

159. Goodnight, Dubbs, and Hart, *Pioneer Days in the Southwest*, 15.

160. "Details for the Old J.A. Ranch (Atlas Number 5381005388)," Texas Historic Atlas, Texas Historic Commission, https://atlas.thc.state .tx.us/Details/5381005388.

161. H. Allen Anderson, "Adair, John George," Handbook of Texas Online, http://www.tshaonline.org/handbook/online/articles/fad03.

162. Goodnight, Dubbs, and Hart, *Pioneer Days in the Southwest*, 23.

163. Harley True Burton, "A History of the J.A. Ranch, II," *The Southwestern Historical Quarterly* 31, no. 3 (January 1928): 234, http:// www.jstor.org/stable/30234997.

164. Ibid., 230.

165. "Chuck Wagon Central," Lone Hand Western, http://lonehand .com/chuckwagon_central.htm.

166. Burton, "A History of the J.A. Ranch, II," 223.

167. Ibid., 229–30.

168. "Largest Herd of Buffalo in Country Preserved on Goodnight Ranch," *The Amarillo Globe*, June 18, 1924, https://allaboutbison.com /bison-in-history/texas-history/charles-goodnight-bison-herd/; Coder, "The National Movement," 13; Goodnight, Dubbs, and Hart, *Pioneer Days in the Southwest*, 28.

169. Burton, "A History of the J.A. Ranch, II," 257.

170. Goodnight, Dubbs, and Hart, *Pioneer Days in the Southwest*, 26.

171. Charles Goodnight, "My Experience with Bison Hybrids," *Journal of Heredity* 5, no. 5 (May 1, 1914): 197–99.

172. James Derr, personal communication.

173. Texas Parks & Wildlife, "Texas State Bison Herd to Once Again Freely Roam the Caprock," news release, Texas Parks & Wildlife, September 6, 2011, https://tpwd.texas.gov/newsmedia /releases/?req=20110906b.

174. Scott Stephen, "James McKay (1828–1879): Métis Trader, Guide, Interpreter and MLA," *Manitoba History* 58 (June 2008), http://www.mhs .mb.ca/docs/mb_history/58/mckay_j.shtml.

175. Ibid.

176. Jillian Overby, "History of Bison: From a Manitoba Perspective," Manitoba Bison Association, http://www.manitobabison.ca/about-the -bison/history-of-bison/; Halbert et al., "Where the Bufalo Roam," 25.

The American Bison Society

177. Documentation of when Baynes died, short biography that includes his parents' names and birthplaces (image), Find A Grave, https://images.findagrave.com/photos/2017/343/178810068_1512968333 .jpg.

178. Raymond Gorges, "Ernest Harold Baynes, Naturalist and Crusader," *The Canadian Medical Association Journal* 19, no. 5 (November 1928), 646, PMC1710098.

179. Hornaday, *Annual Report of the American Bison Society*, 11–12.

180. "Austin Corbin Estate in Newport, New Hampshire," Northern New England Villages, 2014, https://northernnewenglandvillages.com /2014/05/15/austin-corbin-estate-in-newport-new-hampshire/.

181. Mary T. Kronenwetter, "Corbin's 'Animal Garden,'" *Eastman Living* (Fall 2011), http://eastmanliving.com/2011/11/corbin%e2%80%99s-% e2%80%9canimal-garden%e2%80%9d/.

182. Ibid.

183. Ibid.

184. Earnest H. Baynes, "The Corbin Buffalo Herd," in *Fourth Annual*

Report of the American Bison Society (Boston: American Bison Society, 1911), 43, https://archive.org/details/report41911amer/page/n7.

185. Ernest H. Baynes, "History and Proceedings of the Society," in *Annual Report of the American Bison Society 1905–1907* (Boston: American Bison Society, 1908), 1.

186. Theodore Roosevelt, "Message of the President," Office of the Historian, Department of State, December 6, 1904, https://history.state .gov/historicaldocuments/frus1904/message-of-the-president

187. Baynes, "History and Proceedings of the Society," 2.

188. James Daniel Richardson, *A Compilation of the Messages and Papers of the Presidents, 1789–1908, Volume 11 and Index,* (Washington, DC: Bureau of National Literature and Art, 1908), 1171.

189. Dehler, *The Most Defiant Devil*, 91–92.

190. Ibid., 91–93.

191. William T. Hornaday, "The Founding of the Wichita National Bison Herd," in *Annual Report of the American Bison Society 1905–1907*, (Boston: American Bison Society, 1908), 64.

192. "15 Buffalo to Go Back to the Ranges," *The New York Times*, October 7, 1907, https://www.nytimes.com/1907/10/06/archives/15 -buffalo-to-go-back-to-the-ranges-cowboy-rush-here-to-take-part.html

193. Coder, "The National Movement," 157.

194. George Bird Grinnell, "The Last Refuge," *Forest and Stream* 19, no. 20 (December 14, 1882): 382.

195. John Muir, *Our National Parks* (Boston and New York: Houghton, Mifflin and Co., 1901), 335.

196. Paul Fugleberg, "Roundup of the Pablo-Allard Buffalo Herd" (photo, North Lake County Public Library, Polson, Montana, 1908), https://mtmemory.org/digital/collection/p16013coll17/id/101/.

197. William T. Hornaday, "Notes on the Census," in *Annual Report of the American Bison Society 1905–1907* (Boston: American Bison Society, 1908), 75; Lauren Markewicz, *Like Distant Thunder: Canada's Bison Conservation Story* (Gatineau, QC: Parks Canada, 2017), https://www.pc .gc.ca/en/pn-np/ab/elkisland/nature/eep-sar/bison#a9.

198. "Preservation of the Plains Bison National Historic Event," Parks Canada Directory of Federal Heritage Designations, https://www.pc.gc.ca /apps/dfhd/page_nhs_eng.aspx?id=1553

199. Coder, "The National Movement," 266.

200. Ibid., 267.

201. William T. Hornaday, "Census of Living American Bison on January 1, 1908," in *Annual Report of the American Bison Society 1905–*

1907 (Boston: American Bison Society, 1908), 72.

202. William T. Hornaday, "Report of the President on the Founding of the Montana National Bison Herd," in *Second Annual Report of the American Bison Society 1909–1910* (Boston: American Bison Society, 1910), 17.

Yellowstone's Stigma

203. Joel Berger, "Optimism and Challenge for Science-Based Conservation of Migratory Species in and out of U.S. National Parks," *Conservation Biology* 28, no. 1 (2014): 4–12.

204. Peter Ames Carlin, "Buffalo Soldier," *People Magazine*, April 12, 1997, https://people.com/archive/buffalo-soldier-vol-47-no-15/.

205. "Migratory Species," National Park Service, https://web.archive.org/web/20180101000000*/https://www.nature.nps.gov/biology/migratoryspecies/questions.cfm.

206. Daniel S. Licht, "Bison Conservation in Northern Great Plains National Parks and the Need for Reliable Funding," *The George Wright Forum* 33, no. 1 (2016): 18–28.

207. Eric W. Sanderson et al., "The Ecological Future of the North American Bison: Conceiving Long-Term, Large-Scale Conservation of Wildlife," *Conservation Biology* 22, no. 2 (2008): 252–66.

208. Duane Lammers et al., "Bison Conservation Management: Guidelines for Herd Managers," World Wildlife Fund, Inc. (September 2013): 4.

209. Rob Hotakainen, "'The Killing Fields:' Bison Come to Roam. Then They Die," *E&E News*, October 1, 2018, https://www.eenews.net/stories/1060100069.

210. Angus Thuermer, Jr., and Kurt Repanshek, "Yellowstone Bison, America's National Mammal, Stigmatized in Montana," National Parks Traveler, September 2017, https://www.nationalparkstraveler.org/2017/09/bison-west-yellowstone-national-parks-brucellosis-stigma.

211. Mike Volsky, Chief of operations for Montana Fish, Wildlife and Parks, personal communication, 2017.

212. Terry Jones, personal communication, August 2017.

213. National Academies of Sciences, Engineering, and Medicine et al., *Revisiting Brucellosis in the Greater Yellowstone Area* (Washington, DC: The National Academies Press, 2017), https://doi.org/10.17226/24750.

214. Glenn E. Plumb and Rosemary Sucec, "A Bison Conservation History in the U.S. National Parks," *Journal of Wildlife* 45, no. 2 (Spring

2006): 22–28.

215. Western Watersheds Project & Buffalo Field Campaign, *Petition to List the Yellowstone Bison as Threatened or Endangered Under the Endangered Species Act* (Western Watersheds Project & Buffalo Field Campaign, 2014), http://www.buffalofieldcampaign.org/images/about -buffalo/problems-buffalo-face/extinction/Buffalo-Field-Campaign-ESA -Petition-11-13-2014.pdf.

216. Yellowstone National Park press conference with Dan Wenk, August 2018.

217. Mike Mease, personal communication, August 2018.

TRAIN RIDE TO THE FUTURE

218. H.R. Mitchell, "Report on the Establishment of the National Herd in Wind Cave National Game Preserve," in *Seventh Annual Report of the American Bison Society 1914* (Boston: American Bison Society, 1914), 39, https://archive.org/details/report71914amer/page/n3.

219. "The Home of the Bison—The Cultural Foundations of Tribal Affiliations to WCNP," National Park Service, https://www.nps.gov/wica /learn/historyculture/the-home-of-the-bison-the-cultural-foundations -of-tribal-affiliations-to-wcnp.htm.

220. "John Alden Loring," *Wikipedia*, https://en.wikipedia.org/wiki /John_Alden_Loring.

221. John Alden Loring, *Report on Certain Lands in South Dakota Suitable For a Buffalo and Game Reserve* (Boston: American Bison Society, 1911), 17.

222. Ibid., 11.

223. *History of Wind Cave National Game Preserve, South Dakota*, compiled by Clara Ruth (National Park Service, 1921), 27–28; Kim Mogen, *A History of Animal Management at Wind Cave National Park* (National Park Service, 1977); *Department of Interior, Rules and Regulations, Wind Cave National Park, South Dakota* (Washington, DC: Government Printing Office, 1923), 9.

224. "The Home of The Bison—Executive Summary—Wind Cave National Park," National Park Service, 2015, https://www.nps.gov/wica /learn/historyculture/the-home-of-the-bison-executive-summary.htm.

225. Mogen, *A History of Animal Management.*

226. Mitchell, "Report on the Establishment," 47.

227. D.F. Houston, "Letter from the Secretary of Agriculture," in *Seventh Annual Report of the American Bison Society 1914* (Boston:

American Bison Society, 1914), 51.

228. William T. Hornaday, *Popular Official Guide to the New York Zoological Park*, 12th ed. (New York: New York Zoological Society, 1913), 26.

229. "Wildlife Management—Raising Wildlife," National Park Service, 2018, https://www.nps.gov/wica/learn/management/wildlife-management-raising-wild-animals.htm

230. Ibid.

231. Gordon W. Lillie, "Restoring the Bison to the Western Plains," *Cosmopolitan Magazine* 39, no. 6 (October 1905): 651.

232. Hornaday, *Popular Official Guide*, 28.

233. "Wind Cave National Park homepage," National Park Service, www.nps.gov/wica.

234. Gates, et al., *American Bison Status Survey*, 61.

Parks and Bison

235. Freese, et al., "Second Chance for the Plains Bison," 6.

236. Philip W. Hedrick, "Conservation Genetics and the North American Bison," *Journal of Heredity* 100, no. 4 (2009): 411.

237. Halbert et al., "Where the Buffalo Roam," 23.

238. James Derr, "American Bison: The Ultimate Genetic Survivor," (PowerPoint presentation and lecture, Ecological Future of North American Bison conference, Denver, CO, October 24, 2006), https://www.buffalofieldcampaign.org/habitat/documents2/Derr_American%20Bison%20-%20The%20Ultimate%20Genetic%20Survivor.pdf.

239. Hornaday, "The Founding of the Wichita National Bison Herd," 56.

240. *DOI Bison Report*, 45, 55.

241. Elaine Leslie, National Park Service Biological Resources Division Chief, personal communication.

242. Freese et al., "Second Chance for the Plains Bison," 5.

243. Halbert et al., "Where the Buffalo Roam," 28.

244. Freese et al., "Second Chance for the Plains Bison," 5.

Rebounding Across the West

245. Sieg, Flather, and McCanny, "Recent Biodiversity Patterns," 290.

246. Samuell Fuhlendorf, Brady W. Allred, and Robert G. Hamilton, "Bison as Keystone Herbivores on the Great Plains: Can Cattle Serve as Proxy for Evolutionary Grazing Patterns?" (American Bison Society working paper no. 4, 2010): 7, 30.

247. National Park Service, "A Call to Action: Preparing for a Second Century of Stewardship and Engagement," National Park Service, August 25, 2011, 18, https://www.nps.gov/calltoaction/pdf/directors_call_to _action_report.pdf

248. *DOI Bison Report*, 21–73.

249. National Forest Foundation, "Midewin National Tallgrass Prairie: A Shared Vision for Restoration," National Forest Foundation (2011), 2, https://www.fs.usda.gov/Internet/FSE_DOCUMENTS/stelprd3833921.pdf

250. *DOI Bison Report*, 67.

251. Utah Division of Wildlife Resources, "Bison Unit Management Plan: Unit #15, Henry Mountains," Utah Division of Wildlife Resources, 2007, https://wildlife.utah.gov/hunting/biggame/pdf/bison_15.pdf.

252. Dustin H. Ranglack et al., "Genetic Analysis of the Henry Mountains Bison Herd," *PLoS ONE* 10, no. 12 (2015), https://doi.org /10.1371/journal.pone.0144239.

253. *DOI Bison Report*, 65.

254. Bill Bates and Kent Hersey, "Lessons Learned from Bison Restoration Efforts in Utah on Western Rangelands," *Rangelands* 38, no. 5 (October 2016): 263, https://doi.org/10.1016/j.rala.2016.08.010.

255. Ibid., 259.

256. Winona LaDuke, *All Our Relations: Native Struggles for Land and Life* (Chicago: Haymarket Books, 1999), 160.

257. Judith L. McDonald, "Essay: Bison Restoration in the Great Plains and the Challenge of Their Management," *Great Plains Research* 11, no. 1 (Spring 2001): 109.

CONSERVING BISON GENES ON A LARGE-SCALE LANDSCAPE

258. Skylar Peyton, "Home on the Market Range: An Evaluation of Cultural and Economic Barriers to Large-Scale Bison Farming," (thesis, College of Saint Benedict/Saint John's University, May 2018), 58.

259. "U.S. Census of Agriculture," USDA, 2012, https://www.nass.usda .gov/AgCensus/.

260. Derr, personal communication.

261. Ibid.

262. K. Aune, D. Jørgensen, and C. Gates, "*Bison bison* (errata version published in 2018)," IUCN Red List of Threatened Species, 2017: e.T2815A123789863.

263. Freese, "Second Chance for the Plains Bison," 3.

264. Ibid., 6.

265. Ibid.

266. D. S. Licht, *Restoration of Bison (*Bison bison*) to Agate Fossil Beds National Monument: A Feasibility Study*, Natural Resource Technical Report NPS/XXXX/NRTR (Fort Collins, CO: National Park Service, 2014), 51.

267. Ibid., 52.

268. "Blue Mounds State Park and the Minnesota Bison Conservation Herd Welcome New Bull," Minnesota Department of Natural Resources, https://files.dnr.state.mn.us/destinations/state_parks/blue_mounds /yellowstone_fact_sheet.pdf.

269. White, Wallen, and Hallac, *Yellowstone Bison*, 111, 145.

270. "Depopulation of the Great Plains," Wikipedia, https:// en.wikipedia.org/wiki/Depopulation_of_the_Great_Plains#Population _history

271. Deborah E. Popper and Frank J. Popper, "The Buffalo Commons as Regional Metaphor and Geographic Method" (draft accepted by *Geographical Review*, 2013), https://dlc.dlib.indiana.edu/dlc/bitstream /handle/10535/8625/The%20Buffalo%20Commons%20as%20Regional %20Metaphor%20and%20Geographic%20Method%20_%20Great %20Plains%20Re.pdf.

272. Freese et al., "Second Chance for the Plains Bison," 8.

273. Sieg, Flather, and McCanny, "Recent Biodiversity Patterns," 283.

274. Ibid., 288.

275. Ibid., 302–03.

276. "United States National Grassland," *Wikipedia*, https:// en.wikipedia.org/wiki/United_States_National_Grassland.

277. Proceedings and Debates, 86th Cong., 2nd sess. *Congressional Record* 106, part 9 (May 26, 1960–June 13, 1960), 12178.

278. "Niobrara National Park Study, Nebraska" (Draft Special Resource Study, National Park Service, 1995): 14, https://archive.org/stream /draftspecialreso00nati/draftspecialreso00nati_djvu.txt

279. National Park Service, *Niobrara National Scenic River: Final General Management Plan/Environmental Impact Statement,* (National Park Service, 1996), 9.

280. Howard Zinn, *A People's History of the United States, 1492–Present*, (New York: The New Press, 1980), 104.

281. Freese et al., "Second Chance for the Plains Bison," 8.

282. "The National Grasslands Story," U.S. Forest Service, https://www .fs.fed.us/grasslands/aboutus/index.shtml.

283. Jonathan Proctor, personal communication.

284. Elizabeth Gaines, "Creating a Reserve within the Thunder Basin National Grasslands," (MS thesis, University of Montana, 1996), https://scholarworks.umt.edu/etd/7474/.

285. Pleistocene Park: Restoration of the Mammoth Steppe Ecosystem, http://www.pleistocenepark.ru/en/

286. "Scientific Background," Pleistocene Park: Restoration of the Mammoth Steppe Ecosystem, http://www.pleistocenepark.ru/en/background/.

287. "Grasslands," The State of the Birds, 2009, http://www.stateofthebirds.org/2009/habitats/grasslands.

288. Ibid.

EPILOGUE

289. Half-Earth Project, https://www.half-earthproject.org/.

290. Licht, "Bison Conservation in Northern Great Plains," 18.

291. Ibid., 25.

292. Buffalo Field Campaign, "American Bison, A Species of Conservation Concern," Buffalo Field Campaign (2007): 7.

Bibliography

American Bison Association. "Annual Report of the American Bison Association 1905–1907." Second Annual Meeting of the Board of Directors (1908).

Barker, William T. and Whitman, Warren C. "Vegetation of the Northern Great Plains." *Rangelands* (December 1988): 266.

Bates, Bill and Hersey, Kent. "Lessons Learned From Bison Restoration Efforts in Utah on Western Rangelands." Society for Range Management (2016): 263.

Baynes, Ernest H. "The Corbin Buffalo Herd." *Fourth Annual Report of the American Bison Society*. Boston: American Bison Society (1911).

Bechtel, Stefan. *Mr. Hornaday's War: How a Peculiar Victorian Zookeeper Waged a Lonely Crusade for Wildlife that Changed the World*. Boston: Beacon Press, 2012.

Berger, Joel. "Optimism and Challenge for Science-Based Conservation of Migratory Species in and out of U.S. National Parks." *Conservation Biology* 28, no.1 (2014): 4–12.

Black Elk and Neihardt, John G. *Black Elk Speaks: Being the Life Story of a Holy Man of the Oglala Sioux*. Albany: State University of New York Press, 1932.

Brown, Robert D. "The History of Wildlife Conservation and Research in the United States—and Implications for the Future." North Carolina State University (2007): 6.

Buffalo Field Campaign. *American Bison, A Species of Conservation Concern*. (2018).

Catlin, George. *North American Indians*, edited by Peter Matthiessen. New York: Penguin Nature Classics, 1989.

Coder, George D. "The National Movement to Preserve the

American Buffalo in the United States and Canada between 1880 and 1920." PhD diss., Ohio State University, 1975. WorldCat (30223).

Cody, William. F. *An Autobiography of Buffalo Bill.* New York: Cosmopolitan Book Corp., 1920.

Dehler, Gregory J. *The Most Defiant Devil: William Temple Hornaday and His Controversial Crusade to Save American Wildlife.* Charlottesville: University of Virginia Press, 2013.

de Nájera, Pedro de Castañeda. *The Journey of Coronado, 1540–1542,* translated and edited by George Parker Winship. New York: A. S. Barnes & Co., 1904.

Department of the Interior. *DOI bison report: Looking forward. Natural Resource Report.* NPS/NRSS/BRMD/NRR—2014/821. National Park Service, (2014).

Department of Interior. *Rules and Regulations, Wind Cave National Park, South Dakota.* Government Printing Office, 1923.

Easton, Robert, and MacKenzie Brown. *Lord of Beasts: The Saga of Buffalo Jones.* Tucson: University of Arizona Press, 1961.

Feir, Donna, Rob Gillezeau, and Maggie E. C. Jones. "The Slaughter of the North American Bison and Reversal of Fortunes on the Great Plains." Department Discussion Papers 1701. Department of Economics, University of Victoria (2017).

Freese, Curtis, Kyran Kunkel, Damien Austin, and Betty Holder. *Bison Management Plan.* American Prairie Reserve, 2018. https://www.americanprairie.org/sites/default/files/APR_BisonPlan_062018.pdf.

Freese, Curtis, Keith Aune, Delaney Boyd, James Derr, Steve Forrest, Gates C. Cormack, Peter Gogan, et al. "Second Chance for the Plains Bison." *Biological Conservation* 136. (2007): 175–84.

Fuhlendorf, Samuell, Brady W. Allred, and Robert G. Hamilton.

Bison As Keystone Herbivores On the Great Plains: Can Cattle Serve as Proxy For Evolutionary Grazing Patterns? Wildlife Conservation Society (2010).

Gaines, Elizabeth. "Creating a Reserve within the Thunder Basin National Grasslands." PhD diss., University of Montana (1996). ScholarWorks at University of Montana, 7474.

Geist, Valerius. *Buffalo Nation: History and Legend of the North American Bison.* Minneapolis: Voyageur Press, 1996.

Goodnight, Charles, Emanuel Dubbs, and John A. Hart. *Pioneer Days in the Southwest from 1850 to 1879: Thrilling Descriptions of Buffalo Hunting, Indian Fighting and Massacres, Cowboy Life and Home Building.* The State Capital Co. (1909).

Goodnight, Charles. "My Experience with Bison Hybrids." *Journal of Heredity* 5, no. 5 (May 1914): 197–99.

Grinnell, George Bird. "The Last Refuge." *Forest and Stream* 19, no. 20 (December 14, 1882).

Guthrie, Dale R. *The Nature of Paleolithic Art.* Chicago: University of Chicago Press, 2006.

Guthrie, Dale R. *Frozen Fauna of the Mammoth Steppe: The Story of Blue Babe.* Chicago: University of Chicago Press, 1990.

Haines, Aubrey L. *The Yellowstone Story, Volume One.* Yellowstone Library and Museum Association in cooperation with Colorado Associated University Press (1977).

Haines, Aubrey L. *The Yellowstone Story, Volume Two.* Yellowstone Library and Museum Association in cooperation with Colorado Associated University Press (1977).

Halbert, Natalie D. and James Derr. "Patterns of Genetic Variation in US Federal Bison Herds." *Molecular Ecology* (2008).

Halert, Natalie D., Peter J. P. Gogan, Philip W. Hedrick, Jacquelyn M. Wahl, and James Derr. "Genetic Population Substructure in Bison at Yellowstone National Park." *Journal of Heredity* 103, no. 3 (2012): 360–70.

Hedrick, Philip W. "Conservation Genetics and North American Bison." *Journal of Heredity* 100, no. 4 (2009): 411–20.

Herman, Julia A., Antoinette J. Piaggio, Natalie D. Halbert, Jack C. Rhyan, and M. D. Salman. "Genetic Analysis of a *Bison bison* Herd Derived from the Yellowstone National Park Population." *Wildlife Biology* 20 (2014): 335–43.

Hornaday, William T. *Annual Report of the American Bison Society 1905–1907*. Boston: American Bison Society (1908).

Hornaday, William T. *Popular Official Guide to the New York Zoological Park*. New York Zoological Society (1913).

Hornaday, William T. *The Extermination of the American Bison*. Government Printing Office (1889).

Hornaday, William T. "The Founding of the Wichita National Bison Herd." *Annual Report of the American Bison Society, 1905–1907*. Boston: American Bison Society (1908): 64.

Hornaday, William T. "Notes on the Census." *Annual Report of the American Bison Society, 1905–1907*. Boston: American Bison Society (1908): 75.

Hornaday, William T. "Report of the President on the Founding of the Montana National Bison Herd." *Second Annual Report of the American Bison Society 1909–1910*. Boston: American Bison Society (1910): 17.

Isenberg, Andrew C. *The Death of the Bison*. Cambridge: Cambridge University Press, 2000.

Jones, Charles Jess. *Buffalo Jones' Forty Years of Adventure: A Volume of Facts Gathered from Experience*, compiled by Col. Henry Inman. Topeka: Crane & Company, 1899.

Knopf, F. L., and F. B. Samson. "Conservation of Grassland Vertebrates." In *Ecology and Conservation of Great Plains Vertebrates*, edited by Knopf, F. L. and F. B. Samson. *Ecological Studies* (Analysis and Synthesis) 125. New York: Springer, 1997.

Lame Deer, John and Richard Erdoes. *Lame Deer, Seeker of Visions*. New York: Simon & Schuster, 1972.

Lammers, Duane, Kevin Ogorzalek, Tom Olson, John Flocchini, Steve Forrest, Bruce Anderson, Dennis Jorgensen, Alejandro Grajal, Chad Kremer, Tom LeFaive, Jill Majerus, Dawn Montanye, Dan O'Brien, Shane Sarver, and Jim Stone. "Bison Conservation Management: Guidelines for Herd Managers." *World Wildlife Fund, Inc.* (2013): 4.

Licht, Daniel S. "Bison Conservation in Northern Great Plains National Parks and the Need for Reliable Funding." *George Wright Society* 33, no. 1 (2016): 18–28.

Lillie, Gordon W. "Restoring the Bison to the Western Plains." *Cosmopolitan Magazine* 38-39 (1905).

Loring, J. Alden. *Report on Certain Lands in South Dakota Suitable for a Buffalo and Game Reserve*. Boston: American Bison Society (1911): 17.

Malhi, Yadvinder, Christopher E. Doughty, Mauro Galetti, Felisa A. Smith, Jens-Christian Svenning, and John W. Terborgh. "Megafauna and Ecosystem Function from the Pleistocene to the Anthropocene." *PNAS* 113, no. 4. (January 26, 2016).

Marcus, Andrew W., ed. *The Atlas of Yellowstone*. Berkeley: University of California Press, 2012.

Mayer, Frank H. and Charles B. Roth. *The Buffalo Harvest*. Thousand Oaks: Sage Books, 1958.

McDonald, Judith L. 2001 "Essay: Bison Restoration in the Great Plains and the Challenge of Their Management,"

Great Plains Research: A Journal of Natural and Social Sciences 11, no. 1 (2001): 109.

McMaster, Gerald and Clifford Trafzer. *Native Universe: Voices of Indian America*. National Museum of the American Indian, Smithsonian Institution, 2004.

Mech, David, Rick McIntyre, and Douglas Smith. "Unusual Behavior by Bison, *Bison bison*, Toward Elk, *Cervus elaphus*, and Wolves, *Canis lupus*." *Canadian Field Naturalist* 118, (2004).

Mitchell, H.R. "Report on the Establishment of the National Herd in Wind Cave National Game Preserve." *Seventh Annual Report of the American Bison Society 1914*. Boston: American Bison Society (1914): 39.

Mogen, Kim. *A History of Animal Management at Wind Cave National Park*. National Park Service (1977).

Muir, John. *Our National Parks*. New York: Houghton Mifflin, 1901.

National Academies of Sciences, Engineering, and Medicine, *Revisiting Brucellosis in the Greater Yellowstone Area*. Washington, DC: The National Academies Press, 2017.

National Park Service. *Niobrara National Scenic River, Final General Management Plan/Environmental Impact Statement*. National Park Service, 1996.

North American Bird Conservation Initiative, US Committee. "The State of the Birds, United States of America." Washington, DC: US Department of Interior (2009).

O'Brien, Dan. *Great Plains Bison*. Lincoln: University of Nebraska Press, 2017.

Peyton, Skylar. "Home on the Market Range: An Evaluation of Cultural and Economic Barriers to Large-Scale Bison Farming." *All College Thesis Program, 2016–present* (2018): 58.

Pfannenstiel, Robert S. and Mark G. Ruder. "Colonization

of Bison (*Bison bison*) Wallows in a Tallgrass Prairie by *Culicoides spp* (Diptera: Ceratopogonidae)." *Journal of Vector Ecology* 40, no. 1 (2015): 187.

Plumb, Glenn and Rosemary Sucec. "A Bison Conservation History in the U.S. National Parks." *Journal of Wildlife* 45, no. 2 (2006).

Popper, Deborah E. and Frank J. Popper. "The Buffalo Commons as Regional Metaphor and Geographic Method." Draft accepted by *Geographic Review*, 2013.

Punke, Michael. *George Bird Grinnell, Last Stand: The Battle to Save the Buffalo, and the Birth of the New West.* Lincoln: University of Nebraska Press, 2007.

Ranglack D. H., L. K. Dobson, J. T. du Toit, and J. Derr. "Genetic Analysis of the Henry Mountains Bison Herd." *PLoS ONE* 10, no. 12 (2015). e0144239.

Roosevelt, Theodore. *Buffalo Hunting.* Theodore Roosevelt Collection. MS Am 1454.51(2), Harvard College.

Roosevelt, Theodore. *Hunting Trips of a Ranchman.* New York: G. P. Putnam's Sons, 1885.

Ruth, Clara. *History of Wind Cave National Preserve.* Bureau of Biological Survey, USDA, 1921.

Sanderson, Eric W., Kent H. Redford, Bill Weber, Keith Aune, Dick Baldes, Joel Berger, Dave Carter, Charles Curtin, James Derr, Steve Dobrott, et al. "The Ecological Future of the North American Bison: Conceiving Long-Term, Large-Scale Conservation of Wildlife." *Conservation Biology* 22, no. 2 (2008): 252–66.

Schofield, John M. *Forty-Six Years in the Army.* New York City: The Century Co., 1897.

Sheridan, Philip Henry. *Philip Henry Sheridan Papers: Autograph Letters, 1887; Sherman, William T. to Sheridan, 1868 to 1877.* Library of Congress, 1868. Manuscript/mixed material.

Sherman, William T. *Memoirs of General W. T. Sherman*, 2nd edition revised and corrected. New York City: D. Appleton and Co., 1889.

Sieg, Carolyn Hull, Curtis H. Flather, and Stephan McCanny. "Recent Biodiversity Patterns in the Great Plains: Implications for Restoration and Management." *Great Plains Research* 9, no. 2 (1999).

Smits, David D. "The Frontier Army and the Destruction of the Buffalo: 1865–1883." *Western Historical Quarterly* 25, no. 3 (1994).

Snell, S., R. Jackson, and A. Krieger. "Lost and Forgotten Historic Roads: The Buffalo Trace, a Case Study." US Forest Service (2014).

Steinberg, Ted. *Down to Earth: Nature's Role in American History.* Oxford: Oxford University Press, 2002.

Steuter, Allen and Lori Hidinger. "Comparative Ecology of Bison and Cattle on Mixed-Grass Prairie." *Great Plains Research* (Fall 1999).

Stout, Tom. *Montana, Its Story and Biography: A History of Aboriginal and Territorial Montana and Three Decades of Statehood, Vol III,* edited by Tom Stout. Washington, DC: The American Historical Society, 1921.

Tarka, Sarah Anne. "My Brother the Buffalo: An Ethnohistorical Documentation of the 1999 Buffalo Walk and the Cultural Significance of Yellowstone Buffalo to the Lakota Sioux and Nez Perce Peoples." PhD diss., University of Montana (2007). ScholarWorks at University of Montana, 692.

Taylor, M. S. "Buffalo Hunt: International Trade and the Virtual Extinction of the North American Bison." *American Economic Review* 101, no. 7 (2011).

The Glenbow Museum. *Nitsitapiisinni: The Story of the Blackfoot People.* Toronto: Key Porter Books, 2001.

US Department of the Interior. *Rules and Regulations of the Yellowstone National Park*. Washington, DC: Government Printing Office, 1887.

Utley, Robert. *The Indian Frontier 1846–1890*. Albuquerque: University of New Mexico Press, 2002.

Viola, Herman J. *Trail to Wounded Knee: The Last Stand of the Plains Indians, 1860–1890*. Washington, DC: National Geographic Society, 2003.

Volsky, Igor. "Bierstadt and Nationalism." *Hudson River Valley Institute* (February 28, 2007).

White, P. J., L. Rick, and David E. Hallac. *Yellowstone Bison: Conserving an American Icon in Modern Society*. Yellowstone Association, 2015.

Zazula, Grant D., Glen MacKay, Thomas D. Andrews, Beth Shapiro, Brandon Letts, and Fiona Brock. "A Late Pleistocene Steppe Bison Partial Carcass from Tssigehtchic, Northwest Territories, Canada." *Quarterly Science Reviews* 28 (2009): 2734–42.

Zimov, Sergei. "Mammoth Steppes and Future Climate." *Human Environment* 105. http://www.pleistocenepark.ru/files/Science_in_Russia_en.pdf.

Zinn, Howard. *A People's History of the United States 1492–Present*. New York: Harper Collins, 2003.

Zontek, Ken. "Hunt, Capture, Raise, Increase: The People Who Saved the Bison." *Great Plains Quarterly* (1995): 1009.

About the Author

Kurt Repanshek is an award-winning journalist well versed in public lands, wildlife, recreation, environmental, and development issues. After graduating from West Virginia University in 1979, he was hired in 1980 by The Associated Press, initially as a temporary legislative relief staffer, but offered a full-time job late that same year. In 1988, when wildfires swept across Yellowstone National Park and captured the world's attention, he directed and provided coverage of the fires for The Associated Press. He has a diverse journalistic background, having written about the rich biodiversity that lies within Great Smoky Mountains National Park and launched National Parks Traveler, the world's top-rated editorially independent website dedicated to daily news and feature coverage of national parks and protected areas.

TORREY HOUSE PRESS

Voices for the Land

The economy is a wholly owned subsidiary of the environment, not the other way around.

—Senator Gaylord Nelson, founder of Earth Day

Torrey House Press is an independent nonprofit publisher promoting environmental conservation through literature. We believe that culture is changed through conversation and that lively, contemporary literature is the cutting edge of social change. We strive to identify exceptional writers, nurture their work, and engage the widest possible audience; to publish diverse voices with transformative stories that illuminate important facets of our ever-changing planet; to develop literary resources for the conservation movement, educating and entertaining readers, inspiring action.

Visit www.torreyhouse.org for reading group discussion guides, author interviews, and more.

As a 501(c)(3) nonprofit publisher, our work is made possible by generous donations from readers like you.

This book was made possible by the generosity of Furthermore: a program of the J. M. Kaplan Fund. Torrey House Press is supported by Back of Beyond Books, The King's English Bookshop, Jeff and Heather Adams, Jeffrey S. and Helen H. Cardon Foundation, Suzanne Bounous, Grant B. Culley Jr. Foundation, Diana Allison, Jerome Cooney and Laura Storjohann, Robert Aagard and Camille Bailey Aagard, Heidi Dexter and David Gens, Kirtly Parker Jones, Utah Division of Arts & Museums, and Salt Lake County Zoo, Arts & Parks. Our thanks to individual donors, subscribers, and the Torrey House Press board of directors for their valued support.

Join the Torrey House Press family and give today at
www.torreyhouse.org/give.